# Ernest Buckler
## Rediscovery and Reassessment

Marta Dvorak

# Ernest Buckler

Rediscovery and Reassessment

Marta Dvorak

Wilfrid Laurier University Press

This book has been published with the help of a financial contribution from the Publishing Fund of the International Council for Canadian Studies. We acknowledge the support of the Canada Council for the Arts for our publishing program. We acknowledge the financial support of the Government of Canada through the Book Publishing Industry Development Program for our publishing activities.

National Library of Canada Cataloguing in Publication Data

Dvorak, Marta, 1951-
    Ernest Buckler : rediscovery and reassessment

Includes bibliographical references and index.
ISBN 0-88920-354-7

1. Buckler, Ernest, 1908-1984—Criticism and interpretation.   I. Title

PS8503.U2Z66 2001            C813'.54            C2001-930469-2
PR9199.3.B82Z66 2001

© 2001 Wilfrid Laurier University Press
Waterloo, Ontario, Canada    N2L 3C5

Cover design by Leslie Macredie
using a Frederick H. Varley painting, *Open Window*, courtesy of
Hart House Permanent Collection, University of Toronto

∞
Printed in Canada

All rights reserved. No part of this work covered by the copyrights hereon may be reproduced or used in any form or by any means—graphic, electronic, or mechanical—without the prior written permission of the publisher. Any request for photocopying, recording, taping, or reproducing in information storage and retrieval systems of any part of this book shall be directed in writing to the Canadian Reprography Collective, 214 King Street West, Suite 312, Toronto, Ontario M5H 3S6.

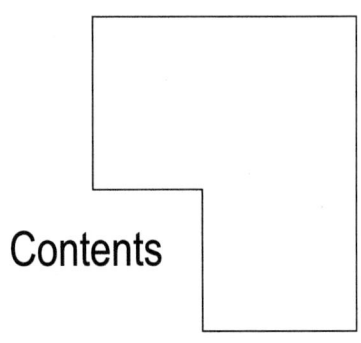

# Contents

Acknowledgments .................................................. vii

Introduction............................................................ 1

**Part One**

*Chapter 1*
"A Literary Giant Scorned?".................................. 15

*Chapter 2*
The Publishing History and
    Reception of Buckler's Major Works ................. 29

**Part Two**

*Chapter 3*
Buckler's Ontological Commitment....................... 63

*Chapter 4*
The Word and the World........................................ 101

*Chapter 5*
Aesthetics and Ethics .................................................................. 127

*Chapter 6*
Arcadia and Death ....................................................................... 153

*Chapter 7*
The Rhetorical Phenomenon: Occupying the Interspace
Where Subject and Object Are Joined by Language ......................... 191

Conclusion ................................................................................. 229

Notes ......................................................................................... 233

Works Cited ............................................................................... 249

Appendix ................................................................................... 261

Index .......................................................................................... 271

# Acknowledgments

I am grateful to the Canadian government's Department of External Affairs for the initial grant that made the research for this book possible, and to the International Council for Canadian Studies for the foreign Canadianists' grant allowing its publication. My thanks also go to those who made the research trip as productive as possible: Claude Bissell for his warm hospitality and encouragement, Andrew Wainwright for the valuable practical advice, Wayne A. Rice, Executor of the Estate of Ernest Buckler, for access to the Buckler papers and manuscripts and permission to make use of all the material, as well as the staff of the Thomas Fisher Rare Book Library who were unfailingly kind and helpful. I am particularly grateful to Lynette Hunter of the University of Leeds, for her invaluable guidance in the early inchoate stages of the manuscript. Her criticism and advice were fundamental in giving it shape. My thanks also go to colleagues from diverse fields in France whose expertise was most illuminating and made certain insights possible: Jean-Pierre Bourdon, Patrick Chézaud, Pierre-Henri Frangne, and Paul Jacopin. I am very grateful to Paul for his unflagging support of my work.

Finally, my thanks go to Sandra Woolfrey for her immediate and wholehearted support of the completed manuscript before handing over the directorship of Wilfrid Laurier Press into the equally competent hands of Brian Henderson.

# Introduction

When The Group of Seven mounted their first public exhibit at the Toronto Art Gallery in May 1920, their forceful, vibrantly colourful paintings of Canadian wilderness shocked an art world accustomed to the European legacy of gentle refined landscapes. Although visitors called the works "disgraceful," fit only for "the ashcan,"[1] and critics in 1932 termed them "a raw upheaval of nauseating colors with pointed rocks and dead trees stuck in at random,"[2] the group slowly awoke part of the Canadian public, used to seeing nature through the lens of another culture, to the fact that an indigenous art and culture were vital to the building of a national identity.[3] Similarly, albeit decades later, in a review of the novels reprinted in McClelland and Stewart's freshly created New Canadian Library series, Constance Beresford-Howe gave a somewhat unenthusiastic evaluation of Ernest Buckler's *The Mountain and the Valley*. She identified the routine of "heavy, ugly farm labour" as making up

---

Notes for Introduction are on pp. 233-34.

the fabric of the novel, which unfolded "with a sense of raw power," but with a style that she qualified as "intolerably oppressive." She complained that so much "portentous imagery is as tiring as being trapped at close quarters with a piledriver." But she acknowledged the novel's distinctiveness and drew a parallel between Buckler's novelistic technique and the Canadian landscape painting that had so outraged critics and public alike: "this is the one Canadian novel I know to share the distinctive quality of some Canadian painting with its simplified, rugged forms, its bold colours and clear atmosphere"(Beresford-Howe 40).

In the catalogue that accompanied their first exhibition, the Group of Seven had declared that "art must grow and flower in the land before the country will become a real home for its people." They created a new space for the Canadian imagination. Similarly, many contemporary writers and critics have expressed the belief that Ernest Buckler was one of the pioneers in creating a distinctive Canadian literature. In a tribute to Buckler organized in 1982, Claude Bissell read out letters from admiring writers that emphasized Buckler's role as an innovator. Margaret Atwood called Buckler "one of the pathbreakers for the modern Canadian novel," adding that all novelists writing today in Canada "are very much in his debt."[4] Margaret Laurence dubbed him "a genuine pioneer in Canadian writing." She argued that he was one of the first authors to write "out of his own perceptions of life and of his own land," one who, instead of taking British or American models, "helped forge a truly Canadian literature."[5] An earlier review from western Canada of a work by Buckler anticipated this appraisal. Although Buckler celebrated the distinctive flavour of his region, the Maritimes, Tom Primrose of the *Albertan* claimed that "Ernest Buckler may have broken ground in Canadian letters which can be cultivated further, even way out West," and insisted that the fictional memoir *Ox Bells and Fireflies* was "a breakthrough or breakaway in the world of Canadian letters" (Primrose 8).

If Buckler did indeed help "forge a truly Canadian literature," it was not by deliberately setting out to do so. He frankly disapproved of yoking art to nationalistic purposes. In a talk he gave on CBC Radio in 1953, he declared:

> it's...interesting to note that all this flapdoodle about the Canadian writer's first obligation being to write like a

> Canadian (however that is), is dying down. If you're a Canadian, and write as honestly as you can about what you know—here or anywhere else—and the result doesn't *sound* Canadian—well, no conscious attitude you strike will ever make it sound so. If you're a Canadian and want to write a distinctively Canadian novel, I'd say: Just trust your natural processes, just trust your natural processes. Don't *try* to write *like* anything—except yourself.[6]

His insistence on artists being themselves, producing a distinctive culture by creating in their own manner, aligns itself with the groundbreaking manifesto that "art must grow and flower in the land before the country will become a real home for its people." The statement actually echoes the words of one of the United States' foremost thinkers, Ralph Waldo Emerson, an influence on Canadian painters and writers from Lauren Harris and Frank Varley to Bliss Carman and Buckler himself.

In the introduction to his first book, *Nature*, nearly a century before the Group of Seven manifesto, Emerson had voiced his young country's need for a national culture in terms with which later generations of Canadian artists and writers could identify: the "foregoing generations beheld God and nature face to face; we, through their eyes. Why should not we also enjoy an original relation to the universe?" (*Nature* 5). In "The American Scholar," Emerson insisted on the importance of each age writing its own books, of each generation writing for the next one, rather than submitting to the tyranny of past dogma (*English Traits* 9). The leader of the American transcendentalist movement, in reaction to the materialists who insisted on "facts, on history, on the force of circumstance and the animal wants of man" (*Complete Essays* 87), advocated the power of thought and will, inspiration, even miracle, and individual culture.[7] He seduced the continent with a style of thinking that gave more authority to intuition than to experience, that made people in the New World feel that anything could be accomplished.

Emerson had a profound influence on North American artists and writers in the nineteenth and first half of the twentieth century. As a result of his teaching, North America could declare itself the champion of simplicity and truth, of the sovereignty of ideas, in opposition to a decadent European civilization in which the "corruption of man" had been followed by "the corruption of language" ("Language,"

*Nature* 37-38). In "long-civilized" nations, Emerson argued, there are hundreds of writers who lead us to believe that they see and utter truths, who actually do not themselves "clothe one thought in its natural garment, but who feed unconsciously upon the language created by the primary writers of the country, those, namely, who hold primarily on nature." When language is in this way adulterated, "new imagery ceases to be created," and "a paper currency is employed when there is no bullion in the vaults" (38). Ironically enough, the country that urged its artists to shake off the dominance of European culture and find their own voice came to dominate Canadian culture in turn, as the Massey Commission reported in 1951 in what amounted to a warning against a takeover by American mass culture. In the first decades of the twentieth century, leading intellectual figures in Canada such as Archibald MacMechan were already calling attention to the imitative quality and lack of inventiveness in a great deal of Canadian writing.

The advent of the transcontinental movement of modernism brought onto the international scene writers who may be considered to be among Emerson's "wise" artists: those who "pierce this rotten diction and fasten words again to visible things" (39) and who create "bullion in the vaults." During the 1920s and 1930s, the innovative formalistic experiments of modernists such as James Joyce, T.S. Eliot, Virginia Woolf, Gertrude Stein, and William Faulkner were at their height. In the United States there was a flowering of cultural nationalism and, simultaneously, a fascination with formalistic effects. Language was developing, was on the move. There was a new aesthetic of language, an interest, particularly in its early stage, in the literary rendering of spoken American English, and so a move toward simplicity, repetition, and even a certain rather liturgical monotony. Yet this was accompanied by the use of multitudinous rhetorical functions and a fascination with the mechanisms of language, of writing itself.

Ernest Buckler's daring use of rhetorical functions, of startling imagery, of what Paul Ricoeur calls "la métaphore vive," places his works firmly within this modernist tendency. Even a small matter such as punctuation can illustrate how Buckler adhered to the modernist questioning of the status of language, of linguistic conventions. A query from John Rackliffe, senior editor at McClelland and Stewart, remarking that in Buckler's manuscript of the future novel *The Cruelest Month*, questions in a dialogue are "punctuated with a comma instead of a question mark," and wondering if these are intentional and should be left alone,[8] calls attention to the deliberate non-use of the question mark initiated by Gertrude Stein and also systematically practised by Faulkner.

Buckler's writing is sophisticated and rhetorically fecund, containing, as with the Faulkner works he so admired, highly figurative and metaphorical language even in dialogue. Claude Bissell reminds us of Buckler's admiration for the diametrically opposed styles of Faulkner and Hemingway, arguing that Buckler felt that "language must be subdued and fashioned to make the reader see and understand the subtleties of human nature. There was no simple way to do this: Hemingway, whom he greatly admired, could do this by cutting language to the bare bones; Faulkner, whom he also admired, could achieve equally splendid results by the full orchestration of language."[9] Buckler himself confessed to his publisher in an answer to an author's questionnaire on his influences: "Maybe when I am tempted to write too fancy I unconsciously feel the ghost of Hemingway rapping on my knuckles: maybe when I get too parenthetical I hear the ghost of Faulkner saying, never mind, that's quite okay."[10] Hemingway probably had his ghostly hands full "rapping Buckler's knuckles." In a letter to the writer Harry Brown, Buckler argued that Hemingway was the first to make it clear that "verbs are where the action is." He self-deprecatingly compared Hemingway's manner of writing so much between the lines with his own style which had "all sorts of adjectives and adverbs tousling around with their hair flying."[11] As he confessed after the publication of his first novel, *The Mountain and the Valley*, Buckler was not particularly interested in verbs or plot. Explaining how he had written his novel, he declared:

> I didn't fret too much about action. For myself, as soon as complications in a book start popping I always feel like muttering to the characters: "Oh, for heaven's sake, stup [sic] scurrying around 'advancing the plot!' Sit still a minute till we get a squint at your insides." For I think that insides are much more important...*and* interesting...than outsides. That action—despite the wire-upper-lip and prose-clipped-with-matscissors school—is far less important than its motivation. ("My First Novel," typescript 2)

His explanation echoes the creed of Henry James, that precursor of modernism, who in the 1908 edition of *The Portrait of a Lady* reiterated the aesthetic concepts of his 1884 essay "The Art of Fiction," declaring himself to be interested "not at all in any conceit or 'plot'" (vi), but in the consciousness of his protagonist, and in the study of memory, imagination, and motive. Modernists such as E.M. Forster would align themselves with James's affirmation that the portrait sketched of his heroine's long "meditative vigil," the simple "representation" of her "motionlessly *seeing*," is as "interesting as the surprise of a caravan or the identification of a pirate" (xvii; James's emphasis). We can detect a close correspondence between Buckler's aesthetic taste and the Forster style, which he described in *The Mountain and the Valley* as having "more to do with the shadow of thought and feeling which actions cast than with the actions themselves" (244). It must also be confessed that the admiration Buckler professed for Hemingway's quite different approach to writing was tempered, to say the least. Among the notes he scribbled to himself, we find the terse sentence fragment, "Reading Hemingway's stories like watching someone squeeze a boil."[12]

William French, then literary editor of the *Globe and Mail*, aptly compared Buckler to a "gemologist," holding words "up to the light to assess their transparency, measure their refractions, probe for their flaws, before deciding to use them,"[13] and Claude Bissell has called attention to Buckler's adventurousness in exploring language, his "boldness in the use of words and complexity of syntax" (*Ernest Buckler Remembered* 65). Yet, a large part of the critical works on Buckler have been biographically or thematically oriented, and have focused on what has been called his sociological and psychological realism, or on his character development. Little attention has been paid to his intense preoccupation with language and aesthetics, or to his tendency to show his own procedures as an artist and to come to terms with the mechanisms of his own creative process, all of which are well within the self-reflexive current of many modernist writers. His protean language with its plethora of conceits and artificially convoluted innovations has never been studied in depth. It will be the subject of my analysis.

Buckler is interested simultaneously in language and in the world. His writing is grounded in phenomenological and ontological concerns; as a trained philosopher, he is preoccupied by the manner in which reality manifests itself to our senses, and with the nature of Being itself. At the same time, he realizes the primacy of language. He adheres to the affirmations of philosophers and linguists such as Gottlob Frege, Ludwig Wittgenstein, and Ferdinand de Saussure, that language (*langue*) re/produces the universe, structuring our perceptions according to its own organization, allowing us to conceptualize all of nature and all of experience. Buckler anticipates Emile Benveniste's affirmation that language represents the highest form of a faculty that is inherent to the human condition: the faculty to symbolize. Consequently, like many other modernist writers, he manifests a fascination with its metalinguistic faculty. He explores the double dimension of language, the fact that it contains both the significance of signs and the significance of its own enunciation. He foregrounds the source of the power of language: its capacity to hold significant statements on significance, and on its own process.

Both dimensions of Buckler's work, linguistic and philosophical, are rooted in aporia: the reader is constantly confronted with the irreconcilable tension between Unity and Diversity that is so reminiscent of "Coleridge's Multëity in Unity" or the "Unity in Variety" proclaimed by Emerson in his essay "Discipline":

> Herein is especially apprehended the Unity of Nature,—the Unity in Variety,—which meets us everywhere. All the endless variety of things make a unique, an identical impression. Xenophanes complained in his old age, that, look where he would, all things hastened back to Unity. The fable of Proteus has a cordial truth. Every particular in nature, a leaf, a drop, a crystal, a moment of time is related to the whole, and partakes of the perfection of the whole. Each particle is a microcosm, and faithfully renders the likeness of the world. (*Nature* 54-55)

Consequently, this book, which addresses Buckler's linguistic and philosophical concerns, will be guided by the interaction between the two spheres, and by the underlying cohesive tension between the Multiple and the neoplatonic prototype of the One.

As a scholar living in France, home of major advances in movements such as structuralism, semiotics, deconstruction, and narratology, I apply close textual analysis to Buckler's work. I shall concentrate particularly but not exclusively on the works, published and unpublished, that have not yet been analyzed or that have been commented on but briefly—till now, critics have focused mainly on *The Mountain and the Valley*.[14] But even though I base my commentary on the elements provided by the text itself, and exclude anecdotes on the author as a man, I also throw light on the text by placing it in the larger context of certain philosophical and artistic currents. My method will involve confronting Buckler's fiction (published and unpublished) with a variety of other texts that are not necessarily direct influences but that can serve a useful exegetic function. My choice of texts does not exclude his own comments, as literary theorist, in his correspondence, essays, or notes made during work in progress.

This introduction will be followed by two chapters on Buckler's literary, educational, critical, and publishing history. Within a writerly framework, I shall give a brief account of his intellectual background and cultural influences, then of the genesis of his eclectic production and its subsequent reception (with respect to agents and publishers, critics and general public) in the United States and in Canada.

Chapter 3 will focus on Buckler's central preoccupation—the nature of Being—and the question of artistic perception and imagination, which mediates between the sensibility and reason. These concepts lie at the heart of Buckler's interest in the transcendental, in the possibilities, limitations, and conditions of knowledge, of metaphysical speculation. I shall throw light on the writer as a thinker by bringing out correspondences with philosophers from Emerson to Merleau-Ponty (who from the 1940s on elaborated a complex exploration of the body and of perception), and I will foreground the aporia in Buckler's texts generated by the confrontation of materialist and idealist currents of thought. Kant's heuristic distinction between the reproductive imagination and the creative imagination will also allow me to study not only how Buckler perceives the world but also how he reiterates, constructs, re/presents the world. Buckler never reduces nature to a spectacle or a representation—we shall see how, in a profoundly Romantic way, it is rather an interlocutor with which the perceiving subject elaborates a dialogue. Furthermore, all the while focusing on the dynamics of aporia, chapter 3 will also explore Buckler's recurrent leitmotifs and systematic recourse to epiphanies in order to arrive at a state of what Merleau-Ponty calls ex-stasis.

Chapter 4 will examine the hermeneutic dimension in Buckler's texts, the relationship between language and the universe that is reflected there, and the way in which the writer reorders the world through *logos*. The relationship of language with the world, argues the French philosopher Michel Foucault, is as much that of analogy as of signifying. Knowledge consists of the restitution of the immense uniform plain of words and of things, in making everything speak. Knowledge involves superimposing upon all the visible marks of the world the secondary discourse of commentary. Buckler adopts the standpoint, elaborated as a linguistic theory by Frege and Wittgenstein, according to which the essence of knowledge is not to see or to show, but to interpret. Foucault's insights on this tradition will provide an analytical framework for my reading. Buckler's stance on language is nonetheless ambiguous: this self-proclaimed farmer sings constant hymns to the artifice of word compositions, yet never ceases to question their adequacy. He celebrates nature and the bookless society of simple farmers and fishermen, yet perceives the universe through the filter of culture. I shall study how the writer thinks and relates to the world in terms of language, actually maps it out in metalinguistic terms. Although Buckler's discourse either overtly or covertly devalorizes artists, and denigrates men's hands that have been "womanized by pen and paper" (*Window* 57), all major human experiences—love, loss, time, death, and even thought—are nonetheless made real, and exist only through language.

Chapter 5 will analyze Buckler's works as heuristic fiction, and will attempt to define the writer's elaboration of an aesthetic philosophy. Like modernist writers as diverse as James Joyce or the French poet Francis Ponge, who set out to "take up the challenge of things in language," like thinkers from Aristotle to Aquinas (who were being reread during the international resurgence of interest in Renaissance studies during the 1930s, propelled by people like Joyce and C.S. Lewis (*The Allegory of Love*), and promoted later in Canada by people like Whalley, Frye, and McLuhan), Buckler pursues the quest for the essence or substance behind *res* and *verba*, thing and thought, putting "the houseness back into the house, the is-ness back into everything there is" (*Window* 111). His aesthetics are grounded in the neoplatonic concept that the beauty of the world is a reflection and projection of ideal Beauty, and that it involves apprehending the supernatural connections that exist between the object and the cosmos, and discerning in the concrete thing the essence, the ontological reflection of the Divine. I shall explore Buckler's Romantic commitment to transmit a vision of ultimate divine truth, to transport the reader to a dimension beyond prosaic reality through revelation of the good. Since the function of beauty is to lead to an underlying truth, and since Buckler believes in the interconnectedness of the good, the beautiful, the true, and the useful (in accordance with Emerson's doctrine of Use), a didactic element is implicit in his work. Consequently, while Buckler fosters love for beauty by re-creating it in language, his writing is grounded in a strong ethical vision, a quest for the universal moral law that, according to Emerson, lies at the heart of nature. For Buckler, the artist's power to create delight by re-creating and transmitting beauty is a moral power. I shall focus on how Buckler's unique celebration of domesticity, of the humble elements that make up the everyday lives of simple people, is a celebration of the good. His texts, we shall see, constitute the social ties that bind the community together and keep its order, whether it be behavioural codes or institutions.

This analysis will be followed by a chapter in which I shall study some of the dominant leitmotifs that generate text. I shall explore the origins and dynamics of the myth of Arcadia, which is an undercurrent in Maritime literature in general, and then the strong presence of death in Buckler's pastoral paradise, notably through the iconographical motif of *Et in Arcadia ego*. Originally a didactic, macabre *memento mori*, the Latin phrase came to take on a contemplative, elegiac dimension through the influence of classical artists like Poussin. Buckler's work, interestingly enough, is fraught with tension between the original grotesque tradition and the soothing classical approach. This will be demonstrated through close textual analysis, notably by examining two early unpublished short stories which were later incorporated into *Ox Bells and Fireflies* and *Windows on the Sea*. The transformations that these pieces underwent reveal a shifting pattern in the writer's aesthetic and philosophical stance.

Chapter 7 will attempt to come to terms with the plasticity of Buckler's language, with its stylistic acrobatics and outrageous combinations. Using the concepts of Merleau-Ponty's "parole parlante/parole parlée" and Paul Ricoeur's "métaphore vive," it will focus on the diverse rhetorical strategies of fusion that channel Buckler's striving toward the One. A close examination of Buckler's recurrent rhetorical devices reveals that the dynamics of his writing involve creating simultaneously, in a paradoxical fashion, a web of ramifications that generate a cross-network of analogies and a corresponding movement from the Many to the One. These tropes constitute the central question in Buckler's work, which is that of aporia. Examining rhetorical devices is a strategy used in many recent studies of aporia, from the early works of Derrida to the current work of Spirat, and the approach is a fruitful one with respect to Buckler. For weaving throughout the fabric of all his texts is a dialectic striving toward synthetic resolution or unity, whether it be in the devices of synaesthesia, enumeration, repetition, paradox, hypallage, or simply the elaboration of convoluted compound words. The metaphor, in particular, plays a central role in Buckler's textual production, as an agent of marvellous transformation, allowing the reader to see one thing under the aspect of another, or to see together, in the same category, what the ordinary gaze does not or cannot associate. Buckler's metaphors do not describe the world—they create a new vision of the world.

To conclude, it is difficult to categorize Buckler's thinking, which is often grounded in Romanticism and Hegelian idealism. Yet the dialectic between his idealism and his desire for the "thingness" of things in all its corporeality, which is central to his work, may be considered problematic by the contemporary reader. Buckler's work may also be considered to be representative of the way mainstream English-Canadian literature of the 1940s-1960s moves from the Romantic to the modernist and, in turn, inflects Canadian postmodernism with a materiality not to be found in the postmodernism of the United States. His texts proclaim the impossibility of ever fully comprehending or articulating the essence of reality. Simultaneously, however, his rhetorical techniques allow him to designate realities for which language does not or cannot provide proper terms, allow him to shatter the frontiers of language and to express the inexpressible.

# Part One

Part One

# "A Literary Giant Scorned?"

Halifax already had its books, newspapers, and magazines when much of the rest of what is now Canada was still unsettled by Europeans. Although Nova Scotia holds a position of chronological primacy in the intellectual development of English Canada,[1] Maritime writers tend now to be marginalized on the literary scene. After the long dominance of Ontario, critics, faced with growing resistance to the hegemony of the centre, have shifted their focus. The gaze has moved westwards, to Prairie and B.C. writers, while writers from Atlantic Canada have remained relatively neglected. Compelling voices have emerged from the Canadian West, along with innovative writing and attractive storytelling, from W.O. Mitchell and Gabrielle Roy to Guy Vanderhaeghe, Aritha van Herk, Thomas King, and Jack Hodgins. But the literature of the Maritimes, widely believed to be a political, social, and cultural backwater, is also rich and heterogeneous—produced by writers such as Frank Parker Day,

Notes for chapter 1 are on pp. 234-36.

Thomas Raddall, Charles Bruce, Hugh MacLennan, and Ernest Buckler, or, among the younger generation, Joan Clark and David Adams Richards, whose novels have the texture and flavour of their East Coast settings.

Having been called "Canada's least-known best writer" (Bissell, "Ernest Buckler: His Prose Reads Like Poetry"), Buckler (1908-84) is best remembered for the 1952 novel that has become a classic, *The Mountain and the Valley*. Margaret Laurence called it "one of the finest novels ever to have come out of this country,"[2] and the poet Alden Nowlan termed it one of the "finest novels in the English-speaking world."[3] Buckler, a modernist writer farmer[4] from rural Nova Scotia, does not gloss over the chronic poverty of a low-income rural area that, during the first decades of the twentieth century, was still without plumbing, electricity, or central heating, often without the car, the radio, or the telephone. His work nevertheless reflects a deep love of the land, and is grounded in the pastoral myth of Arcadia, which, as Janice Kulyk Keefer has pointed out, is a *topos* of Canadian Maritime literature in general (16). Like his contemporaries Gabrielle Roy, Sinclair Ross, and W.O. Mitchell (who shares striking similarities with Buckler, both writing for magazines, television, radio, and the theatre, for instance), Buckler wrote his novel of the land at a time when an increasing amount of Canadian fiction began to reflect the population shift to the cities and to use urban settings.[5] But his book contributed to establishing a Canadian sense of identity and self-worth, and to changing Canadian literature "from a colonial clone—what Northrop Frye, in his famous conclusion to *The Literary History of Canada: Canadian Literature in English* (1965), called 'a poor naked *alouette*' (821)—to an internationally recognized bird of plumage" (Pell 13).

Buckler went on to write a second novel, *The Cruelest Month* (1963), that disconcerted some critics and enthused others, and a fictional memoir, *Ox Bells and Fireflies* (1968), whose lyrical simplicity seduced reviewers and readers alike. In collaboration with the photographer Hans Weber, he also produced a book of prose poems entitled *Nova Scotia: Window on the Sea* (1973), and a collection of satirical prose and verse, *Whirligig* (1977), which startled many critics but won the Stephen Leacock Award for Humour the following year. In these works, which I shall be examining closely in the following chapters, he often anticipated the best of the postmodern Canadian fiction that would follow, by blurring the borders between genres, mixing documentary and fiction, narration and lyrical description, essay and poetry.

Buckler was eclectic. He also wrote plays, short stories, essays, reviews, and newspaper columns—he had a regular column in 1947 and 1948 in *Saturday Night*, in which he wrote on a variety of social, political, and economic issues. Today's public is completely unfamiliar with his plays, since most of them were broadcast by the CBC in one-time-only performances. Like the early plays of Robertson Davies, Buckler's early theatrical pieces often resemble the "nimble acrobatics"[6] of Noel Coward's work, which the young writer so admired. They were light love stories consisting of a concatenation of verbal jousts and witticisms. "Excerpts from a Life," to take but one example, is a one-act play in four scenes. In each scene the heroine, a playwright, receives a proposal of marriage from a different man. Her light banter has a satiric edge. It attacks the young Buckler's favourite targets: institutionalized religion ("I haven't anything against religion—the church has it safely muzzled now, but personally I prefer intelligence"); the myth of progress ("So many know a little and so few know so much. I venture there was more in the head of Mr. Plato than could be distilled from the entire modern cranium"); and overly lyrical or mawkish love poetry ("You flatter too well to love well. Love, like vegetables, is dumb").[7] This last striking simile in particular is illustrative of a paradox that will run through all of Buckler's works—a certain rhetorical mastery coupled with a distrust of words. I shall examine this attraction for and denigration of language in chapter 4.

Some of Buckler's radio and television plays are dramatic adaptations of parts of his novel *The Mountain and the Valley*, or of his published or unpublished short stories (even rejected ones). *Three's a Crowd* was produced within the framework of *The Canadian Theatre of the Air*, which, according to the announcer in the opening routine of the script broadcast by the CBC in May 1942, featured "Canadian actors and actresses in plays by Canadian authors."[8] Many of these radio and television dramas played ironically with the conventions of light comedy and romance. *Four on a Match*, broadcast the preceding year in the same series, was based on an early, unpublished short story, "Five on a Match," and deals with the romantic embroilments of two Varsity roommates who woo twin sisters until eventually the Jack ends up with the Jill (yes, one of the roommates is called Jack, and one of the sisters, originally his roommate's fiancée, is called Jill). In *Four on a Match*, an athletic girl saves a budding playwright in a reversal of the classic runaway horse scene: "She dashed right up alongside Spitfire and grasped his head, holding her own horse's reins in her teeth."9

Not all of Buckler's scripts are so playful. His script for "Choose Your Partners, or Artist's Life," a thirty-minute television comedy, was an adaptation of the rather facetious story "Choose Your Partner," published in the *Atlantic Advocate* in 1962, in which there seems to be little or no ironic distancing. A struggling young writer and his dissatisfied wife exiled in the countryside are visited by their old beaux from the city. Their wistful longings for other, greener pastures, or for what might have been, give way to the realization that they are all better off with the partners that they have. The pat ending of this formulaic story is neatly reinforced by a *deus ex machina*. In a mechanical mirror image of the rejection slip that arrives at the beginning of the play, the story ends with the arrival of an acceptance letter offering the young writer the astronomical (at the time) sum of $500 for his short story.

*A Singing in the House,* produced by John Hobday with the Halifax Theatre in 1960, was a rather clumsy adaptation, necessitating long interventions on the part of a narrator, of "The Stars Were Bright," a sentimental short story with religious overtones about a woman giving birth alone on Christmas Eve. A mysterious woman, whom the reader is brought to suppose is the Virgin Mary, inexplicably appears to comfort her. A truncated version (truncated for reasons I shall examine further on) had been published fifteen years earlier in *Saturday Night*, under the title "Yes, Joseph, There Was a Woman, and Her Name Was Mary." In the script entitled *The Stars Were Bright*, Buckler had pencilled in several dates, indicating that the CBC television version was broadcast on 20 December 1954 and that CBC-Halifax broadcast the material as a radio play in December 1959.

Referring to the radio and television productions of his work, in particular to *The Stars Were Bright,* and *By Sun and Candlelight* which was also produced in Halifax, Buckler acknowledged a certain saccharine dimension, but admitted that he needed the income: "Both these half-hour plays are quintessentially corn niblets, with sugar added…but, hell, a buck is a buck."10 Many of these dramas, catering to the taste of the time, are indeed excessively sentimental, even mawkish, but some of them are sentimental in the best sense of the term, an idea I will discuss further on with respect to his short stories. *By Sun and Candlelight*, a dramatization of the lives, love, and work of Elizabeth Barrett and Robert Browning, first appeared within the framework of the CBC's *Play of the Month* in June 1961 to celebrate the one hundredth anniversary of Barrett's death. Running through the play is a leitmotiv underlying much of Buckler's work, one that I shall explore in chapter 4 on the word and the world: that of the writer struggling to write—the "shadow-merchant in the thistle-down of words."[11]

Buckler's short stories began appearing in Canadian and American magazines such as *Esquire, Saturday Night,* the *Atlantic Advocate, Collier's, Maclean's, Chatelaine,* and *Reader's Digest* in the 1940s. In two stories that appeared in the *Trinity University Review* as early as 1933 and 1934, Buckler was already practising genre crossing. "No Second Cup" was part sketch, part narrative.[12] Then Buckler had his first story, "One Quiet Afternoon," accepted in 1940 by *Esquire*, which in the thirties had become one of the central literary magazines in which most of the leading American writers—Scott Fitzgerald, Dreiser, Dos Passos, Sinclair Lewis, Ezra Pound, e.e. cummings, Hemingway, Dorothy Parker, Tennessee Williams—as well as one Canadian, Morley Callaghan, appeared. "One Quiet Afternoon," elements of which would reappear in *The Mountain and the Valley*, was a meditation on what lies under the surface of things, and on the relationship between the inner and the outer. In the years that followed, "The First Born Son" appeared in *Esquire*, and half a dozen stories in *Saturday Night* alone. W.O. Mitchell, fiction editor of *Maclean's*, published "Penny in the Dust" in 1948, and the following year Buckler's story "The Quarrel" won the first prize of $1,000 in *Maclean's* fiction contest. Buckler would go on to publish almost forty short stories over the next couple of decades, many of which I shall examine. The Buckler Manuscript Collection at the University of Toronto contains many others I shall also look at, either original stories or, as is often the case, different versions (with different titles) of a story. "Puss in the Corner," for example, which was taken by *Esquire* but never used, is a rather witty deflation of clichés that the young author elsewhere had respected. In a version of the Chandleresque one-liner, the narrator says of a quiet girl at a party, "I found out why she hadn't been dancing. She couldn't," and adds the syllepsis "Though she wasn't standing in the first place, she fell silent anyway."[13]

Although Buckler's private journal discloses a hostility to institutionalized religion[14] that we have already glimpsed in the play "Excerpts from a Life," there is an important spiritual dimension in his work, and many of his short stories contain heavily religious overtones or even make explicit biblical parallels. One has only to look at the versions I have mentioned of "Yes Joseph, There Was a Woman...," or at the story published in *Saturday Night* in 1943, "On the Third Day," which is set at Easter and which draws a parallel between Christ's Resurrection and a young husband and father whose plane has just crashed. In the same vein, among Buckler's unpublished early material is the short story set in France, "Unto the Hills," in which the protagonist, Jacques, a young man shot by German soldiers on a Friday, is even more heavyhandedly made into a Christ figure.

Fourteen of Buckler's published short stories were selected and brought together by Robert Chambers in 1975 in a single collection entitled *The Rebellion of Young David and Other Stories*. They include a series of stories that appeared in *Maclean's* that are meditations on childhood, on family relationships, and on the magic of the ordinary. Although Buckler earned the support and encouragement of fiction editor W.O. Mitchell, his short stories have received little critical attention. They nonetheless hold an important place in Buckler's literary history, and in Canadian literary history in general, which is why I shall examine many of them in the following chapters. William French, literary editor of the *Globe and Mail*, was already wondering in 1972 why such a "literary giant" was not receiving more critical attention (23). There are still relatively few full-length critical works devoted to Buckler.[15] And oddly enough, with the exception of *The Mountain and the Valley*, all of the publications of this author, who has repeatedly been hailed as one of Canada's best writers, have been allowed to go out of print.

## Buckler's Intellectual and Cultural Environment

To understand Buckler's writing, it is helpful to place it within the context of a certain intellectual and cultural environment. Buckler was a profound thinker who studied philosophy in the second half of the 1920s, and who came into contact with many influential Canadian figures. A brilliant student, he qualified for university by the age of twelve, a phenomenal achievement in a virtually bookless rural society. After working from the age of twelve to seventeen, he enrolled at Dalhousie University in Halifax, where he obtained a BA in mathematics and philosophy in 1929. During the years that Buckler studied there, Hugh MacLennan was a fellow undergraduate, as was Ernest Howse, who later became a learned preacher and a moderator of the United Church, and with whom Buckler kept up a correspondence. Archibald MacMechan, who had just published his influential book *Headwaters of Canadian Literature* (1924), among the first extended critical studies on Canadian literature that were not mere surveys, was a professor at Dalhousie, giving lectures notably on Carlyle.[16] Among the visitors to the university could be found figures such as Bliss Carman, Charles G.D. Roberts, and Wilson MacDonald.

In 1929, Buckler accepted a fellowship to pursue an MA in philosophy from the University of Toronto. Also enrolled in philosophy and English at the University of Toronto that year, but as an undergraduate, was Northrop Frye, who would go on to study theology. Harold Innis, the prolific thinker whose explorations of social structure and the human condition influenced countless academics in various disciplines, had been on the teaching staff of the University of Toronto since 1920. The dean of Trinity College, where Buckler was a resident, was the Reverend George Frederick Kingston, who would become archbishop of Nova Scotia and Primate of Canada. Buckler pronounced his admiration for Kingston in an early essay reprinted in the collection *Whirligig*, affectionately referring to him as "Freddie" Kingston (Buckler, "Best Place" 12). His principal tutor of philosophy was George Sidney Brett, of whose "giant intellect" Buckler was in awe ("Best Place").

These years in Toronto awakened his literary interests, in particular the opportunity of seeing professional theatre productions at the Royal Alexandra with excellent actors such as Katherine Cornell, Basil Rathbone, Edith Evans, and Orson Welles. Entries in his private journal show that the young Buckler was particularly dazzled by the quick facility for words of Noel Coward, whom he found brilliant to the point of wondering "that he did not get ahead of Bacon and write Shakespeare."[17] In the same journal entry, in which he confides that he is drafting a letter to the playwright, he confesses, "My only criticism of his genius that I can honestly suggest is that his brilliance is too effortless to be praiseworthy." Although he wants to inform Coward of his admiration, he decides not to ask him to read his play, although he is sure he would like it. Coward probably would have liked it, for the plays Buckler churned out in these early years, as we have seen, were romantic comedies consisting of light banter and (often facetious) witticisms.

Among the essays Buckler submitted for his MA[18] was "Prichard's Criticism of Kant's Theory of Knowledge," on Kant's distinction between sensibility and understanding, as well as Kant's doctrine of space (a form of perception). In "Hobbes to Herbart," Buckler explored the schools of association and apperception. Some essays focus on Idealism, such as the one entitled "Progress of Idealism from Kant to Lötze," or the one on Benedetto Croce, who follows the Hegelian tradition, offering a common ground where neo-idealists and neo-realists can meet. Others, like "Relation of Leibnitz to Locke," focus on empiricism and theories of knowledge, while still others, like "Plato's Myths and Their Significance," are metaphysical explorations of pure matter and pure form. "Spinoza's Conception of Experience and Its Evolution" is a search for an abiding object of love behind the illusory, transitory, and unsatisfying mirage of appearances, in the apprehension of which should consist the highest intellectual, moral, and spiritual perfection. This preoccupation, as we shall see, will provide the groundwork for his later fiction.

In "Aristotle's Psychology of Conduct," Buckler explores Aristotle's notion of *akrasia* (*akrates* signifying "without force" or "powerless"). The essay shows that the young Buckler is already interested in "the actions of those who know what is right but who fail to act upon the good," who lack "strength of will."[19] We shall see how Buckler's early short fiction often revolves around these notions of knowledge and will, based on the Socratic idea, handed down by Plato to the stoics, that Reason is the organ of morality, that morality is an affair of knowledge. Even in a later novel like *The Cruelest Month*, the underlying notion is that to see the good is to know it and to do it. Yet, other texts by Buckler, like *The Mountain and the Valley*, are tinged with the Christian doctrine of the Fall, which wounded Reason and weakened the will: for the protagonist David, knowing the truth will not suffice, for the will is weak and action is hard.

Buckler's student essays, as well as later pieces, some published, some unpublished, reveal the author's deep interest in metaphysical considerations, in design and free will, and in the questions of matter and form, of perception and being, that have always preoccupied idealist and neo-idealist thinkers. The concept of perception, particularly, continues to function throughout as a catalyst in Buckler's work. But as Claude Bissell has pointed out, Buckler "always retained a contemptuous attitude towards philosophical speculation that ignored epistemological questions."[20]

Buckler was offered a further fellowship by the University of Toronto to pursue a doctorate, but severe health problems sent him back to the family farm in the Annapolis Valley. The following year, he returned to Toronto and began working for a life insurance company, all the while keeping up his ties with the university and the graduate students he knew. But after five years of living in the city, chronic migraine and dissatisfaction with city life (both recurrent leitmotifs in his texts) once more took him back to the family farm, where he was needed particularly since the death of his father in 1932. Buckler returned to live with his mother and began the routine that would be his for the rest of his life, of farming during the day and writing at night.[21] He submitted a piece to an essay contest the prestigious *Coronet* magazine was running in January 1938 and won the $100 first prize. The prize represented the first cash he had earned from his pen, and was doubly welcome on a farm that essentially provided mere subsistence.

Buckler never derived more than a meager income from his writing, remarking in his humorous piece "Muse in Overalls" that "[t]he average writer's income is roughly that of a Burmese coolie" (*Whirligig* 86). He confided in the early 1950s to the assistant editor of *Esquire* that he lived "from pen to mouth on the perpetual brink of insolvency,"[22] and wryly remarked in an interview three decades later that "all the yachts you could build with your Canadian royalties you could sail in your bathtub."[23] He was actually repeating a remark he had made in 1953 after the publication of his first novel, when he expressed satisfaction at the critical reception and sales in the United States, but regretted that in Canada, where the critical reception was also very good, he could "detect no brush-fire of popular enthusiasm."[24] The validity of the bathtub observation at such a later date indicates that even in the last quarter of the twentieth century, it was still difficult for Canadian authors to live solely on the income of their writing. As his longer fiction generally took him years to write, Buckler depended on his radio dramas, short stories, and articles for most of his income. He often referred gratefully to the supplementary income derived from the CBC, for programs such as the series of fifteen-minute readings from *Ox Bells and Fireflies* done in the late sixties by the well-known actress Evelyn Garbary.[25] In a similar fashion, the three Canada Council grants that he received helped him to complete his books by reducing the pressure to sell essays to magazines.

After Buckler's death, *Books in Canada* published an article by H.R. Percy. Its blurb read: "More than just a farmer who happened to write, Ernest Buckler (1908-1984) was the author of one of the pinnacles of Canadian literary achievement" (11). Referring to the much-repeated quotation by Buckler, "What I happen to be is a farmer who writes, not a writer who farms,"[26] Percy praised Buckler for having recognized a certain way of life "with rare percipience in so young a word-dreamer," as the only one in which "his literary aspirations could take root and flourish." According to Percy, Buckler saw that "the grist for his literary mill lay right there in the Annapolis Valley where he had been formed, among earthy scenes and 'real' people," and that if "he was to render that fast-vanishing life with the uncompromising precision that was its due, he must be in direct and constant contact with it." Six years of city life and "city grubbing" were enough to convince Buckler, Percy argued, that "anything he might write there would be facile and, ultimately, worthless."

I shall examine in a later chapter how Buckler's relationship to work and to the land generated his texts. Suffice it for the moment to remark how in his letters, in total contrast to Faulkner, who bought the plantation Rowan Oak in 1930 and thereafter cultivated the image of a gentleman farmer, Buckler often mentioned, even detailed, his daily labour on the farm. By deliberately naming the individual acts and gestures that make up farm work, he gave them an undeniable reality. For he made it clear that he wrote only in the evenings with whatever energy he had left,[27] and that his days were taken up threshing, seeding, splitting, kindling, milking, bedding down cows, calving, fixing fences, and so forth. In the opening paragraph of "My First Novel," describing the six-year-long process of writing *The Mountain and the Valley* (see note 1, chapter 2, p. 236), he facetiously confessed that in the morning, his "colons (were) really sluggish," and that his life as a writer "really began after supper," when he "slugged it out with the muse for exactly three hours." A letter to the executive editor of his

American publisher Henry Holt, declining an invitation to go to New York on a promotional visit to launch *The Mountain and the Valley*, reveals how his duties as a farmer interfered with and held priority over his tasks as a writer: "There is harvesting, cows, fall fencing, cows, undelegatable family responsibilities, fear that maybe I'd be immediately struck tongue-tied once I *did* get there, allergens, cows...."[28]

The touch of humour, of self-derision, does not attenuate Buckler's message; in fact, it reinforces it. Exactly in the same way, in one of the satirical pieces in *Whirligig*, Buckler insists in an Emersonian fashion on the primacy of the land over culture, although he makes his point with the clever use of a trope combined with alliteration in the following synecdochic comparison: "in any clash between a squash and a sonnet, the squash wins every time." (86)[29] In the same piece, "Muse in Overalls," he deromanticizes living and working on the land, deflating the idealized and romantic notions that we tend to entertain about artists living in the country. He points out that, rather than peace and quiet "amidst Nature's glories" with no impediments to inspiration, reality is composed of "boredom, exhaustion, seasonal slaveries, droughts, hurricanes, flue fires, fencing, hornets..." (84). And just as E.M. Forster uses the cow metaphorically in the opening passage of *The Longest Journey* to represent the confrontation between materialism and Idealism (see the extract quoted in chapter 3, p. 65), so too does Buckler. His cow incarnates, through a humorously anthropomorphic corporeality, the sober, unsentimental, even grinding materiality of farming as action, as act. Buckler informs us that

> cows hate a writer. They'll go to any length to thwart him. As surely as the rain shower knows the exact moment it can drench the hay en route from the field to the barn, a cow knows when you have a deadline to meet. That's the day your gentlest Jersey will suddenly change nature, taunt some cranky Herefords on the next marsh into pitched battle—and draw you away for a whole forenoon of arbitration (and restoration of the barbed wire) between them. (84)

Buckler had read little in the way of major literature as a boy: he confessed to his publisher Henry Holt that in his early years he "never dreamed that anyone ever wrote a book but Zane Grey."[30] Even as an undergraduate he did not enjoy authors such as Dickens or Thackeray who were on the compulsory reading list.[31] He did have a love for Thomas Hardy, which he kept in later life, confiding to a correspondent the secret of his attraction, revelatory of what would become his own writer's quest: "I know of no other place where one gets such intolerably moving pictures of the exquisite melancholy at the heart of things."[32] Although he lived in almost complete isolation on his farm in the Annapolis Valley, the child prodigy now become an adult acquired an extensive knowledge of contemporary literature as well as of the classics, thanks to the miraculously well-stocked travelling lending library from Annapolis Royal. He admitted to Don Cameron he could not live without it, and that it brought to his door everything "from Aeschylus to Mailer" (Cameron, "Interviews," 5). Buckler read voraciously: the librarian Diana Lockhart confided to Claude Bissell that his "appetite for books was both prodigious and exotic" (*Ernest Buckler Remembered*, 9). In "My First Novel" Buckler explained how his contact with other writers, with literature and culture, consisted of the visits of the "Godsent Bookmobile," "Which brought me almost anything I wanted: Hemingway, Henry James, Dylan Thomas, Faulkner, Proust, Mailer....In batches of twenty, sometimes" (3).

That Buckler was familiar with the classics as well as with his contemporaries is evident in the interview with Don Cameron, to whom he confessed his doubts about any contribution he could make to the literary scene when the literary giants had already said everything: "Shakespeare has said it consummately, Dante has said it consummately—so what are *you* going to do?" (8). Buckler's literary allusions range from the ancient to the modern in letters such as the one addressed to Arnold Gingrich, publisher of the literary magazine *Esquire*, in which Buckler referred once more to the "marvellous itinerant Bookmobile that stocks everything from fragments of Sappho to Robbe-Grillet,"[33] or the letter to Don Cameron in which he ruefully admitted facing some "formidable competition" from Jane Austen, and admiringly quoted some "outrageous" lines from *Northanger Abbey*.[34] In a letter to Holt describing his book in progress, *The Cruelest Month*, Buckler explicated the reference of his title: "(You know: 'April is the cruellest month/Mixing memory and desire', etc etc.")", he added, "Do you like Eliot? I do—if he didn't *look* as if he'd be so hyperfinicky with his own excreta."[35] There is also the example of his letter to Diane Mew, assistant editor at McClelland and Stewart, concerning the page proofs of *The Cruelest Month*, in which he requested that they insert two additional quotations to the epigraph page already containing the above quote from T.S. Eliot's *The Wasteland*. It was for "telling and elucidatory effect" that Buckler wished to add two quotations from John Dryden and Shakespeare, namely "Men are but children of a larger growth," and "Motley's the only wear."[36] Diane Mew agreed that "the Dryden and Shakespeare would be most applicable but felt that the book "was sufficiently lucid and penetrating to a discerning reader for such signposts to be unnecessary."[37]

In contrast to writers like Faulkner who read and reread only great classical authors such as Shakespeare, and who claimed to read none of the works of their peers, Buckler read almost everything published by his contemporaries. Claude Bissell argues that Buckler devoured modern fiction, poetry, and criticism, claiming that in his correspondence with him, Buckler "referred to almost every significant contemporary novelist, usually with a distinctive and illuminating comment" (*Ernest Buckler Remembered* 12). The entries in Buckler's private journal from 1936 on also make casual but frequent references to a wide range of writers from Kafka, Camus, and Giono to Shaw, Eugene O'Neill, and Gertrude Stein.

The older Buckler kept up with and greatly appreciated the work of younger Canadian novelists. He admired Margaret Laurence, calling her a "superlative writer" who was "reliably excellent."[38] Complimenting her on *The Diviners*, he wrote to her: "whereas most other writers are merely shadow-merchants cultivating the little window-boxes of adjectives, adverbs, and similar candytuft, you get right down to the very roots of the human herborium."[39] He was also in awe of Margaret Atwood, confessing that when he met her for the first time he was "terrified of her" because she wrote "so well and so piercingly."[40] The qualities he admired in her reveal his demands on himself as a writer: he remarked on her penetration, on the "felicity" of every word and line, the "induplicable sleight-of-heart in seeding the most un-preening observation with generations of Truth."[41] He wrote to compliment her on her poetry, arguing that "It discloses with such shocking immediacy the very is-ness of what is that one is led to thoughts of the sun's absolute knowledge or a mountain's or a river's. Or blood's."[42] Thanking her for sending him a copy of the just-published *Surfacing*, he praised her "stunning achievement," her "firecrackerish string of aperçus": "Hold most books in your hand and they're objects simply:

print on paper. Hold this one and you're in the presence of a living body—breath, blood, and bone."⁴³ On the other hand, the writing of his contemporary, Robertson Davies, was not to his taste. Calling Davies "the poor man's Ustinov," Buckler admitted in a letter to Max Ferguson in which he congratulated the latter on winning the Stephen Leacock Award, that Davies was "clever enough," but he confessed that Davies set up a "curious bristling" in him, and that he could not appreciate a word he wrote "except grudgingly."⁴⁴

Finally, we should keep in mind the fact that Buckler was not only a writer but also a theorist or professional reader, and that his reviews of newly published books appeared regularly from the late1930s on in the *New York Times Book Review,* the *New York Herald Tribune Book Review,* the *Los Angeles Times,* the *Globe and Mail* (notably in the "At the Mermaid Inn" column), and *Esquire,* among others.

His first paid review was for the *New York Herald Tribune Book Review* in 1939, but *Esquire* was actually the first magazine to publish his criticisms, which arrived through the back door, as it were. In 1937 he began to send in a succession of long letters to the publisher, exhaustively reviewing the most recent issues, and they appeared in the readers' column "The Sound and the Fury." The criticisms were brash, often flippant, as in his appraisal of George Jean Nathan's play *The Avon Flows:* "All I can say is, Mr. Nathan can't write Shakespeare like Bacon did" ("Buckler, like the Brook" 10), or his dismissal of Scott Fitzgerald: "Any of his work published in the last ten years has been, as far as his early alleged genius is concerned, quite posthumous" ("Thinks Dos Passos Opaque" 178). They delighted not only the editor, Arnold Gingrich, who eventually devoted a whole editorial to Buckler's contributions, but also the readers. The writer and editor Manuel Komroff wrote an admiring letter to Buckler, advising him to turn his letters into critical articles: "The ten-pins fall in all directions and great names mean nothing. It is lively and most unique. It hits with explosive force. The big ones are not bled white, they just turn white and stay that way."⁴⁵ In his memoir, Gingrich informs us that his readers began to save their issues and read them "only after Buckler's exegetical comments on them had appeared in subsequent numbers" (253). Furthermore, they wrote in to say they would "rather read what Buckler said about the issues than read the magazines themselves," and that Buckler was "worth Hemingway, Fitzgerald, Dos Passos, Dreiser and all the rest put together" (253).

# The Publishing History and Reception of Buckler's Major Works

The account of the genesis of Buckler's production (beginning in the 1930s) and its subsequent reception in the United States and in Canada would be useful even outside of a study of textual evolution. Exploring, understanding, and confronting the reactions to Buckler's texts of his professional environment (agents, editors, publishers, and critics), as well as of his general readership, makes it possible to assess his work not only in the light of certain philosophical and aesthetic currents, but also with respect to the tastes of his time (which vary, interestingly enough, from the United States to Canada). These tastes, and the writer's need to conform to certain trends in order to publish and to earn a living can actually account for certain choices of subject matter, narrative approach, and even style, that many a critic through a contemporary, and therefore distortional, evaluative lens has decried.

---

Notes for chapter 2 are on pp. 236-40.

Finally, an account of Buckler's publishing history is representative of the evolution of the Canadian book industry, which in turn is representative of Canadian cultural history, and its double, perhaps undissociative, dimension of domination by, and resistance to, American culture in its economic, political, and social spheres.

## *The Mountain and the Valley* (1952)

*The Mountain and the Valley*, which took Buckler over ten years to complete,[1] was originally published in the United States on 27 October by Henry Holt and Company, because Buckler's agent at the time was an American, Harold Ober, who also handled Faulkner and Scott Fitzgerald. In Canada, both Macmillan and McClelland and Stewart had expressed interest in the work-in-progress, but Buckler trusted his agent to help him make an impact on the substantial American market and then create an overflow in Canada through an associated domestic publisher. Jonathan Leff, the assistant editor at Henry Holt, enthusiastically wrote to Buckler what the novel meant to him:

> a story of the Simple Life as it is lived in Nova Scotia; a carving of characters in bold, bold relief, then bared to the most minute detail; a remembrance of things past of unusual depth; an overwhelming stream of figures of speech, images of uncanny perception; a skill of successfully mixing viewpoint—and still "writing from the inside," a wistful, sometime somber, sometime gay story of loneliness, and of Man's groping for identity.[2]

Clarke, Irwin had the Canadian rights to the novel but, in spite of the excellent reviews that the novel received, their promotion and marketing strategy was unenthusiastic. In a letter to his American publisher, Buckler asked if there was any way to "dent Clarke, Irwin's apathy about distribution of "The Mountain and the Valley" in Canada" and confessed his doubts as to whether there was "any way of jolting these babies out of their Olympian indifference."[3] Buckler complained that "it was ages" before the Canadian distributor "began to sprinkle around what few copies they *had* ordered." They did not make the books available in time for the mid-November Book Week but were "all sold out at the height of the Christmas trade." Buckler can be excused for looking at Mr Clarke with incredulity when the publisher assured him "with absolute solemnity, that his original order of 250 for all Canada had not been *really* a cautious one," particularly when Holt had sold 7,000 copies in the United States, and when novelist and critic William Bird had assured Buckler that if Macmillan of Canada had been "handling the thing it might have sold 10,000 copies" in Canada. Adding to Buckler's regret was the fact that he considered Macmillan to be "the only publishers in Canada worth a tinker's damn" and that they had been "very anxious to get Canadian rights for The Mountain and the Valley from the beginning." The rights were eventually re-negotiated and McClelland and Stewart came out with a new edition in 1961. By 1972, the New Canadian Library edition had sold 28,000 copies and was in its fifth printing.

Prior to its publication by Holt, several publishers had initially rejected the novel, arguing that it would fail critically and financially because of its alleged lack of action. The Atlantic Monthly Press had taken a first option on it, but ultimately declined to publish after readers' reports claimed that the style was "over-elaborate" and that there was a "lack of narrative movement."[4] The director, Dudley Cloud, explained to Buckler that the American market was poor terrain for first fiction, and that fiction in general was rarely profitable: "We cannot sell a novel of more than 100,000 words for less than $3.00 unless we can foresee a simply astronomical sale. I am sorry to say that I don't think any publisher could hope to break even on *The Mountain and the Valley*."[5] Offering to send him the readers' reports, Cloud advised Buckler to "concentrate on [his] short stories for awhile to build up [his] story-telling technique," which was his "principal deficiency."[6] Similarly, Buckler's New York agent informed him that *The Mountain and the Valley* had been rejected from the Harper Prize Novel Contest because, according to the readers' reports, it was not "successful in depicting characters and their actions."[7] Random House, too, had refused, in spite of "genuflections to occasional passages," judging that there was not "quite enough narrative drive and interest to hold out promise of successful revision."[8]

Nevertheless, the reception in the United States as well as in Canada for Buckler's first novel was ultimately overwhelmingly favourable. It was on the *New York Times*' "Bear in Mind" list for five weeks. The novel touched a chord in critics and readers alike. They approved of Buckler's opposition to contemporary fiction's "relentless insistence on the grimy underpelt of everything" that the author liked to attribute to the influence of writers such as Beckett. He would go on to affirm, "This is an infernal and senseless world, to be sure, but this poor man's Peale still thinks there are still some things in it to celebrate."[9] To the delight of his readers, celebrate he did. The writing is unique if only because the sphere of domesticity that is celebrated there with such sensitivity had until that time been the focus largely of women writers. In describing his own reaction to the novel, Sinclair Ross summed up well the reader's feeling upon finishing *The Mountain and the Valley*: "After a poignant and beautiful picture of a family, the ties and loyalties and tensions, and, above all, the silences, it is the measure of your achievement, of the insight and compassion with which you bring your people to life, that its dissolution hurt so much."[10] Ross's perception of the silence that Buckler paints is an astute one, and reminiscent of his beloved Faulkner's love of silence.[11]

Reviewers of *The Mountain and the Valley* marvelled at the writing, praising "a style pregnant with beauty, amazing details and wealth of color, so that the reader lingers over each sentence, to savor fully its significance and wonder about its aptness."[12] William Arthur Deacon proclaimed the novel, "a true fruit of Freud and James Joyce's Ulysses" [sic] and found it "beautifully written—each word chiselled with loving care."[13] Another reviewer remarked that the novel was "as fresh, as vibrant, as spring sap in a silver birch," and that Buckler's "sensuous imagery [was] unusually evocative" (Porterfield 4). David Anderson Ramsey, in a review for a North Carolina newspaper, declared *The Mountain and the Valley* to be a "brilliant first novel," and praised Buckler's ability "to evoke mood, to portray character, and to picture environment—to say things exactly, as one of his characters expresses it."[14] Ramsey was so enthusiastic about the novel that he did something that professional reviewers rarely do: he wrote to Buckler to thank him for "one of the most rewarding reading experiences" of his life.[15] Buckler himself, in a letter to his American publisher Henry Holt about his second novel-in-progress, mentioned how Arthur Phelps had given a trans-Canada broadcast in which he labelled *The Mountain and the Valley* "surely the best writing in the form of a novel ever to come from Canadian hands."[16]

Although Buckler's first novel was published at the same time as many other excellent novels by established writers, including Steinbeck's *East of Eden*, American critics took notice, mentioning Buckler in the same breath as D.H. Lawrence, Thomas Wolfe, and Hemingway, as in Sterling North's column in the *World-Telegram and Sun*, New York, in which he paid homage to two novelists: "To Hemingway, for his comeback with *The Old Man and the Sea*, and to Ernest Buckler, a Nova Scotian farmer, who against tremendous odds, loneliness, poverty and back-breaking labor has come through with a fresh and exciting first novel (qtd. in French, "Ernest Buckler" 23)." The critics particularly appreciated the novel's complexity and original voice. The *Boston Sunday Post* pointed out that its rural characters were "not the simple country louts of so much American fiction,"[17] and compared Buckler to Willa Cather in his feeling for imagery and angle of approach. The *Los Angeles Times* found remarkable Buckler's "brilliant, vibrant delineation of scene" (Merlin). The reviewer from the *Miami Herald* gave the author a unique place in North American writing, arguing that Buckler's "interweaving of people and places, of men and women with their environment, is a technique that is often found in European writers, almost never in authors of this hemisphere."[18] The *Washington Star* drew attention to Buckler's "brilliant gift of drawing images," which "needle almost every paragraph with a shock of recognition," and recommended taking the rich mixture in short bites "to savor its full flavor" (Sartwell). The *Boston Herald* claimed the novel had "all the proportions of stupendous, pounding tragedy" and that its characters stood out "as though limned with an etcher's tool" (Fran Blake).

Buckler's novel achieved popular as well critical success. A fairly dependable indication of the former is the fact that *Reader's Digest* went on to publish a five-page condensation of the novel's first chapter for its home market, and then in 1969 asked for Commonwealth and foreign rights for chapter 16. Almost two decades after its publication, Buckler wrote to Pamela Frye of McClelland and Stewart following receipt of his royalty statement, pleased at how well *The Mountain and the Valley* was still selling. He expressed amazement that "even the violentest young" seemed to like what he labelled a "terribly old-fashioned novel."[19] He recounted how a professor at the University of New Brunswick had sent him quotes from the exam papers of his classes in English literature, in which the students "came over all nearly *lyrical* over it. And they were *engineers* yet!" In an earlier letter to Don Cameron, Buckler had expressed similar surprise at the novel's continued success with students, and clarified what he meant by the term old-fashioned: "[n]ot much screwing, not much violence, no detailed blow jobs...quite out of the modern stream."[20]

Yet not all readers expressed enthusiasm for the novel. Buckler was amused to see that for every person in Canada who welcomed the novel's "frankness," there was another who recoiled "from any mention of Life's—which is to say, his own—basic impulse, s-x."[21] In a letter to Jack McClelland ten years after the publication of the novel, Buckler evoked some "amusing" incidents with respect to the novel's reception among local readers: "[a]ctual burnings by the pathologically prim were reported." Buckler remarked that "it was often the very types whose own sexual life and lingo was the untidiest who took exception to the book's frankness."[22] Many readers continued, decades later, to be shocked by Buckler's treatment of sex as a natural function. An article dated 20 March 1970 from the *Canadian* in Charlottetown recounts that parents complained to the education minister, Gordon Bennett, that a novel denounced by MLA Keir Clark in the PEI Legislature as being "very low, vile and degrading" was nonetheless required reading for the Grade 11 students of Montague Regional High school. The parents asked to have *The Mountain and the Valley* withdrawn from the curriculum.

The American publishers who had rejected *The Mountain and the Valley* had not done so for questions of prudishness, and although they criticized what they saw as a lack of narrative movement, they did sense that Buckler was "trying to articulate the inarticulate."[23] Buckler, who argued that his characters, representing "a psychological cross-section of life in a small Nova Scotia village about the time 1910-43" were "no less unintricate for being inarticulate,"[24] reversed tactics for his next novel, *The Cruelest Month*.

## *The Cruelest Month* (1963)

Significantly enough, even before the October publication of *The Mountain and the Valley*, Buckler had sent his American publisher his ideas for his next novel:

> I am half inclined to try a novel with a setting somewhere like Greenwich[25] (which I know well), with characters more

> articulate, if not more complicated, than the characters in the present book. (It is sometimes rather limiting to have to avoid all observations in dialogue which wouldn't come naturally to a rural spokesman.)

Buckler went on to protest that he did not mean to write about

> those chatterboxes which so many of the bright boys nowadays go in for, who keep flapping their tongues (and their wrists) at each other all the time about filigreed little whimsies that couldn't be closer to nothing—but well-rounded people with a certain urbanity (in the best sense of the word) about their outlook.[26]

I shall deal in chapter 4 with Buckler's ambiguous relationship with language, so perceptible in the above passage. In the meantime, we can note that the value judgments underlying the pejorative lexicon censure pure verbal skills as sterile and, indeed, lacking virility. For, in Buckler's cultural environment, real men don't talk, and in his notes on *Window on the Sea*, he disparages city men whose hands have been "womanized by pencils."[27]

Interestingly enough, the young Buckler's early short stories and radio plays were peopled with these "chatterboxes," undoubtedly modelled on the facetious dialogues of the Noel Coward plays he had so admired. A few years later, Buckler would admit to Claude Bissell that he realized that this admiration belonged to "callow and totally mistaken enthusiasms," which would be revealed now that he had sold his papers to the University of Toronto Library. He explained, "When my generation were all young buds and thirsting for 'sophistication,' we thought that Noel Coward epitomized it."[28] There is nonetheless still some "flapping of tongues" even in his second novel, and a good deal of forced "sophistication," whether the "little whimsies" making up the subject of talk be ironic or not. The characters thrown together belong to two separate worlds. There are the highly educated, highly articulate characters who talk like books, and the characters who are inarticulate, even illiterate. The two camps and their interaction embody, as I shall demonstrate in chapter 4, Buckler's ambiguous relationship to language, which is ostensibly placed at the positive pole on the axis of values, but simultaneously devalorized by various authorial devices. Buckler's desire to walk down both sides of the street at the same time caused him to write three different versions of the ending which revolve around the decision of Paul, the main protagonist of *The Cruelest Month*, to marry his illiterate housekeeper, Lettie. We see from a letter he wrote to his editor Jack Rackliffe that Buckler was torn between the original ironic ending, with its "you can't win twist," and the desire to "protect" the uneducated Lettie, at whose expense the irony is constructed.[29] Determined to show Paul she too can talk "proper," Lettie watches her conjugations and tells Paul, proudly, that they will go and see the doctor "Just as soon as you've *drank* your coffee" (298). The alternative "straight" ending lamely had Lettie succeed in correcting herself in an anticipated conversation with Paul: "Now remember," she cautioned herself out loud. "'Isn't it a lovely morning!' *Isn't*." But finally it was the original ironic ending that was left.

Although publishers' reports had noted the difficulty in *The Mountain and the Valley* of articulating "the inarticulate," the manuscript of the new novel disconcerted agents and publishers precisely because its characters were so (over)articulate. Ivan Von Auw Jr, Buckler's agent at Harold Ober Associates, expressed perplexity at "so many characters [being] introduced in so many places and time sequences,"[30] and objected to the point of view shifting from the third to the first person. Henry Holt, followed by Doubleday, refused to publish it, objecting to (although this was already 1960) "the disjointed narrative, the jumps in time," and the "awkwardness of Buckler's style."[31] Doubleday refused to enter it for the Canadian Novel Award, claiming that in spite of "some really effective scenes," the novel as a whole did not quite "come off."[32] The novel, which contains small sections of narrative taken from the short story "The Harness" (later to be included in the collection of short stories under the title "The Rebellion of Young David"), does at times lack a certain cohesion. Buckler meanwhile had slightly revised the manuscript, confiding to his agent that he was aware that *The Cruelest Month* was "largely a novel of ideas and that such [were] not especially marketable." He admitted to Von Auw that the manuscript had taken so many years and involved "so many tussles" that he could not make any "sweeping changes in content" but that he would be "willing to make almost any concession to a publisher who'd clear it off the boards" for him.[33] In the end, Von Auw refused to handle the manuscript, then called "The Cells of Love," finding the style "frequently irritating."[34]

But when McClelland and Stewart brought out the New Canadian Library edition of *The Mountain and the Valley*, they enthusiastically expressed interest in publishing the new novel, which as I shall demonstrate, is not only a novel of ideas, but a profoundly moral and didactic work. Ironically, John Rackliffe, the senior editor, expressed fervent appreciation for the very elements that his American counterparts found disconcerting or irritating. In a letter to the author, he called the manuscript "an astonishing book," and went on to say:

> The book is a truly marvellous piece of work. One keeps being hit by it—as one was continually hit by THE MOUNTAIN AND THE VALLEY, though the two books are in so many ways utterly different. That is one thing, indeed, that is impressive; this book could not remotely have been predicted or extrapolated from the earlier book. You deserve all kinds of congratulations—and straight priase [sic] and applause. And I feel honoured to be amond [sic] the first to have the good fortune to tender them. It must be—can you relish and appreciate it yet?—a magnificent feeling to have come out on the other side, with a piece of work so rich and so complex.
>
> ...The book, in this sense, has not one moment, and not one sentence, which is sluggish or groping or clumsy or imprecise.[35]

Rackliffe's only tentative criticism was that the book might be *too* brilliant. He wondered if the reader would not crave some relaxation of the tension, some neutral "passage work"

> which would permit him to unwind a notch or two, to stop being perpetually on his toes? I.e. does he say, "Surely [the characters] can't all always be this subtle, this intense, this perceptive? They must have their moments of unawareness, moments when their reply to a brilliant statement is not an equally brilliant statement of their own but instead a well-meaning but languid "Huh?"[36]

When shown the galleys of *The Cruelest Month*, Claude Bissell wrote to Jack McClelland to admit certain flaws: "the writing is much more involuted and metaphysical than it was in the first novel, and it would be greatly improved by deletions and revisions." Bissell nonetheless maintained that Buckler was Canada's "finest artist in prose." He argued: "He is the only Canadian novelist who writes in depth and who makes a consistent effort to get below the surface. He looks at the world under a powerful microscope and, although the detail is often irritatingly complex, it is cumulatively effective."[37] Canadian reviewers agreed with Bissell, it would seem. After the novel was published, the *Montreal Gazette* claimed Buckler could "say more in one page than most authors say in a whole book," recommending the book as one "to be enjoyed again and again for pure pleasure" (James). The *Winnipeg Tribune* maintained that *The Cruelest Month* contained "some of the most evocative prose ever, in brilliant descriptions of and response to nature's moods, and sometimes ruthless baring of motive and impulse in the man and woman of today." The *Tamarack Review* claimed that the "magic" was "in the richness of the texture and the freshness and fidelity of the revelation of relationship."[38]

In spite of the favourable reception in Canada, no American publisher would agree to publish the novel for the American market, although Buckler expressed a willingness to make any required changes.[39] One after the other, World Publishing; Charles Scribner's Sons; Little, Brown; Random House; Harcourt, Brace and World; George Braziller; and Atheneum Publishers, all declined. The board of Holt once more refused to publish the book, considering it "a minor offering."[40] The New American Library of World Literature called it too "subtle" to be successful as a hardcover, and explained that it could not be reprinted as a mass market publication without hardcover success.[41] The editorial department of Little, Brown found the novel too "slow-going" to be successful in the American market.[42] Hiram Haydn, editor of Harcourt, Brace and World, also pointed out that "the quiet nature of this book [would] make it very difficult to sell on the American market."[43]

Just as W.O. Mitchell had done before him, Buckler faced a divergence in taste between the Canadian and American markets—one that had come about in the space of one decade—along with an evolution in marketing strategy, if not taste, within the American market. The quiet and slow-paced quality of Buckler's first novel had not stopped it from being successful in the United States; Buckler's second novel would not be given a chance.

The exclusion from the American market ultimately compromised Buckler's chances of success in the Canadian market. For in a letter to Buckler's agent at Harold Ober Associates, who was trying to arrange for simultaneous publication of *The Cruelest Month* south of the border, Jack McClelland explained a few grim truths concerning the dependence of the Canadian publishing industry on its American counterpart:

> It is greatly to an author's advantage to have simultaneous publication in the U.S.A. and Canada. There are a number of reasons for this. Firstly, there is the undoubted fact that the spill-over of American publicity helps Canadian sale. American publications, such as *Newsweek*, *Time* Magazine, and so on all have comparable circulation in Canada....The spill-over is useful. Unfortunately there is little or no effect the other way. It also seems to be true that the spillover of publicity if the book is published later in the United States doesn't serve much useful purpose. Why this should be I don't know, except that because of the nature of the trade today the book, if it is a novel, is usually, as far as the Canadian bookseller is concerned, dead by that time for practical purposes.[44]

McClelland went on to explain the advantage, for everyone concerned, in Canadian and American editions being produced from the same type, creating economies of scale and reducing the retail price of the book. His final argument for simultaneous publication was his impression that American publishers tended to be more enthusiastic when they were publishing a book that had not already appeared in North America, remarking that McClelland and Stewart had seldom made a sale to an American publisher when the book had already been published.

This was to be the case with *The Cruelest Month*. The novel sold only about 2,000 copies in Canada, and quickly went out of print. But it was not the only iron in Buckler's fire.

## *Ox Bells and Fireflies* (1968)

In 1952, before the publication of *The Mountain and the Valley*, in the same letter to the associate editor at his American publisher in which he mentioned his ideas for his next novel, which would be *The Cruelest Month*, Buckler was thinking even further ahead. He described a project that would, one and a half decades later, lead him to dispense with plot altogether, and abandon the form of the novel for the fictional memoir or philosophical prose poem, resulting in *Ox Bells and Fireflies*. He informed Henry Holt that:

> some day I'd really like to do astraight [sic] repertorial account of the "mores" of village life as I've known it here. With a literal, attemptedly more humorous (though still sympathetic and understanding) approach than the novel has. There are thousands of intriguing things about their ways and speech and customs that the novel didn't even hint at.[45]

Buckler's description of the final text, completed sixteen years later, eerily echoes the above announcement of the tentative project, formulated in 1952. In the Author's Questionnaire that Buckler filled in for his publisher in 1968 for promotional purposes, he described *Ox Bells and Fireflies* in strikingly similar terms:

> The overall purpose of the book is to give a comprehensive picture, descriptive and analytical, of Nova Scotian village life at the time of my childhood and later, in the vicinity of historied Annapolis Royal. This way of life, with all its distinctive customs, institutions, values, tasks, recreations, idioms of speech and behaviour, atmospheres and textural variety, has now vanished forever. I have tried to triangulate it, so to speak, within the mingling stream of heritage, material change and social mutation. Using fact, incident and character as the prisms of theme.[46]

We can nevertheless note the unfortunate shift of aspect (from the incomplete aspect "there are," "as I've known" to the perfect, completed, punctual mode of "at the time of," "later") which attests to the loss of a world in the space of a decade and a half, a loss made explicit by the use of the verb "vanished" and irrevocable through the adverb "forever."

In this final description of this work, which he himself calls "a fictional memoir," Buckler theorizes on the hybridity of his genre. "The backbone is literal fact; but whenever a touch of the imaginative (which is quite different from the imaginary) seemed to focus the truth clearer than any clinical photography of strictly literal detail, I have tried to supply it." Buckler's distinction between the imaginative and the imaginary is evocative of the famous distinction that Faulkner made between fact and truth—"Facts have nothing to do with truth." In an interview he granted to Don Cameron, in which he discussed the factual dimension of *Ox Bells and Fireflies*, Buckler insisted, like Faulkner, that "fact is no good novelistically," and that "fiction probably can construe the circumstances better than fact baldly states." He maintained that "fiction is so often not only more emphatic, but it's *truer* than fact" (Cameron, "Interviews" 9). His fictionalized fact allowed him to avoid the flaws of both "the dreary documentary" and the "wispily elegiac excursion into the 'happy valley' of childhood." When Buckler was looking for a new American agent, he sent the manuscript still entitled "Fireflies and Freedom" to Josephine Rogers of Collins-Knowlton-Wing, a subsidiary of Curtis Brown, Ltd., with the following description: "It is not really a novel, but a memoir sometimes cast in imaginative form, the kind of novelistic non-fiction on which I think Capote is quite wrong in his claim to have registered the first patent."[47]

Although Rogers agreed to take on the book, publication of the manuscript proved once more to be an arduous task. Buckler's agent, Ivan Von Auw Jr, had declined to take it on, explaining that he did not "see it making much of an impact on the American market."[48]

Jack McClelland meanwhile agreed enthusiastically to publish the work. In his acceptance letter to Buckler, he described his personal reaction upon reading the text: "It gave me more pleasure, more enjoyment, more emotional involvement than anything that has come my way in a very long time. It's superbly well-written, and I truly believe that in this work you have got right to the core of life in a way that has seldom been achieved."[49] McClelland expressed astonishment at Von Auw's reaction, and was confident that he could help Buckler find an American publishing house that would be delighted to publish the manuscript. He reassured Buckler that his publication of the book was not "contingent" on finding an American publisher to publish simultaneously, but that this would be greatly to Buckler's advantage as well as to that of McClelland and Stewart. This echo of McClelland's analysis of the power wielded by the American publishing industry in the 1962 letter to Buckler's agent I quoted previously impels us to conclude that not much had changed in the way of commercial dependence in the intervening five years.

The manuscript of "Fireflies and Freedom" was refused by three American publishing houses. Dodd, Mead wrote to Buckler's agent acknowledging that the book contained "a great deal of charm and sensitivity" and that the author wrote "convincingly of his part of the world." But the book seemed to them to be "rather too special"[50] to justify taking it on. Harcourt, Brace and World appreciated the "lyric passages of real quality" and the "wholesomeness" of the memoir, but found the writing "uneven."[51] Scribner's explained that it could not manage anything so "abstract" or "nostalgic," implying that the book leaned toward the kitsch. "There is a lot of poetry and feeling in it," Anne MacDermot wrote. "Almost too much. Like solid crème de marrons."[52]

In the end, Alfred A. Knopf, which Buckler delightedly proclaimed "the finest house of all,"[53] agreed to publish in the United States for precisely the same reasons that Scribner had declined. In a warm acceptance letter to Buckler, Angus Cameron declared that as an old Indiana farm boy, he had experienced a shock of recognition when he read the manuscript. He declared that there was a receptive audience for books in that "field," that "there are a great many people around who remember a simpler world and an even greater number of people who don't remember it but are interested in it." Cameron believed that Buckler's book was "the most evocative book of that lost world."[54] In a subsequent letter, he assured Buckler that there existed an "identifiable market [in the United States] for books that recover our agrarian past."[55]

After expressing delight with the book, Cameron nevertheless made some suggestions for revisions. He pointed out that in the series of vignettes, anecdotes, and character sketches making up the structure of the book, "Children," the Mark and Laura episode, did not seem to belong. He claimed that "it seemed that the whole piece had been imported as if perhaps it had been written originally for another purpose."[56] Cameron was right: it had been imported. The rather clumsy piece felt tacked on because it was one of three unpublished variants of a story, including "Hares and Hounds" and "The Day before Never," written under the pseudonym Owen Swift. The latter story was identical, except for the opening sentence and the names of the characters, to "Children," which in turn seemed to be the embryo to the David–Effie relationship in *The Mountain and the Valley*. Cameron prevailed, and the piece was cut from *Ox Bells and Fireflies*. Nevertheless, in spite of Cameron's keen eye for detecting tonal shifts, Buckler did successfully incorporate into the book much of his earlier material.

"The Bars and the Bridge," published in the *Family Herald* in April 1958, for example, became the chapter "A Man," the principal modification consisting in a shift from first-person narration to third. "A Little Flag for Mother," published in *Farm Journal* in May 1963, became the chapter "A Woman." "The Balance," an unpublished short story, was revised to become the chapter "Another Man," which also contained echoes of "Snows of Christmas, Snows of Spring," another unpublished story. These stories all reflect a theme that provides the dynamics for a number of Buckler's texts, and that I shall examine closely in the following chapters: the theme of the outsider, the bleak marginality of those who have no partners and no children.

We can also note whole chunks of *Ox Bells and Fireflies* in *Christmas in Canada,* the cantata for chorus and narrator that Buckler wrote in collaboration with the composer Keith Bissell, the world premiere of which was performed in December 1967 in Halifax. But here it is more likely that Buckler dipped into his manuscript of *Ox Bells* to nourish his script, than the reverse.

Cameron's suggestions for revisions also focused on Buckler's distinctive technique of chaotic enumeration, which I shall analyze in chapter 7, and which he referred to under Buckler's own terms as the "bare recital of selected details."[57] Cameron questioned the "sometimes seeming arbitrariness" of the use of this technique and remarked that its overuse could be "a kind of substitute for incorporating some of the impressions more fully." Wondering if there was not "[t]oo much of a muchness," he suggested certain cuts and redistributions, pointing out that when they are overdone they "destroy the illusion of identification" and become "noticeable as devices." But when Buckler himself suggested certain cuts, notably certain chapters that might be too sentimental,[58] Cameron dissuaded him, arguing that they were not sentimental but "filled with sentiment."[59]

Wishing to capture Buckler's "atmosphere of scene and object" in what was already a cross between essay and narrative, poetry and prose, Cameron decided to include in the book some atmospheric headpieces and a few tailpiece spots, and invited suggestions for the artist. Buckler liked the idea of an interaction with drawings, which "could give a subtle lead-in to the text and heighten its penumbra," and suggested that the artist draw from the recurrent images in the text, or any of "the other basic eternals which are the bread, wine and salt of country life. Sparse in detail, but a kind of synecdoche."[60]

When the book was published, these recurrent synecdochic images touched a chord in most reviewers, who praised Buckler's poetic prose. Although balking at the richness of the imagery, Kenneth Bolton, in a review for a Saskatchewan newspaper, found resemblances to Dylan Thomas in Buckler's lyrical "poetic sensitivity."[61] In the *Albertan,* Tom Primrose from Alberta hailed Buckler as Canada's own

Robert Frost or Carl Sandburg. He argued that *Ox Bells and Fireflies* was "poetry of the same kind as Robert Frost's, rural, close to the land, natural, about the everyday things of life which may pass unnoticed until someone with a sense of poetry in the soul draws our attention to them" (8). Claude Bissell, freely acknowledging certain flaws, called attention to the innovative quality of the writing: "the style is metaphysical—a rarity in the flat landscape of our prose. There is some overreaching, places where the words refuse to be twisted or bent to support the thought. But there are many triumphs, passages of great and poignant beauty." He went on to label *Ox Bells and Fireflies* "one of the most important Canadian books of this century" ("Masterly Return"). The writer Harry Brown dramatically described the powerful impact of the book, with the confession: "I was sent sprawling by the first of a series of emotional hammer-blows that kept sending me to the canvas again whenever I struggled to my knees and, after I'd reached the end of the book, left me dazed for a solid week."[62]

Jack McClelland expressed shock that *Ox Bells* had not been selected for final consideration for that year's Governor-General's Award, claiming that the book was "not only perhaps the finest piece of Canadian writing published in 1968, but also [wa]s one of the finest books ever written and published in this country.[63]

The sensuousness of the writing, its ability to re-create the world of touch and smell, was also detected by many a reviewer on both sides of the border. Ed Wellejus, in the Erie, Pennsylvania, *Times* described how the book brought to the reader with "a sudden stabbing immediacy...an odor acrid or delicious, a remembered vagary of wind or sun, the timbre of a voice" as well as the "true look of the men and women who peopled the Nova Scotia of the author's boyhood" ("The Bookshelf"). William Ready from Hamilton's McMaster University Library, recommended the book to all libraries, arguing that it imparted "a sure wild beauty, a bitter-sweet quality like verbena," and claiming that the "fecundity of the earth possessed the writing."

For other reviewers, however, this 'fecundity of the earth' was inappropriate, and the same prudishness that we detected in the reception of *The Mountain and the Valley* once more manifested itself:

> The book could be called earthy in places. Buckler is a frank writer who does not gloss things over. At first some of the

> passages come as a bit of a shock. One's reaction may be, "Oh, Lord, not here, not in this book I've been enjoying so much [sic] does sex have to be brought in like any other modern book?"
>
> ...[T]he frankness is blended with humour most of the time...but surely there are some books in which raw sex doesn't need to be dealt with. (Primrose 8)

This prudishness was quite ironic, considering that it was just such an attitude that Buckler implicitly condemned by overtly praising his Norsteaders' natural attitude to sex, and their ability to "pierce the sham and shirring that becloud and barnacle a thing's honest password" (*Ox Bells* 170). For Buckler's characters, sex was "never an open subject" but neither was it "one so underground that it moldered or grew nightmares of itself." Their approach was a balanced, healthy one: the inevitable "sniggering" was done openly, with little that was "sidelong or septic." Sex was wisely seen as a "blend of comedy and sheet lightning," with sometimes the lightning uppermost, sometimes the comedy—"what can be more comic than people with their mouths together like guppies,' sprawled in the pose of grasshoppers?" (169). It is no doubt this attitude, which refused to romanticize physical love, which painted the beauty of sensuality and of the flesh all the while gently mocking the vicissitudes of the mating dance, that disconcerted certain readers and critics, happily a minority.

Others were enchanted by Buckler's language, by what James Richmond of Savannah, Georgia called the "pure beauty which spins cobwebs," by the "lush and rich style" (the Kansas *Wellington*), the "exquisite imagery" (*The Houston Post*).[64] Richmond even announced that an excerpt from the book was to appear in a digest of books.[65] But the novelist and playwright Harry Brown was perhaps not so pessimistic in his judgment of the Average Reader, when he prophesied poor reception for *Ox Bells and Fireflies*: "When it comes to books as fine as this, literacy is not enough. The Average Reader, so-called, simply lacks the sensitivity, as well as sufficient spiritual reserves, to be allowed to read this latest work of Mr. Buckler."[66] An anecdote that Buckler recounted to a great number of his correspondents and interviewers[67] certainly confirms Brown's appraisal. It concerned the dubious compliment of an admiring reader from Cape Breton, who wrote Buckler: "I enjoyed your book. The print was so clear." Brown's evaluation of the average reader's tastes and competence was certainly correct as far as sales of *Ox Bells and Fireflies* were concerned. Two pieces from *Ox Bells* had reached a mass audience by appearing in the huge *Reader's Digest* book *In Search of Canada*, a compendium of text and pictures that was published in 1971. But four years after the publication of *Ox Bells*, the book had sold less than 3,000 copies in Canada.

## *Nova Scotia: Window on the Sea* (1973)

In 1970, Buckler informed Angus Cameron of Knopf that he was collaborating with a photographer on a collection of prose sketches and photographs. Buckler noted that his text would be "not so much echoing but contrapuntal prose."[68] Jack McClelland was enthusiastic about the manuscript, but delayed publishing it, hoping that an American publisher (he had Viking in mind), would also pick it up. Buckler explained to Cameron that the Canadian publisher was stalling in order to obtain simultaneous publication, because "shared sheets" reduced costs.[69]

When Buckler finally sent the complete manuscript to Pamela Frye, senior editor at McClelland and Stewart, he explained his attempt to create a subtle interaction between text and photograph. As he had indicated to Cameron, he had refused to try for close parallel, discarding the method he described as "the primer 'A is for Apple' idea," where the picture was on one page and opposite it "something, in effect, like 'This is a tree....'" Rather, he tried to find ways other than "direct duplication" for the text and the pictures to "fit each other." His purpose was to express mood, a "geography of the spirit," rather than the usual "pasty/toothpasty 'travelogue' prose." He was convinced that his text needed to be almost as "dense" as poetry, and would spend a whole day over one line "to get this kind of compactness" that was more "allusive than spell-out-y."[70]

Buckler and Hans Weber, the photographer, exchanged letters over a period of years during which they discussed questions of format, structure, development of theme, pending contracts with publishers, and problems of editing. In one letter, Buckler described to Weber the "pointillist thing" he was trying to "bring off" in their book—namely, to "drag objects in and hope that their, if you like, penumbra, will summon to the reader's mind (do I dare to say 'heart') a whole constellation of feeling."[71] In an earlier taped conversation in which Buckler and Weber discussed their collaboration, each giving his reactions to the other's work, the writer said he had tried "to drop as many words with their implications" as Weber had "dropped" photographs. He illustrated his idea with "fence stakes," which give an entirely different feeling "leaning against the February dusk" than when "they're standing up straight with their perpendicularity." Weber nevertheless expressed apprehension that people might be inclined to find the text reiterative. Buckler retorted that the apparent reiteration was absolutely deliberate and that it is only when reiteration is inadvertent that you "fall flat on your ass." He pointed out his strategy of using the same "bare-stripped nouns" over and over again to give the reader an intuition: "you stick it [the noun] in obliquely and hope it will make a sediment of the constants." Weber agreed that "nouns with photographs" were better than "the clausal thing," and remarked that his own photographs tended to be nouns. Buckler pointed out that if his prose had a fault, it could be accused of being "too adjectival," but that it was balanced by the photographs which were nouns that beckoned.[72]

The taped conversation between the writer and the photographer makes it clear that the work, which they intended to call "Nova Scotia: Lamps and Latitudes," was already well advanced by 1968. When Weber asked Buckler to change his ending, the writer balked at making any "wild structural changes" or "major rewriting," saying that "when you've worked at something so long, it gets set like cement," adding that "a line takes me a day you know." Nevertheless, Weber persuaded Buckler that the ending needed "an injection of adrenalin," and suggested taking a small earlier section of dialogue between a small boy and his father about a gigantic stone the boy's grandfather had once lifted, and bringing it out at the end. The new ending would have the advantage of closing on the powerful words "No, never," and of once more evoking numerous photographs (boy and man, man and horse, boy walking through graveyard, and so forth). Buckler admitted that he had been "abstracting too much," that a "down-to-earth dialogue" at the end was indeed desirable, and that "'never' is a hell of a good word to end on" (Tape 2). When asked by Weber if he thought people would be "put off" by his strong emphasis on feelings, on the heart, Buckler replied, "I'm afraid they will be. But I think the tide is turning" (Tape 2).

Pamela Frye was convinced that the project would be a marvellous book that would "sell like hot cakes."[73] We learn that she had initially shown him some slides and jotted down his reactions, which she then typed out (not without difficulty, for the notes she had taken in the dark looked like "a report from a hysterical Ouija board") and sent to him as the basis for some text.

In an earlier letter to Frye, Buckler had confessed to having "plugged" into material from *Ox Bells and Fireflies*, out of a "lack of confidence."[74] Indeed, the vignette that begins "Gram, what makes so many cracks in your face?" in *Ox Bells* is reproduced in only a slightly amplified form in the fourth chapter of *Window on the Sea*. It anticipates one of the photographs that follow (not directly), that of an elderly woman with a strong, deeply lined face. Or rather, when the reader turns to the photograph, the pictorial image triggers in the reader's mind the earlier narrative fragment, in the way Hans Weber described, of "small threads" (Tape 2) that are not readily apparent being linked up. But Buckler did not specify to Pamela Frye that he had recycled earlier short stories as well. He claimed he had cast chapters 3 and 4 in the form of a story for purposes of immediacy, for "a sort of shifting of gears" destined to avert possible monotony. The embryo of *Window on the Sea*'s "Man and Snowman" was an early unpublished story, "The End Came Quietly At...," which Buckler called in a letter of submission "a study in the enormously misunderstood quiescence of the very old." The story evolved into "The Snowman," also unpublished, but more interesting and complex than the abridged and yet rhetorically amplified version published in *Window on the Sea*. These variants will be examined closely in chapter 6.

Buckler asked Weber what he thought of his having cast the third and fourth chapters of *Window on the Sea* in the form of a short story. The photographer admitted to having been puzzled initially, then won over by the "poignant" dimension that brought out "those important things that are on the balance between being lost or kept" and that worked well with photographs. He felt that these chapters drew on all the "lacework" at the beginning and tied it together (Tape 2).

When Pamela Frye finally received the manuscript, her reaction was a physical one of "pleasure and pain." She wrote Buckler that the sentences set up "such a singing in [her] head that it became a whole orchestra."[75] She particularly admired the harmonious interaction of the two genres, the way the "visual word" matched the "speaking image."

Apprehensive that McClelland and Stewart would back down from publishing *Window on the Sea* if there was not a simultaneous American run, Buckler's agent, Josephine Rogers of Collins-Knowlton-

Wing, endeavoured to find an American publisher. In the undated Author's Questionnaire that Buckler filled out for New York–based Crown Publishers Incorporated, he included a 300-word description packed with metaphors from the just-completed *Window on the Sea*:

> I was aiming with all my guts to celebrate the country I love and to show, in every packed illuminative sentence, how its unique personality and inhabitants comprise (without compromise) the last bastion of integrity…against the speciousness of modernism wherein the soul-emptied man, numbed beyond numbness, finds not even the wishbone of spirit to test his teeh [sic] on in its asphalt carcass.

Called on to justify the merits and unique nature of his book, Buckler claimed that, unlike most illustrated books, in which the text and the photographs were "redundant translations of each other," his text and Hans Weber's pictures joined hands and supplemented each other in a much subtler way. Josephine Rogers was confident of placing this book on Nova Scotia on the American market because of its paradoxical "appeal of universality." She explained, "it may be about Nova Scotia in particular, but in theme, it's so universal that it seems to me what you've put together are essays in life."[76] Nevertheless, one publisher after another declined. Viking, initially interested, decided that the book was too costly and that the photographs were not of top quality.[77] Alfred A. Knopf also eventually refused, but in the end Clarkson Potter informed Buckler that they would publish it the following spring.[78]

Buckler had just received the galleys for *Window on the Sea* at the end of January 1973 when *Maclean's* informed him that they wished to commission a "picturable article"[79] on Nova Scotia. Buckler did the project, once more collaborating with Hans Weber, marvelling at the photographer's ability to capture the abstract. The article, entitled "This Side of Paradise, Nova Scotia (Home Is Where You Hang Your Heart)," appeared in *Maclean's* in September 1973, and was reprinted four years later in the *Reader's Digest* under the title "My Places of Peace." The *Maclean's* article was accompanied by a preface by Gregory Cook praising Buckler's "photographic essay" in which "you risk the dizzying perspective at the mountain's height, share his valley's river-depth of loneliness, feel the cemetery's sigh-end of death, and know the homely freedom of things, like the kitchen stove" (40).

By June 1973, *Window on the Sea* had become number one on the Nova Scotian Best Seller list, but was subsequently allowed to go out of print.

## Buckler's Short Stories

The idea of publishing a collection of Buckler's short stories was originally the idea of Margaret Laurence, and was raised during a meeting with Robert Chambers of Trent University, who was working on a critical study on Buckler and Sinclair Ross. Chambers agreed to send McClelland and Stewart a proposed selection. When he did so, he pointed out to Jack McClelland that the volume, *The Rebellion of Young David*, would be about the same size as the selection of Sinclair Ross short stories *The Lamp at Noon and Other Stories,* published in the New Canadian Library series.[80] McClelland subsequently sent the selection to Buckler for approval. He announced to Buckler in June 1974 that there was to be no introduction in the hardbound volume, unless the author decided to write one himself, but that Margaret Laurence was to write an introduction to the New Canadian Library edition, which they planned to publish the following year.

Jack McClelland already had material that Buckler had sent him the previous year for what would later be the collection of satirical verse and prose, *Whirligig*. Explaining that this other manuscript needed more material, and that they were having difficulty imposing some form of unity on it, McClelland advised Buckler to publish the collection of short stories first, which would be "much welcomed by the college and school market"[81] as well as by Buckler's admirers. He summed up the evolution of reception and sales with respect to short fiction in the mid-seventies in a realistic manner that nevertheless ended on a positive note: "I am not going to pretend that things have changed and that collections of short stories sell well. They don't, but I think the reception for them today in Canada is better than it was even 5 years ago."[82]

The collection *The Rebellion of Young David* contains fourteen of the the sixty or so stories that Buckler wrote. Those that were included, as well as those that were published elsewhere, have often been treated by critics as origins of his later fiction. Alan Young, in "The Genesis of Ernest Buckler's *The Mountain and the Valley*," has examined how Buckler transformed earlier short story material into his first novel.

Buckler also made use of earlier short stories to construct his other longer works, *The Cruelest Month* (notably "The Harness"), *Ox Bells and Fireflies* (notably "The Bars and the Bridge," "The Balance," and "Snows of Christmas, Snows of Spring") and *Window on the Sea*. The earlier versions of *Window on the Sea*'s "Man and Snowman," as I have pointed out, were two unpublished stories, "The End Came Quietly At...," and "The Snowman," which will be compared with the later variant in chapter 6.

Things are further complicated by the fact that Buckler often fed on one short story to build another. "The Christmas Order" is not merely a variant on the same theme as the stories "The Bars and the Bridge" and "By Accident": it contains whole chunks of text from the latter story. Another problem is Buckler's habit of modifying merely his titles while leaving much of the rest of the story intact. "The Ring" is an early, almost identical version of "Cleft Rock with Spring," which was included in *The Rebellion of Young David*. The story "Snow Apples" was published decades after the original story was completed (1978) in the *Review* under the title "The Orchard." The rather mawkish, clumsy story "By Accident, (or) A Pocketful of Rue," later shortened to "The Accident," was beautifully rewritten and reborn as "The Christmas Order." This revised version finally appears in *The Rebellion of Young David*—as "Last Delivery before Christmas"—totally intact except for the inexplicable excision of the first paragraph of "The Christmas Order," an exploration of memory.

Some stories benefited immensely from cuts and revisions. "In Times Like These" is a story with a twist at the end, when the reader learns that the young married couple who are the protagonists are actually Henry VIII and Anne Boleyn. The dialogue is stilted, the narration trite, and the external focus clumsy. But in "A Sign of the Times," the version published in *National Home Monthly* in 1950, Buckler edited out the most jejune elements.

Although the themes of many of the stories revolve around the simple elements that make up domesticity, a number of the stories (like "Glance in the Mirror," "It Was Always Like That," or "It Was That Tune") are reflections on language and the artist—on the hard and lonely task of writing. Unfortunately, such pieces were often rejected because magazine editors deemed that stories about writers did not interest their readers. With respect to "Glance in the Mirror," one editor pointed out to Buckler that his error was having made the husband a writer, but that for their readership the basic situation in the story was a good one, since it involved "a sensitive man married to a rather superficial female."[83] Yet correcting the "error" would have involved destroying the bedrock of the piece, which fundamentally explored the (debilitating/destructive) relationship between love and art, between marital and artistic commitment.

We need to take into consideration the compromises and concessions that Buckler, along with other contemporary writers, had to make to editors determined to render all material accessible to the largest possible readership. The example of W.O. Mitchell springs to mind: Little, Brown, the original publisher of *Who Has Seen the Wind* in 1947, cut the novel by about 7,000 words so that it would fit the format of one of their popular series (under 300 pages for a consumer price of under $3).[84] Ironically, even the subsequent reprintings by Macmillan of Canada reproduced the revised version instead of the original manuscript.[85] With respect to Buckler and his "family stories," John Butler regretted that the writer should have on several occasions been willing to sacrifice artistic integrity to expedite publication. He quotes a letter from Buckler to *Good Housekeeping* giving them permission to start a story on page four of his manuscript should they find "the lengthy establishment of mood at the beginning...unnecessary." He also quotes B.K. Sandwell, the editor of *Saturday Night*, who demanded massive deletions in a piece that Buckler had submitted: "I will buy 'The Stars' for $50 for next Christmas *if you can get it down to 3000*. Don't retype; I can have that done here. But it deserves a better market" (Butler, 5). The piece that Buckler agreed to cut massively was "The Stars Were Bright," deemed appropriate for a Christmas issue because of its mystical dimension. The truncated version, published in 1945 under the title "Yes, Joseph, There Was a Woman; She Said Her Name Was Mary," lost the fullness and beauty of the husband-wife relationship that Buckler had created by exploring the inner thoughts of his characters through alternating inner focalization. It reduced the original poetic creation to a caricature.

The grimly ironic ending that we find in Buckler's original typescript of the story "Glance in the Mirror," also disappeared completely from the version ultimately published in 1957 in the *Atlantic Advocate* and reprinted in the collection *The Rebellion of Young David*. In a period of about ten years, Buckler had suggested three possible endings to the story, all of them ironic. Already in 1950, in a letter to W.O. Mitchell, who was then fiction editor at *Maclean's*, he offered to rewrite it, to alter the female character, and give the piece a happy ending should the editor find the current one "too grim."[86] When Buckler submitted it years later to the *Atlantic Advocate*, he told the editor that it was a "somewhat ironic and off-trail story" but that since they were aiming at a rather sophisticated readership, they would surely not want "the 'formula' piece with the built-in slushy ending."[87] Nevertheless, the variant that he sent them was not the version with the sharpest irony, but a soothing version with only a tinge of ambiguity, in which the destructive dimension is drastically toned-down. The original ending, implying that a superficial wife cannot share the silence of her artistic husband and therefore destroys the artist in him, finds an echo in an interview in which Buckler made a generalization about women and marriage that is surprising, to say the least, for someone, even of his generation, who was in constant contact with talented women writers, artists, and thinkers. When asked by William French why a man who wrote "so eloquently about the family and its pleasures" should never have married, Buckler replied that he "wouldn't want to impose any woman's life on a writer's life. He might have it on the tip of his tongue to be Shakespeare, a phrase out of the compost heap of everything he's ever experienced, just as she says 'Christ, the carrots are done, are you going to sit there on your ass much longer?'" (French, "A Literary Giant Scorned?")

While Buckler at times had to tone down his irony, on other occasions he subsequently added irony. The story "The Balance," which had been rejected for publication, was accompanied by a letter from Buckler suggesting an alternative ending, which this time was the ironic one: the irony consisting in the fact that "the coercion of habit in the lonely man would be stronger even than the revelation."[88] This alternative ironic ending was the one Buckler would choose when he reused the story in the chapter "Another Man" in *Ox Bells and Fireflies*. The resolution, reflecting the complexity and imperfection of human nature, was the opposite of the one that unfolds in the brightly optimistic "Last Delivery before Christmas," published in *Chatelaine* and reprinted in *The Rebellion of Young David*, in which the protagonist also has a dramatic insight on a major flaw but here manages to act upon it.

Buckler had persevered with the writing of his short fiction despite the discouragement of many rejections. The story "Humble Pie," for example, before being published in 1960 in *The Advertiser*, had already been rejected almost a decade earlier by the *American, Chatelaine, Collier's, Country Gentleman, Everywoman, Family Circle, Farm Journal, Good Housekeeping, Maclean's, Red Book,* the *Toronto Star, This Week,* and *Woman's Day.*[89] But the refusals did not necessarily mean that the pieces submitted were not good enough—on the contrary, they were often too good. After having rejected a piece as being unsuitable for *Saturday Night,* B.K. Sandwell bent the rules and accepted a humorous sketch that he knew would not be appreciated by the majority of his readers:

> It is so damned good that I can't make up my mind to pass it up. As a matter of fact, the one thing against it is that it is a little too damned good for S.N.—too literary. But there will be a fair percentage of its readers who will get its flavor."[90]

A simile used by Sandwell aptly expresses the problematic superiority of Buckler's writing: "It would be like putting a string quartet to perform in a band shell in the open air, with fireworks going on half a mile away."[91]

Three decades later, commenting to Jack McClelland on Chambers's selection of stories for *The Rebellion of Young David,* Buckler expressed a preference for his original titles, "The Harness" and "Mary Redmond" rather than "The Rebellion of Young David" and "The Dream and the Triumph" (although the stories had already appeared in *Maclean's* and *Chatelaine* in 1951 and 1956, respectively, under the later titles). He was apprehensive mainly about what he perceived as the repetitive aspect of the stories that had been selected. But in a letter to Margaret Laurence, he thoughtfully justified the writer's recourse to variants of the same as being legitimate: "just as the Eskimoes have fifty different words for 'snow,' so fifty similar subjects may become fifty different ones, according to the angle of light or perspective," and remarked that if his observation were not true "then all one would have to do to write everything that has ever been written would be to put down 'man, woman, life, death.'"[92]

Although he understood how the story fit into the arrangement, he also expressed the fear that "A Present for Miss Merriam" might verge on the over sentimental.[93] Although in his work with Hans Weber, Buckler had been adamant about the importance of coming back to the heart, when he eventually received the advance copies of *The Rebellion of Young David* his apprehension turned into acute embarrassment at what he judged to be the stories' "nakedness." He wrote to Claude Bissell to apologize for what he called the "molasses of sentimentality," which he put down in rather crude terms as a form of selling himself to the demands of the market, or "whoring":

> at that time, it was impossible to market a story that didn't have an overall—to use a terrible word—"upbeat" (Just as today you can't possibly sell a story that isn't made up of soot-picking, nullity and/or kinky fucking.) I suppose it was whoring on my part, to keep the market in mind, but when one is starving, one does strange things.[94]

It is true that some of the short stories are sentimental in a heavy-handed way. The original title of the story "The Accident," for example, was "By Accident, (or) A Pocketful of Rue." Its facetious pun is already revelatory of the clumsy story of a boy who thinks he caused his father's death, who resents his new stepfather, and who is brought to a reconciliation after his parents envisage taking him to a psychologist. Clumsy or not, the story, which provided a basis for certain elements in *The Cruelest Month*, certainly corresponded to the tastes of the time. It was published in *Chatelaine* in 1960, and the following year was adapted for the Halifax Theatre and broadcast on the CBC.

But other writers did not share Buckler's severe judgment. W.O. Mitchell, who did not hesitate to refuse Buckler's submissions to *Maclean's* when he detected flaws, had a very high opinion of that writer's short stories in general. With respect to "A Penny in the Dust," the first short story by Buckler that *Maclean's* accepted for publication, W.O. Mitchell assured him that the story was "quite moving without being mawkish or sentimental," and that he had done "a lovely and sensitive job in showing the relationship between the child and the father."[95]

Mitchell's choice of the term "sensitive" is a significant one. Using the same distinction I made in the preceding chapter when I briefly dealt with Buckler's plays, in particular *By Sun and Candlelight*, it can be argued that the short stories are sentimental in the best sense of the term. In more than one interview, and notably with Don Cameron years later, Buckler would point out that there is "a very very thin line between sentiment and sentimentality" and that while "blatant *sentimentality* is a different thing altogether," in his opinion "*sentiment* is just fine" (Cameron, "Interview" 5). Angus Cameron, senior editor at Knopf, made the same distinction, using it to dissuade Buckler from cutting the pieces "A Man" and "A Woman" from the manuscript of *Ox Bells and Fireflies*. Cameron argued as we have seen that they were not sentimental but filled with sentiment. Finally, while sentiment has been out of fashion for the last few decades, more and more readers today will tend to agree with Buckler when he said: "I think heart is a big word, because it has the same letters as earth....Heart is what we live by, I don't think we live by mind, I think we live by heart" (Cameron, "Interview" 5).

## *Whirligig* (1977)

When Buckler initially sent McClelland and Stewart his manuscript of satirical verse and essays, it was still entitled "Shakespeare Wrote Bacon or Seen Through Different I's," but was referred to by Buckler in his correspondence as "Hamlet, or Oh Dad Poor Dad," in honour of one of its pieces "Hamlet, or Oh Dad Poor Dad, I'm Hung Up In Ma's Closet and I'm Feeling So Sad." Other titles such as "The Great Phallusy" or "Advice Not Taken, or Ann Landers, Meet Moll Flanders"—the latter a spoof of *Hamlet* in the form of a letter written by Ophelia to Ann Landers—illustrate his fondness for word play and flippant intertextuality. Buckler had been thinking for years of publishing a collection of his comic verse and essays, which he had written on subjects as varied as bestsellers, bores, opera, Christmas cards, religion, contraception, politics, party lines, philosophy, and the vicissitudes of writing.

In a letter to the photographer Hans Weber, Buckler quoted from a letter he had received from Claude Bissell encouraging him to steam ahead with his humorous book although he was working on the manuscript of *Window on the Sea*. Bissell had argued that the stodgy, heavy Canadian literary scene was in need of a "witty, undogmatic" book: "Canadian Literature—a little heavy and doughy, what with Callaghan's mashed potatoes and MacLennan's sinewy beef—needs light and digestible fare."[96] Bissell knew the material well, for as he explained to Jack McClelland when the latter consulted him about the manuscript, Buckler had been showing him his humorous pieces at regular intervals over the years.[97] Although Bissell made it clear that many of the prose pieces went back "a number of years" and that Buckler had been working on the verse "on and off for some time," Buckler claimed otherwise in a letter to his New York agent, Josephine

Rogers: "The major pieces are brand new. Others are rewrites from the magazine and radio field of some years back. E.g., 'Puss in the Corner' was taken by *Esquire* (though never used). A section of 'The Mouths of Babes' appeared in the *Atlantic Monthly*. A few originated in scripts for the CBC. Etc." Buckler argued that "in most of these cases the piece [had] been so revised and updated as to be nearly a fresh article."[98]

He later confessed to Jack McClelland that three pieces—"Non!," "Bestsellers Make Strange Bedfellows," and "Marriage, TV Style,"— had all appeared previously in the *Atlantic Advocate* (the latter appeared as far back as 1956 under the title "The Eruption of Albert Wingate"), but insisted that they were all "updated."[99] If we compare the opening sentences alone of "Marriage, TV Style" and "The Eruption," we can see how Buckler has tightened the narrative, edited out superfluous traces of narratorial voice, and moved from the abstract to the concrete, and from the general to the particular. The earlier piece began with the generalization, "Every man carries in him a potential volcano of some sort."[100] The *Whirligig* version was more physical, immediately plunging into the eloquent corporeality of a comparison: "Cora Wingate outweighed her husband Albert by some fifty pounds" (93).

Light hudibrastic verses that often read like mediocre imitations of Ogden Nash are among Buckler's earliest attempts at writing. Among the papers in the Buckler Manuscript Collection, there is a handwritten poem spoofing Palmolive soap advertisements, labelled in pencil "First attempt at humor 1933," with the final rhyming couplet:

> Ivory suffices for the Pope
> But God demands Palmolive soap.

Among his earliest material are satirical essays, doggerel, and sketches with titles that many readers would label 'corny,' such as "The Hearse-and-Bogey Doctor," not reproduced in *Whirligig*. Much of this material has verve and flair. Some of it, like the aphorisms in "The Dragnet," or the poem "Casting Suspicion on an Adage," was published as far back as 1938.[101] Pieces that are undated can sometimes be placed in time thanks to historical references, such as in the rather lame poem "Moot Question":

> When Berlin whistles,
> Rome must dance.
> But who at Vichy
> Wears the pants?

In his letter to Jack McClelland about *Whirligig*, Claude Bissell admitted that the book would be "uneven," with a blend of strength and weakness. He felt that Buckler's *forte* was satire, that the best material dealt with the immediate scene, and that the successful verses were "those with a satirical edge that touch[ed] upon specific social absurdities." He advised McClelland to place the "humorous squibs" that did not "come off" as end-pieces or to place a few between each prose piece.

When McClelland explained to Buckler in his letter of 26 June 1974 that they were having difficulty in finding some form of unity for the material, Buckler protested, "I had thought that in a collection of this sort, 'unity' (as in a novel) is impossible—if not deliberately to be avoided."[102] He argued that variety, such as alternating prose pieces and verse, might "relieve the monotony of a 'one-note' theme," and pointed out that other humorists such as White, Thurber, or Benchley hopped from subject to subject "like a jumping bean." In any event, no two editors at McClelland and Stewart had agreed on which type of essay to favour. Some of the philosophical essays were cut in the fear of appearing too "donnish." The book's editor, Diane Swift, cut three pieces including the philosophical essay "By Guess or By God." Although "Alienated: A Dateline" has a superficial resemblance to the latter essay, it is merely light word-play engaging in no deep philosophical thought. But in Swift's evaluation, "By Guess or By God" competed with "Alienated," which she found a brilliant and entertaining piece. Similarly, it was deemed that the average reader was only mildly interested in the trials and tribulations of the writer: "A Wasted Life" was cut with the claim that "A Muse in Overalls," "Artist's Life," and "Leave Your Leisure Alone" were better representations of the theme, although the latter two pieces had little to do with the subject. Most significant among the material that was quietly edited out was political satire that was deemed either too controversial or too prone to become outdated, such as Buckler's "Vietnamese Folk Songs":

> Baa baa Nixon
> Have you any bull?
> Yes sir yes sir three bags full
> One for the Senate, and one for the House
> And one for the little boy we burned up in Laos.[103]

Among other material that was edited out was "I Wish I Were You," a spoof of a serious theme or undercurrent in Buckler's work that echoes the short story "The Doctor and the Patient":

> The painter wishes he could sing, the singer he could paint,
> There's scarce a man but longs to be what he so plainly ain't...[104]

Some of the material that was cut was used in the *Globe and Mail*. For instance, the piece "Confessions of a Neurotic, or Take a Psychiatrist Out to Lunch" was published in the *Globe* in November 1977 under the title "Going Crazy, Pal?" The satire set in the House of Commons, "Is There a Chaplin in the House?," which appeared in the *Globe* under the title "A House, A House, My Kingdom for A House" in January 1977, was reluctantly cut by McClelland, who informed Buckler that it was one of his favourite pieces but that it would rapidly become outdated if the government went over.[105]

In his Introduction to *Whirligig*, Bissell anticipated that the book would come as "a surprise to Buckler readers" and as "a disconcerting aberration to critics, who like their authors to move in a straight line, with an upward flourish at the end" (7). And he was right. Although *Whirligig* won The Stephen Leacock Award for Humour in 1978, the book was not on the whole well received. Moreover, it was never published in the United States. In the early 1970s, Buckler's American agent, Josephine Rogers, had warned him that the manuscript was not right for the U.S. market, explaining that "national tastes do differ."[106]

Reviews of the book ranged from the wildly enthusiastic to the scornfully dismissive. There were those who felt that Buckler had proved he excelled in yet another genre. For Louis MacKendrick, writing for the *Windsor Star*, the pieces were "lighthearted and delightful froth" that were nonetheless "pithy observations of human nature, in essays and verses both sharp and sympathetic."[107] He appreciated the energy and invention, even the "atrociously bad/good rhymes" and the "vulgarly riotous doubletalk," arguing that Buckler's "knee-slapping corniness" succeeded where "self-indulgent subtlety will not."

William French, on the other hand, called *Whirligig* both a "tantalizing book," because it showed that Buckler in top form was "a humorist to reckon with," and a "frustrating book," because he did not reach that form often enough. French ended his review in the *Globe and Mail* by hoping Buckler would go back to "playing his concert grand"

("Unbuttoned" 45). The *Toronto Star* called the material "highly disposable." Ken Adachi argued that the book was "an agreeable waste of time" and that, although there were a few "gems," for the most part the humour was "forced and the babble banal."[108] The *Brantford Expositor* was somewhat milder. Gerald Huntley allowed that Buckler had "the itch to write" but pointed out that "unfortunately there are some itches that cannot be properly scratched, and a few of these should not have been." He felt that the first pieces were belaboured and mediocre, but that the best material near the end was "refreshingly hilarious."[109]

In the *Ottawa Journal*, Dorothy Bishop reminded readers that Buckler had called himself "the poor woman's Woody Allen." She remarked that "some of the light-hearted stuff [was] clever," other pieces put "permanent chuckles in the memory," and some was "chaff that would scarcely have been printed if it hadn't been a Buckler."[110] If Josephine Rogers was right in saying that 'national tastes do differ,' reviews of *Whirligig* show that personal tastes also differ widely. A piece that one critic would denounce as not even remotely funny would be the piece that another liked best.

Buckler was not above earthy self-criticism with respect to his own humorous pieces. In a 1968 letter to writer Max Ferguson in which he congratulated him on having won the Stephen Leacock Award, Buckler bowed to his colleague's superior talent with the raunchy analogy: "I am stuffed with words, like dry bread dressing up a goose's ass—but none of them is as brilliantly dead-on and amusing as yours."[111]

# Part Two

# Buckler's Ontological Commitment

> The greatest delight which the fields and woods minister, is the suggestion of an occult relation between man and the vegetable. I am not alone and unacknowledged. They nod to me and I to them.[1]
>
> —R.W. Emerson, *Nature*

Like many North American artists and writers in the first half of the twentieth century, Buckler was undoubtedly originally influenced by Emerson and his transcendentalist movement, which in turn was influenced by and interacted with the European Romantics. Emerson maintained a privileged relationship with Coleridge, Wordsworth, and Carlyle, who also believed in the reality of a supersensuous realm of being, and who shifted the term "sublime," used in the eighteenth century to designate objects of

Notes for chapter 3 are on pp. 240-42.

overwhelming vastness or power, to connote that state of mind arising in contact with the transcendent and infinite. For as Emerson admits in his essay "The Transcendentalist," his alleged "new views" are not new, but "the very oldest of thought cast into the mould of these new times," and "what is popularly called Transcendentalism…is Idealism" (*Complete Essays*, 87). Because ontological idealism such as Kant's defines the universe in terms of phenomena, and posits that existence is relative to the mind's perception, its inherent logic tends toward an ultimate and total fusion of subject and object, perception and percept, mind and universe, that Buckler finds attractive. It refuses any distinction between the external and the internal, between mind and matter, thought and thing. Shelley, who was read religiously in the English-speaking world in the second half of the nineteenth century and the first half of the twentieth century,[2] remarked in his manifesto *A Defence of Poetry*, that "All things exist as they are perceived; at least in relation to the percipient" (1085). In the final chapter of *The Mountain and the Valley*, the protagonist David seems to melt into nature, to attain such fusion:

> (in the reverse of what happens when you stare at a pattern of lines until suddenly the pattern moves off the page and cleaves to your retina), as he looked at the frozen landscape it was as if the outline of the frozen landscape *became* his consciousness: that inside and outside were not two things but one. (281)

The debate between materialism or objectivity and idealism or subjectivity is a central preoccupation of many of Buckler's contemporaries. In an interview with Don Cameron, W.O. Mitchell explains that he too as a young man was interested mainly in philosophy. Having been told by his instructors that he had to choose between materialist empiricism and idealism, "between the world of passion, appetite, the many, and the world of one," Mitchell thought of himself for a long time as "a Platonist, with Presbyterian overtones," but as would be the case with Buckler, later realized that "there could be no closed systems in art" (Cameron, "W.O. Mitchell," 52). His enduring aesthetic philosophy nevertheless contains distinct, even insistent, Emersonian overtones. Mitchell affirms that "the only justification for art is that this particular narrative, these particular people, shall articulate some *transcending* truth that *transcends* region and *transcends* a given time, and that it shall have meaning and significance that *transcends* the actual in the world of the many" (51, emphases mine).

Significantly enough, E.M. Forster is explicitly brought to our attention by Buckler in *The Mountain and the Valley*, when David discovers Forster's writing to be "more rapturously adventurous than any odyssey of action," and is uplifted by the recognition of "the absolute truth" of Forster's perceptions (244). In the opening passage of Forster's *The Longest Journey*, first published in England in 1907, but not until 1922 in the United States, some university students debate the existence of a reality beyond the consciousness by focusing on a cow:

> "The cow is there," said Ansell, lighting a match and holding it out over the carpet. No one spoke. He waited till the end of the match fell off. Then he said again, "She is there, the cow. There, now."
>
> "You have not proved it," said a voice.
>
> "I have proved it to myself."
>
> "I have proved it to myself that she isn't," said the voice. "The cow is *not* there." Ansell frowned and lit another match.
>
> "She's there for me," he declared. "I don't care whether she's there for you or not. Whether I'm in Cambridge or Iceland or dead, the cow will be there."
>
> It was philosophy. They were discussing the existence of objects. Do they exist only when there is some one to look at them? Or have they a real existence of their own? It is all very interesting, but at the same time it is difficult. Hence the cow. She seemed to make things easier. She was so familiar, so solid, that surely the truths that she illustrated would in time become familiar and solid also. Is the cow there or not? This was better than deciding between objectivity and subjectivity. (1-2)

But Emerson's brand of idealism is a subtler one. In his essay "Idealism," he claims that in his utter "impotence to test the authenticity" of the report of his senses, it makes little difference "whether Orion is up there in heaven, or some god paints the image in the firmament of the soul" (*Nature* 59-60), for in both cases it is equally useful and venerable. Unlike the characters in *The Longest Journey*, Emerson does not deny the sensuous fact, the solidity of the cow, but he refuses to see that alone. Colouring all of Buckler's works is a stance rooted in Emerson's admission in "The Transcendentalist" that he does not deny the presence of a particular table, chair, or the walls of a room, but that he looks at these things "as the reverse side of the tapestry, as *the other end*, each being the sequel or completion of a spiritual fact" (*Complete Essays* 88).

The encounter in the final pages of *The Mountain and the Valley* between the sensitive protagonist, David, and the pragmatic neighbour, Steve, is thus a metaphorical one, a confrontation between materialism and idealism. In the character of David, Buckler incarnates the vision beyond *eikos* (appearance or perceptible reality): "as he looked at the frozen landscape it was as if the outline of the frozen landscape *became* his consciousness: that inside and outside were not two things, but one—the bare shape of what his eyes saw" (281). This standpoint is in direct contrast to that of Steve, who saw only the trees and the fields, saw them as mere external objects devoid of significance, empty as it were: "He saw the trees and the fields. Yet in a way he didn't see them at all. A tree was a tree, a thing for the axe. A field was a field. You hauled across it when it was frozen, ploughed it when it was soft. That's all there was to it" (283). We shall see more closely how Buckler, like Emerson, "takes his departure from his consciousness, and reckons the world an appearance" (*Complete Essays* 89), adopting a "metaphysical" measure of the world, namely, not the size or appearance of things, but the *"rank"* that they take in his consciousness. Buckler is attracted to Emerson's standpoint according to which mind is "the only reality, of which men and all other natures are better or worse reflectors," and thought is the Universe (89).

In both *The Mountain and the Valley* and in *Ox Bells and Fireflies*, the reader is made to feel that the human act of lighting the lamp is the direct cause of the coming of night. In the following sentences, "the lamp was still lit, the day hadn't really begun" (*Mountain*, 67) and "My mother has not lit the lamp. That would make it really dark outside" (*Ox Bells* 39), the two events are separated by a comma or a full stop, and not joined by any connector implying causality. And yet causality is inferred through simple contiguity, through the dynamics of the logical error singled out by scholasticism under the term *post hoc, ergo propter hoc*. As Roland Barthes argues in "Introduction à l'analyse des récits," the groundwork of narrating is the confusion between consecutiveness and consequence. We inevitably tend in any sequence to interpret what comes *after* as having been *caused by* (10). Instead of "the lamp was lit because the day hadn't really begun," we infer that "the day hadn't really begun because the lamp was still lit." Similarly, we infer that the mother does not light the lamp because that would not only signal nightfall, but trigger it. For those reading Buckler's texts, just as for his narrators, lighting the lamp will cause night to fall just as putting out the lamp will cause daylight to come. Thought is the universe in an even more direct fashion when the boy narrator in *Ox Bells and Fireflies* creates the world through his gaze:

> My eyes follow the sky's single cloud, the shape of a wing. I see creation in it. I don't move. I see a squirrel moving on the ground. A partridge. A snail. There is no one there to see them but me. *I have created them*....And then I see the raspberries in the old chopping. There are bushels of them, huge and ripe. No one has discovered them. *I have created them*. (295-96; emphases mine)

But I shall argue that Buckler does not completely adhere to this immaterialist stance, and that materialist currents of thought invalidate and undermine his idealist position in an endless dialectic.

The belief that there is a relation between the mind and matter, that for those who know how to look, the universe becomes transparent, the light of higher laws shining through it, has existed since the dawn of civilization, argues Emerson in his essay "Language" (*Nature* 43). His debt to neo-Platonism is evident when he declares that "there seems to be a necessity in spirit to manifest itself in material forms" and that "day and night, river and storm, beast and bird, acid and alkali, preexist in necessary Ideas in the mind of God" (43-44). He refers to material objects in the terms of a French philosopher he omits identifying, as kinds of "*scoriae* of the substantial thoughts of the Creator, which must always preserve an exact relation to their first origin," adding that "visible nature must have a spiritual and moral side" (44). In Buckler's world, nothing is inanimate. The humblest, most prosaic objects breathe, speak, and participate: "Things (the teakettle, the sled tongue, the well curb) broke the seal of inanimacy, showed they could be made friends of, spoke the unspoken history of each occasion they had ever had a part in each time they were looked at" (*Ox Bells* 87).

A similar breathing of life into inanimate materials is one of the characteristics of fellow modernist writers such as Katherine Mansfield, who also seeks to evoke the essence of reality, all the while proclaiming the impossibility of ever fully comprehending or articulating it. In "Prelude," published in 1920 in the collection of short stories *Bliss*, the protagonist, Linda, is simultaneously witness and creator of the wallpaper coming alive:

> She turned over to the wall and idly, with one finger, she traced a poppy on the wall-paper with a leaf and a stem and a fat bursting bud. In the quiet, and under her tracing finger, the poppy seemed to come alive. She could feel the sticky, silky petals, the stem, hairy like a gooseberry skin, the rough leaf and the tight glazed bud. Things had a habit of coming alive like that. Not only large substantial things like furniture, but curtains and the patterns of stuffs and the fringes of quilts and cushions. (*Selected Stories* 53)

The inanimate things that live and breathe in Buckler's texts echo such modernist passages, in which everything comes alive "down to the minutest, tiniest particle" (54). But Buckler's pantheistic reverberations are already to be found in Wordsworth's *Prelude*, which represents the universe as an organic, living whole:

> I heard among the solitary hills
> Low breathings coming after me, and sounds
> Of undistinguishable motion, steps
> Almost as silent as the turf they trod (Book I, 322-25)

in Byron's *Childe Harold's Pilgrimage:*

> Are not the mountains, waves, and skies, a part
> Of me and my soul, as I of them? (Canto III, 707-708)

or in Shelley's *Prometheus Unbound*, with its "breathing earth" (II, 2, 52) and neoplatonic concepts:

> And lovely apparitions,—dim at first,
> Then radiant, as the mind, arising bright
> From the embrace of beauty (whence the forms
> Of which these are the phantoms) casts on them
> The gathered rays which are reality—
> Shall visit us (III, 3, 49-54).

These very notions shape Buckler's ethos, as he himself reveals in the undated Author's Questionnaire that he filled out for Crown Publishers, who were on the point of publishing *Window on the Sea*. The following comments, inspired by a love of his Nova Scotia, show how deeply he is attuned to, and prepared to align himself with, the philosophical views of his Romantic predecessors:

> Here's [in Nova Scotia] where you can find the elementals made correlative to your every feeling. When, for instance, God (or whatever the hell you like) is sunsetly at it again, striking His superlative sets from moment to moment, without rehearsal, each consummately perfect...there's where you can see yourself *represented*....In Nova Scotia, *the universal is (even more than Blake saw it), seen in the particular;* and if you are made small by the comparison, you are also made great (...) by feeling (even if unconsciously; what the hell does the how of it matter?) that *you are pantheistically a part of the whole universe*[3] (second and third emphases mine).

The explicit reference to Blake announces the kinship Buckler feels with the Romantics and their characteristic of seeing the grand in the small, the abstract in the concrete, the universal in the particular. In *Auguries of Innocence,* Blake wrote

> To see a World in a grain of sand,
> And Heaven in a wild flower,
> Hold Infinity in the palm of your hand,
> And Eternity in an hour. (209)

The kinship is evident in *Ox Bells and Fireflies*, whose nature is imbued with spirituality. The boy narrator wanders through "the Sabbath naves" and sees "the holiness in the August light" (296), sees "the entire Mystery in the crows," and feels "the oracle" in the moss beneath his feet (297). The kinship is announced more explicitly in the supplementary answers to an Author's Questionnaire that Buckler filled out prior to the publication of *Ox Bells*. In the questionnaire, the writer points out how in the fictional memoir he has tried to

> underline the omnipresence of the far in the near (maps of Tasmania on the cow's brockled sides); the universal in the particular (all geometry in the owl's eye); the macrocosm in the microcosm (whole galaxies in a pasture of wild flowers);

> the duplicate rendering of every mood in some physical object or cast of nature (all sadness in the swinging of an unhinged November gate)...the infinite clusters of varying determinants of behaviour in the infinite variants of weather or season; the translatability of the senses one into another (songs the colour of poppies, roofs the sound of sleep). The interlocking and cross-pollination of all things, tangible or intangible.[4]

I shall look more closely at these specific techniques of Buckler's in chapter 7. For our purposes here, suffice it to note the similarity between Blake's "Heaven in a wild flower" and Buckler's "whole galaxies in a pasture of wild flowers," a variant consisting in the slight transformation from singular to plural.

Buckler's adherence to a pantheistic worldview in which every particle is related to the whole, explicitly proclaimed in the *Window on the Sea* Author's Questionnaire, is also clearly reminiscent of Emerson's "Unity in Variety," discussed in the introduction, which in turn echoes Coleridge's "Multëity in Unity." In his influential *On Principles of Genial Criticism*, Coleridge declares that "[t]he beautiful, contemplated in its essentials, that is, in *kind* and not in *degree*, is that in which the *many*, still seen as many, becomes one"(443, emphases in the text). He posits the beauty inherent in an old, dirty coach-wheel, imputable to "how the rays proceed from the centre to the circumferences, and how many different images are distinctly comprehended at one glance, as forming one whole, and each part in some harmonious relation to each and all" (443). Buckler's fellow writer W.O. Mitchell certainly also adheres to this stance, declaring that "the abstract or the universal has to grow out of the particular" (Cameron, "W.O. Mitchell" 58). The stance clearly governs Buckler's tastes as a reader and critic: in a letter to Harry Brown, he praises the writer for two new books, in particular for his "whole flood of perceptions that tap the particular into the universal."[5] For Buckler as a writer, a belief in the existence of close interrelationships or correspondences is evident in many a passage in texts such as *Ox Bells and Fireflies*. We witness the fusion not only of the natural and the cultural, as when the blood of the boy narrator "springs with the hallelujah of downstairs and outdoors" (9), but also of the micro and the macro, as in the following passage: "I listen to the brook, and my own flesh and I are such snug and laughing brothers that I know we are forever mingled with the sun's pulse (or the wind's or the rain's) and forever unconquerable" (12). It is also manifest in a short story like "Snow Apples," later entitled "The Orchard," in which the voice of an older narrator evokes his childhood meditations on a young sister who had died before he was born. Seeing his mother still mute with grief after having stumbled across a box of the little girl's keepsakes, the boy notices that the air is quieter than silence, and that "there was none of that 'whispering' together of things growing side by side in the fields. Things seemed oblivious to them*selves*. The leaves of the pear tree moved, but without *deciding* to. Even the stones, which have their own way of speaking, were deaf and dumb."[6] The wiser voice of the older narrator intervenes with a retrospective analysis: it was not the hush of sadness, for sadness "is active." The boy had lost that miraculous fusion, that sense of completeness or oneness with the world around him, that the very young can have. It was "simply the first time [he] had found out about *distance*, the cruelest word in the language" (*Orchard* 29). But the protagonist recovers his vision of an organic universe in a passage that transmits through personification a unifying vision that transcends *eikos:* "The 'nowness' came back to the stones. Everything in the day heard its own name and answered to it. It was as if something you'd taken to be an object had turned out, on nearing you, to be a face" (*Orchard* 29).

The transcendental belief in a universal soul of which everything living is a part, in which "every man's particular being is contained and made one with all other," is expressed exquisitely by Emerson in "The Over-soul," published in 1841 in his first series of essays, which were almost immediately issued in England with a preface by Carlyle. Emerson declares:

> We live in succession, in division, in parts, in particles. Meantime within man is the soul of the whole; the wise silence; the universal beauty, to which every part and particle is equally related; the eternal ONE. And this deep power in which we exist and whose beatitude is all accessible to us, is not only self-sufficing and perfect in every hour, but *the act of seeing and the thing seen, the seer and the spectacle, the subject and the object, are one.* We see the world piece by piece, as the sun, the moon, the animal, the tree; but the whole, of which these are the shining parts, is the soul. (*English Traits* 138, emphasis mine)

The fusion of subject and object, the internal and the external, the individual and the universe, the micro and the macro, the many and the One, had already been proclaimed by Schopenhauer in his major work, *The World as Will and Idea*, published in 1818. His famous phrase "clear eye of the world," referring to artists who manage to divest themselves of their personalities and to remain *"pure knowing subject,"* as well as "a clear mirror of the essence of the world" (109), is the culmination of an exposition of idealism that is remarkable in its clarity, and that urges us to give up our recourse to the light of scientific reason and the study of phenomena, and to turn our spirits toward the power of intuition. It calls on us to fill our consciousness with the visible contemplation of a natural object that is physically present, and claims that the individual who does so

> *loses* himself in this object...i.e. he forgets his very individuality, his will, and continues to exist only as the pure subject, the clear *mirror of the object*, so that it is as if the object alone were there without anyone there to perceive it, and he can no longer separate the perceiver from the perception, but *the two have become one*, because the whole consciousness is filled and taken up with one single sensuous picture. If the object has to such an extent passed out of all relation to something outside it, and the subject out of all relation to the will, then what is known is no longer the individual thing as such, but the *Idea*, the eternal form....The person rapt in this perception is thereby no longer individual...but he is a pure, will-less, painless, timeless subject of knowledge. (102; first two emphases mine)

This text describing the fusion of subject and object, and the subsequent phrase "we are only that *one* eye of the world which looks out from all knowing creatures" (121), doubtless inspired the striking remark by Emerson, who comments on the transformation that comes over him in the midst of nature: "I become a transparent eyeball. I am nothing. I see all. The currents of the Universal Being circulate through me; I am part or particle of God" (*Nature* 13).

Certain passages in Buckler's texts owe a debt to both Schopenhauer's and Emerson's ocular metaphors. There is the description in *Ox Bells and Fireflies* of the hunt when "your body became one great eye searching for the wild graceful deer that walked toward you with its death in its nostrils" (114). There is the affirmation that earth and sky "were such a constant in the field of vision that it seemed as if they lived, no less directly than the images of kitchen chairs, within the eye itself" (87). There is the description of the "hen's eye, occult as a fish's," that the children watched to see if they could "catch the lightning wink with the single lid that moved *up*ward instead of downward." The description ends with a commentary that is quite Emersonian: "[w]e stared, in fact, into the eye of everything. Flesh or plant or matter" (45). Finally, the unifying leitmotiv of the circle, as in the evocation of the "circles of sun, and moon, and breakfast plate, and clothing eyelet, and date stamp on the treasured letter…and the pupil within the eye that sees them all" (233). The epilogue of *The Mountain and the Valley* also include such metaphors, particularly in the description of the frozen landscape from David's point of view as being "one great white naked eye of self-consciousness, with only its own looking to look at" (281).

## Liminality

Buckler centres his writing round the notions dear to Schopenhauer, of perception/reflection, of the mirror,[7] of an eternal and perfect form: Idea, essence, or representation. But ultimately he distances himself from the Schopenauerian notion, stemming from Kant, of the world as representation, as mere thought constituted from the depths of our acosmic subjectivity.[8] It is not I through the power of my gaze who causes the world to appear, but rather the world which offers itself up to me, as soon as I show myself attentive. Because perception is always linked to the incarnated body's position in space and time, I am part of the spectacle; I see because I am in turn visible. The object of my gaze is the visible image of what I am as beholder; I can see my own eyes in the eyes of the Other. My gaze and the visible meet and mingle, as do the sea and the beach, to borrow the heuristic analogy that Merleau-Ponty makes in *Phénoménologie de la perception*, and that Katherine Mansfield, in "At the Bay," published in 1922 in the collection of short stories *The Garden-Party*, makes use of to create her universe of ambivalence, her omnipresent liminality,[9] to explore the boundaries of internal/external, self/Other, illusion/reality: "there was nothing to mark which was beach and where was the sea" (*Selected Stories* 203). This liminality, derivative of a philosophical stance, is also conceptualized and put into practice by W.O. Mitchell, who insists that art, like life, is made up "of contradiction, of dilemma, of *not either/or but of both*" (Cameron, "W.O. Mitchell" 52; emphasis mine). Not for nothing does fellow modernist Buckler have his boy protagonist David in *The Mountain and the Valley* choose to sit on the top beam of the haymow to watch, safely out of reach, the milling neighbours and the flailing legs of the temperamental ox being shod. For in this strategic, privileged position, the protagonist is "*in* it, but *above* it and *outside* it at the same time" (59).

Perception is made up of a multiplicity of sensations that come together in infinite combinations, reflected in the writing strategies I shall examine in chapter 6, such as Buckler's synaesthesia, or his daring word-combinations, like the "*glint-leoparding*, never for two seconds the same, of ground and running water by light and shade striking on them through a canopy of moving leaves" (*Ox Bells* 116). The thing perceived is not a stable, definitive reality, but a fluctuating significance. Perception allows meaning to be constructed in an allusive fashion; perception is Being at a distance.

In one of the numerous litanies in *Ox Bells and Fireflies* celebrating the small details of the ordinary, Buckler sketches the marvel of what puts the man "at the core of all the green he looked at, what shielded him from all the grays—because it so mingled his presence with the woman's and the child's that each had the companion seeing of the other at the back of his own seeing eye" (184). We recognize Buckler's stance in Merleau-Ponty's affirmation in *L'OEil et l'esprit* that acting and being acted upon are so little distinguishable that we can no longer know who sees and who is seen, who portrays and who is portrayed.

But the beholder does not melt into or fuse with the object any more than the object fuses with the subject, for then the vision would vanish even as it was being generated, and the subject would not be able to contemplate itself in the act of contemplating, as David does in *The Mountain and the Valley* ("with only its own looking to look at"). Only Steve, who sees merely the trees and the fields and not beyond to their Being, would, as Buckler tells us, "never look at the eye of his own watching" (283).

Like Merleau-Ponty in *Phénoménologie de la perception*, published in 1945, Buckler seems to be positing that we reveal the world because we are an integral part of it. For the perceiving subject, nature is not simply a spectacle or a representation. Since the relations between things or their aspects are always mediated through our body, the whole of nature is the staging or performance of our own life, or rather an interlocutor with which we elaborate a dialogue. In Buckler's texts the subject and object share a quasi-identity, a kinship based on the notion of participation. As with Merleau-Ponty, the object of the gaze is not a separate entity that is indivisible, but a sort of channel or passage between exterior and interior horizons that remain open, that brush against other elements, part of the ephemeral modulations and crystallisations of the cosmos. The philosopher does not set out to minimize the role of the human being in the elaboration of truth, but insists that what is original, in the primary sense of the word as signifying first, is not the *cogito*, but the "there-ness" or Be-ing of the universe. In a twist on the conventional idealist stance, Merleau-Ponty posits that human beings do not *produce* the sight—they *are* the sight; they are not simply viewers, but also part of the visible, part of the Be-ing that offers itself to the gaze.

Buckler's stance seems to coincide with the concept advanced by Merleau-Ponty, that humans and the world originate from the same matrix and are irrevocably woven together, bound, supported, and nourished by a Being that is not a thing but a contingency, a latency. We are not so far from Emerson, who argued that although we tend to see the world piece by piece, these "pieces" are in effect shining parts of the whole, of the world soul. But unlike Emerson with his immaterial "Over-soul," Merleau-Ponty in *Phénoménologie de la perception* names his Being "la chair" or the "flesh" of things, the substance that glues the pieces together, that binds the components of the universe. For Merleau-Ponty, consciousness is not the pure thought of the Cartesians, but an incarnated consciousness, with a body anchored in the world. Buckler too, constantly underlines the fact that we are made up of the same matter as the universe, that our bodies have the same composition as the other components, both visible and invisible, of the world. This common flesh or shared matter, far from being an obstacle, is on the contrary the means of commun(icat)ion. An attentive reader will remark an illustration of the incarnated consciousness in a passage from *Ox Bells and Fireflies* that we have already looked at: "I listen to the brook, and my own flesh and I are such snug and laughing brothers that I know we are forever mingled with the sun's pulse (or the wind's or the rain's) and forever unconquerable" (12).

Merleau-Ponty conceptualizes the philosophical stance that emanates from Buckler's evocation of the narrator's flesh. The philosopher argues that the "thickness" or solidity of the body, far from being in conflict with that of the world, is the only means we have to get to the heart of things, through the procedure of making us into world and, its inverse, of making things into flesh.

This common flesh or shared matter, Merleau-Ponty continues to argue, links us not only to other human beings, but also to the world of the past, the present, and the future. Buckler's texts function in just such a way. We have seen how the boy narrator in *Ox Bells and Fireflies* claims to create the world through his gaze. It is interesting to note, however, that apart from the traces of a conventional idealist stance visible in the phrase that is repeated, refrain-like, "I have created them," there is an echo, or rather a proleptic parallelism, "I see creation in it," that contradicts the claim of extemporaneous creation and hints at an anterior creation, an original or divine creation, an existence prior to the moment of (his) viewing. The motion of the boy's eyes, the movements of his body in space, link him with the world he moves in and fuses the perceiving subject not only with the visible world, but also with time itself. Or rather, through a favourite strategy of Buckler's, this fusion gives the impression of arresting time, of connecting with the past and the future to form eternity. When the boy enters the woods, he tells us, "I am in the very depths of the afternoon. The afternoon and I are Now's all" (295). When he sees a great rock of the side of the road, he tells us, "I see the everlasting in it," and the religious nuance of the noun anticipates the sentence a few lines later that develops the ahistorical, metaphysical dimension: "I see creation in it." I shall examine more closely Buckler's manner of dealing with time later in this chapter, when I explore the writer's frequent recourse to the epiphany, and subsequently in chapter 5 in my analysis of the theme of Arcadia, as well as in chapter 7, when discussing the rhetorical device of anamnesis.

In Buckler's texts, the gaze envelopes, wraps itself around visible things in a harmonious, seemingly pre-established relationship, and it is difficult to know which is in control, which is the initiator. The writer's approach is an oddly corporeal blending of idealism and materialism, reminiscent of the French modernist poet Francis Ponge, who in the metaphysical texts groping for the ontological core of existence, paradoxically insists on the materiality of objects. In 1948, Ponge proposed to the reader a journey through a trapdoor to the heart of things: "Je propose à chacun l'ouverture de trappes intérieures, un voyage dans l'*épaisseur* des choses" (176, emphasis mine). (See the epigraph, chapter 4, p. 101.) This heart or core in the "thickness of *things*" ("epaisseur") finds a correspondence in the "thickness of *words*" ("l'épaisseur sémantique des mots"). Merleau-Ponty clarifies such an oddly corporeal blending of idealism and materialism by making an analogy with a hand. My hand, which touches tentatively, exploring objects and surfaces, is simultaneously touched by my other hand, feels and is felt, from both within and without. It opens out toward the other, yet remains accessible to the other, of which it is an integral part. It is touching and touched. It is touching touching, when the touching subject becomes the touched object.

## The Visible and the Tangible

The same interdependency exists between the motion of our eyes and the changes that they produce in visible objects. The visible, too, belongs to the domain of the tactile. Because the same body sees and touches, the visible and the tangible are interlinked. Every movement of our eyes, every movement of our body in space takes place in the same visible world that we explore, and inversely, everything that can be seen occupies somewhere a tactile space. This straddling or overlapping, in what amounts to epistemological synaesthesia, was posited in no unclear terms in *An Essay Towards a New Theory of Vision* (1705) by Berkeley, a philosopher whom Buckler admired:

> having of a long time experienced certain ideas, perceivable by touch, as distance, tangible figure, and solidity, to have been connected with certain ideas of sight, I do upon perceiving these ideas of sight forthwith conclude what tangible ideas are, by the wonted ordinary course of Nature like to follow....It is thought a great absurdity to imagine that one and the same thing should have any more than one extension, and one figure. But the extension and figure of a body, being let into the mind two ways, and that indifferently either by sight or by touch, it seems to follow that we see the same extension and the same figure which we feel. (20-21)

For Buckler, as for Berkeley, seeing is being in contact with a thing; looking amounts to feeling through one's gaze (just as Buckler's protagonists "touch" the world with their eyes, or as the second-person narrator, and consequently the implied reader as well, feels that his presence fills exactly the space that his eyes encompass [*Ox Bells* 94]), and the one who looks cannot be a stranger to the world gazed upon.

Like the countless artists who have painted themselves in the process of painting, adding how they are seen to how they see things, in their attempt to arrive at a total or absolute vision, Buckler often resorts to ocular metaphors, or imagery based on the mirror or the circle. The mirror, argues Merleau-Ponty in *L'OEil et l'esprit*, is a huge round eye, an extrahuman gaze that symbolizes the artist's eye that reflects the world. In the short story "Glance in the Mirror," when the writer-protagonist's superficial wife enters the room to persuade him to start a business and stop "wasting" his life "puttering around with a few old words," she instinctively glances at her image in the mirror. When she asks to read the text he has been working on in which he describes how an insensitive wife can destroy a writer, destroy his voice, he gives it to her defiantly, thinking "go ahead, look in this mirror for a change" (*Rebellion* 137). Rather like the mirror in Romantic poetry that is a truth-revealer, the text within a text here is the mirror that reflects a deeper reality, the writer's eye that sees beyond surfaces.

I have already alluded to Buckler's abundant use of the circle. Readers will find many an example, from the concentric circles of Ellen's rug in *The Mountain and the Valley*,[10] and the breakfast plates in *The Cruelest Month* that Letty looks at "as if their simple circularity were something splendid" (297), to more structural forms. The short story "The Doctor and the Patient" has a circular structure with a twist at the end—the psychiatrist has the mirror symptoms of the patient, identical but reversed. The story "Short Circuit" functions like a giant round, hopping from one character to another around the planet, through the intermediary of a $2 bill that circulates from hand to hand.

The eye, the mirror, the circle, have metaphysical resonances. They recall a passage from an essay by Emerson entitled "Circles," which focuses specifically on their correspondences and their ontological significance:

> The eye is the first circle; the horizon which it forms is the second; and throughout nature this primary figure is repeated without end. It is the highest emblem in the cipher of the

> world. St. Augustine described the nature of God as a circle whose center was everywhere and its circumference nowhere. (*Complete Essays* 279)

We have seen how in Merleau-Ponty's theoretical framework, the visible and the tangible are closely intertwined. In Buckler's texts, along with the omnipresence of the gaze, the importance of the senses, of the tangible, cannot escape notice. In his fictional memoir, as in his first novel and numerous short stories, he creates a paradise of the senses. In *Ox Bells and Fireflies*, bliss is that moment of going to bed on a cold winter night when "your feet touched the hot flatiron wrapped in an old sweater under the blankets and you felt sleep stun you with its first delicious blow" (52). In *The Mountain and the Valley*, pleasure is also the deliciousness of a hot stick of wood in a cold bed, as well as the smell of Christmas fruitcakes lying on inverted pans. It is touching the "chestnuts in the quick dust as if their chocolate shapes shining in the cold leaves held in them the smoothness of all the days that were gone" (54). The sensuality of the pleasure is accentuated through the recurrence of the voiceless consonants and the sibilant consonant as well as through the use of consonance and alliteration that resonate in the reader's mind like a caress. In the "chocolate shapes" there is also a hint of synaesthesia, a synergetic relationship established between the different modes of sensation of taste, touch, and sight.

And yet, once I have completed this theoretical framework, I shall demonstrate in my analysis of Buckler's treatment of the *topos* of Arcadia, how paradise is constructed through virtuality, through form and not matter, through the ethereal rather than the material. For Buckler, like his fellow modernists, was aware that perception is an open synthetic process, forever incomplete. He may have been acquainted with the phenomenological studies of Edmund Husserl, who pointed out that we never see the six sides of a cube simultaneously. We see two full sides, depending on where we stand, plus one or two others emerging. As we move, they will come into view, but the first ones will disappear. What we call the cube is merely the synthesis of a multiplicity of successive apparitions that we assemble into a unit. The object is never truly perceived in its unity and integrality: the "reality" of a thing is exactly what slips away from our perception.

This is what fascinated modernists and continues to fascinate postmodernists. The true subject of many of these artists is vision itself.

Emily Carr's painting journal, later published under the title *Hundreds and Thousands: The Journals of an Artist*, reveals that, like Picasso and Braque in their period of analytic cubism, she was exploring perception itself, the difficulty of holding objects in visual space. She concerned herself with the structure of seeing, as well as with the process of fabricating vision, analyzing how to convey space and movement onto a flat, two-dimensional, rectangular surface, and drawing attention to the ordering, to the thought process.[11]

In the same way, David Hockney's experiments with collages and Michael Snow's formalist works in the field of visual arts, his blending of the genres of photography and film, as well as his cerebral and playful writings, are reflections on perception, an exploration of the process of seeing and of the processing of information. Hockney, too, argues that vision "consists of a continuous accumulation of details across time and synthesized into a larger, continuously metamorphosing whole," pointing out that "the general perspective is built up from hundreds of micro-perspectives. Which is to say, memory plays a crucial role in perception" (Weschler 63). I shall come back to these notions when I deal with Buckler's "pointillist" writing technique, but for our immediate purposes, I find it useful to refer to the introduction to the exhaustive *Histoire de la peinture*, in which art critic Pierre Francastel explores the transformation that the concept of image has undergone. He points out that

> [a]u lieu d'être envisagée comme devant permettre le report sur la toile d'une réalité extérieure à l'individu—artiste aussi bien que spectateur—elle a été conçue comme liée à un phénomène de conscience et de vision intérieure, psychologique avant tout. On est passé de la vision en Dieu au Moyen Age et de la vision dans la Nature, à la vision dans l'esprit de l'homme. Par où s'est trouvée encore ruinée l'ancienne conception du symbole. Le symbole, qui jadis était l'objet représenté, est devenu lui aussi la sensation. (28)

Essentially, Francastel argues that the image in our modern era is no longer envisaged as the transfer to a canvas of a reality external to the individual—the artist or the viewer—but is closely linked to the phenomenon of consciousness and inner vision. There has been a shift from God and Nature to vision in the mind. Among the consequences of such a transformation, Francastel remarks, can be found the destruction of the former conception of the symbol. Formerly the represented object, the symbol, too, has become the sensation. We have seen the important role of sensations in Buckler's texts, just as we cannot have failed to remark the importance of touch in Mansfield's magical, organicist transformation of the poppy in "Prelude" in the sequence I evoked earlier. When the picture comes alive, the protagonist can *"feel* the *sticky, silky* petals, the stem, *hairy* like a gooseberry skin, the *rough* leaf and the tight *glazed* bud" (53; emphases mine)—a total of five different sensations linked to the tactile in the space of a single sentence whose subject is allegedly visual. One cannot help thinking of Merleau-Ponty's insisting that the visible is not a film without substance or thickness, but that latent in the precise form of all things is a certain texture.

Now, as ideas and influences flow not only from country to country, but also from one field to another, from one genre to another, Francastel's observations seem aptly to describe the whole of modernist production, which in turn laid the groundwork for postmodernism. He argues that the shifting of the notion of object from the domain consisting in the observation of occurrences considered to be realities external to humans, to the domain consisting in the differentiation of their cerebral or psychological activities, has been the most momentous event of the twentieth century. The remark that follows is a remarkably synthetic one, encompassing the evolution of literature and the humanities:

> Dans le même temps, la littérature, notamment le roman et la poésie, a suivi la même route, sans parler des sciences humaines qui, toutes, ont pris non pas le spectacle de l'univers mais le cerveau de l'homme comme matière de leur information. On ne cherche plus à définir, aujourd'hui, l'homme par son aventure, mais par l'évolution de son esprit. (29)

Francastel calls attention to a significant parallel between the visual arts, literature, and the humanities in general. All these fields take their subject matter no longer from the spectacle that the world offers, but from the human brain. They define human beings no longer in terms of "adventure"—that is, in terms of what happens to them—but in terms of the evolution of their minds. Once more, Buckler's allusion to Forster in *The Mountain and the Valley* springs to mind, particularly the protagonist's declaration that Forster's perceptions are "more rapturously adventurous than any odyssey of action" (244). Modernist writers such as Forster, Mansfield, Virginia Woolf, Faulkner, and Buckler accomplished in literature what the Impressionists and post-Impressionists accomplished in the visual arts: they set up a whole new concept of art, an art that strives toward an understanding of the role and power of the human beings who produce it and those for whom it is intended. They in turn would inspire new generations of artists such as Steve McCaffery—one of the members, along with bp nichol, of the performance group the Four Horsemen—who cited as an influence in his experimental homolinguistic translations, the cubist approach of writers like Gertrude Stein. He explained in his notes on his homolinguistic translation of Stein's *Tender Buttons*, that he had preserved her "cubist perceptual method" and that her "method of observation and description" had become his "method of reading and translating."[12]

## A Celebration of Form

If subjectivity, inner consciousness, and perception are the key notions governing modernist production, we must not forget something that Buckler constantly keeps in mind: the fact that all perception is perception of a form. Meaning emerges from the senses through the manner in which the elements are combined, and it is the contingent arrangement of matter that gives it its intelligibility. When we look closely at an Impressionist painting, all we see at first is a confused mass of colours. Then forms begin to emerge, an organization announces itself. "Brute" perception does not offer up to us objects with precise, stable contours, but with allusive or suggestive ones that require a certain analysis on the part of the viewer. This is not a deficiency in our perceiving consciousness, but a fundamental trait of Being that offers itself up in each object as a surface full of promise, rich in potential. The form that gives an object its contours is not a definitive given, but rather a formation, a disorder that is taking on form. That is why modern painters tend not to paint static lines that limit objects within stable contours, but rather mobile lines in the throes of gestation, for, as Klee puts it, the line no longer contents itself by imitating the visible—it now *makes* visible, sets up for our eyes the genesis of things.

The very concept of form is indeterminate, even nebulous. Umberto Eco points out that over a period of centuries, the term "form" that initially indicated what was visible on the surface, came to signify what is dissimulated underneath (12). We tend to forget that for the ancient Greeks, the term ειδοζ (*eidos*) significantly meant both "essence" and "form," as well as "quality," as distinct from "matter." Ideas were "the permanent, essential *forms* of the world" (Schopenhauer 110, emphasis mine). The Idea or Form is the stable view of the instability of things, as Bergson explains in 1907 in his *L'Évolution créatrice*. The philosophy of Ideas thus takes its point of departure in the Form, which is the very essence of reality. The Form is posited in an immobile eternity, independent of time and space, and of our perception: it is form as archetype. In his essay "Idealism," Emerson claims that it is "the animal eye" that sees "outlines and colored surfaces" but that, if Reason is stimulated, outlines and surfaces "become transparent, and are no longer seen; causes and spirits are seen through them" (*Nature* 60). Similarly, protagonists in Buckler's texts, right from his very early material, learn to look behind *eikos* or icon, appearance or image. In the unpublished short story "Would You Know It If You Fell Over It?" the gifted child who fails in all his aspirations learns that people are "shallow breathing shells" and that even language and speech are "mere mirages put on the mask of reality."[13] In *The Mountain and the Valley*, an epiphanic sequence is evocative of the hidden faces of Husserl's cube: planning the book in which he will find the words to express the "single core of meaning" (298) in all things, David proposes to relate the country people "just as they are," convinced that "people will see that there is more to them than the side that shows" (300). He realizes that people's faces are just the way they are, because of "all the *feelings* behind them"[14] (292-93).

Nevertheless, in his essay "The Poet," Emerson deplored the shallowness of doctrines of beauty that did not acknowledge the "instant dependence of form upon soul" (*English Traits* 167), judiciously quoting from Spenser: "For, of the soul, the body form doth take,/For *soul is form*, and doth *the body* make" (173, emphases mine). Buckler's conception of form is also a complex one, grounded in aporia, evoking simultaneously the universal forms of Plato's Ideas and the solid corporeality of the body.

Recurrently found in Buckler's texts is a celebration of pure form. As Claude Bissell remarked in his homage to the writer-philosopher, whose first love was mathematics, when Buckler was searching "for the ultimate metaphor in perfection, he invariably fell back on mathematics. 'It's the only clean thing in the world,' he once observed." Bissell added that "in the writer's finest poetic passages," he seemed to "see the whole world as *a vast equation* in the mind of God that only the supreme artist can hope to solve" (emphasis mine).[15] In *Ox Bells and Fireflies*, we can find whole passages of enumeration dedicated to shapes, often presented in precise mathematical or geometrical terms. The writer proceeds in a seemingly arbitrary, chaotic manner, guided by loose association of ideas. But the similarity of shapes that the writer evokes, the contiguity of seemingly disparate elements, creates a relationship of equivalence, a network of correspondences between nature and culture, between animal, vegetable, and mineral, between human and non-human:

> The *perpendiculars* of bulrush and crane leg. The *triangles* of deer track and trowel. Pears and wombs. Scrota and walnut shells. *Cloud-shaped* rocks and rock-shaped clouds. The *rectangles* of door and grave. The *cornu*copias of Morning Glory and gramophone *horn*. Fox *hearts* the *shape* of strawberries. *Cones* of hackmatack and the *cones* that the sand makes in the road when the child sifts it between his palms in the spellbound afternoon. (232-33, emphases mine)

As with the rectangle of door and grave, suggesting that death is but yet another exit, or perhaps entrance, Buckler makes repeated use of circularity, as I have mentioned above. The circle is of course the form that is cosmic, immobile, finite yet infinite, at all its points eternally the same, perfection itself. It is the archetypal figure excluding chaos, embodying the sacred. According to Emerson in "Circles," it "symbolizes the moral fact of the Unattainable, the flying Perfect" (*Complete Essays* 279). But the search for perfect lines, forms and patterns is intricately woven throughout the fabric of all of Buckler's texts. Perfect forms are connected, even fused, to moments of intense happiness, flashes of bliss or ecstasy, due to the simple nature of be-ing. The boy narrator's father in the story "The Bars and the Bridge" is an expert at creating with his plow pure lines that incarnate beauty and perfection: "even without pacing or markers, the free-hand rows of his garden came out as beautifully straight as if they'd been done with a chalk-line" (typescript, p. 2). In the unpublished short story "The Christmas That Faced Both Ways" (an early version of "Goodbye, Prince"), the child narrator waits to make sure his mother has "embedded the once-a-year walnut kernels in a *per-*

*fect pattern* on top of the fudge she'd just turned out into the pans, so that they'd come out in the *exact centre* of each square when it was out" (typescript, p. 2) In *Ox Bells and Fireflies,* the boy narrator, in total symbiosis with the domain of the cultural (his mother churning butter *inside* the kitchen) and the natural (the sun *out* in the yard "sifting" through his hair), watches his mother "press the shining butter into the mould that has the *pattern of acorns* carved on it" (10) by his father.

From the pattern of acorns on a humble butter mould, Buckler will go on to sing the mystical beauty of the homely boiled egg, peeled carefully so as not to spoil its "glistening perfection of geometry" (43). There are so many beautiful, infinitely varied forms to describe that the writer often contents himself with simply naming, rather than describing. The following passage from *Ox Bells* illustrates the technique of chaotic enumeration that I shall analyze in chapter 6:

> Hummingbirds' nests. Bears' dens in the caverns walled by ancient wood rocks. Volcanoes of the burrowing mole...
>
> Blades of grass, blades of wind. Tines of fork, tines of sun...
>
> Wings, paws, hoofs, beaks...
>
> Beechnut and pyramids, small fortresses, spider webs...
>
> Lion's paw and sheepkill. Ganders and hornpouts. Sunrises and sunsets. Moonlight and microcosms...
>
> And the man's knowing that for each saving instant that brimmed him whole his wife had one of her own. (116-17)

What Buckler does in such passages is to re-present or re-create the world by naming its micro-components. For the simple act of naming an object, as Merleau-Ponty explains, is to tear it away from the dimension of the individual or particular, and to see in it the representative of an essence or category.[16]

In the writer's exploration of perception, I have shown how, somewhat like modernist and postmodernist painters and artists, Buckler plays with the role of memory. The passages of chaotic enumeration illustrate how Buckler, like Kant, identifies perception with the imagination, and makes a distinction between the reproductive imagination and the creative imagination. For Buckler, as with Kant, the imagination seems to be a mediator between sensibility and understanding. We perceive or have an intuition of something,[17] which becomes stored away in our memory. When we wish to re-present it, we do not see it as if it were present; we see it through our imagination—Kant's reproductive imagination. Kant's distinction in *Critique of Pure Reason* (1781) between the reproductive and creative forms of Imagination[18] (the latter being the prolongation of the former, involving a constructive, structuring process, an elaboration) was the development of the two types of Imagination posited since the Renaissance. It was then taken up in almost identical terms by one of the most influential Romantic thinkers and critics. Coleridge in his *Biographia Literaria* distinguished between the primary and the secondary Imagination. Like Kant's reproductive imagination, Coleridge's primary Imagination is the "prime Agent of human Perception," while the secondary Imagination, an "echo" of the former, different only in degree and mode of operation, "dissolves, diffuses, dissipates, in order to re-create" (452). The concept was taken up by many writers such as Edgar Allan Poe and through him, in turn, Baudelaire, who admired his work and introduced it to his compatriots by translating it into French.

Through his stark enumerations, Buckler in effect (re)presents the world. Elsewhere in his texts, he prolongs and develops the things perceived, no longer contenting himself with re-activating the images already existing in his and our memories, but staging them. The creative imagination takes over and reiterates, constructs, and re-presents the world, in the sense of a representation that is a *mise en scène*, a performance or production. With Buckler, "the sudden enormity of the plainest object or its leopardry stops the mind, as when you see pictures of an elephant or a python or a secretary bird and the mind is stopped by the fantastic made suddenly more real than anything plausible" (*Ox Bells* 217). The imagination in this way mediates between life and conception. At times Buckler offers us a simple representation reduced to its basic element, the image. This recourse to Coleridge's primary Imagination calls to mind that the Romantic poet held it to be "a repetition in the finite mind of the eternal act of creation in the infinite I AM" (452). While doing this already amounts to making a weighty ontological statement, elsewhere Buckler shows that a full representation also entails a conception and a *mise en scène*. We shall see more clearly in the following chapter how, like many major thinkers elaborating an aesthetic philosophy, Buckler realizes the ultimate inadequacy of a mimetic presentation and the need for a cultural dimension of thought.

Buckler's recurrent technique of chaotic enumeration is nonetheless a fundamental step in his complex attempt to apprehend the nature of being in its organic wholeness and process. By naming the micro-components of the world, Buckler is re-creating the universe, reproducing the act of creation itself. For the ancient Greeks, the term κοσμοη (*cosmos*) signified order, beauty, the universe—in other words, the totality of things regulated by a rigorous order and therefore beautiful. The love of beauty, as we shall see further in chapter 5, is a source of pleasure, and beauty is closely linked to order, the exact-ness of the forms of things. In Buckler's wondering description of a humble daisy, the precision and complexity of its patterns evokes a divine plan, a perfect cosmic design:

> The daisy with its tens of white tongues encircling the thousand grains of gold mounded at its centre. Each speckling, or roundness, or pointedness, or wallpaper scrolling, or shading of color into color was as perfectly in pattern as if a draftsman's lifetime had gone into the making of it. There was not a pinpoint of earth where this infinite variety did not spring up side by side, yet not the smallest member of it without a purity of diagram to dumfound [*sic*] gods or worlds. (*Ox Bells* 106)

In an essay entitled "Beauty," Emerson remarks how "the primary forms, as the sky, the mountain, the tree, the animal give us delight *in and for themselves;* a pleasure arising from outline, color, motion, and grouping" (*Nature* 19). The resemblance of the following litany with Buckler's passages, such as the chaotic enumeration quoted from *Ox Bells*, is striking, leading us to infer an influence rather than simple coincidence:

> Almost all the individual forms are agreeable to the eye, as is proved by our endless imitations of them, as the acorn, the grape, the pine-cone, the wheat-ear, the egg, the wings and forms of most birds, the lion's claw, the serpent, the butterfly, sea-shells, flames, clouds, buds, leaves, and the forms of many trees, such as the palm. (*Nature* 19)

Buckler's enumeration, like Emerson's, is a form of ontological vehemence, to borrow a term from Paul Ricoeur. The French philosopher argues, "Dire 'cela est,' tel est le moment de la *croyance, l'ontological commitment* [*sic*] qui donne sa force 'illocutionnaire' à l'affirmation"

(313). Indeed, if it is often true, as John L. Austin pointed out in his work on the speech act, that to tell is to act, it is judicious of Ricoeur to expand the notion of the performative to affirmations of being. When Buckler announces "This is," or "that exists," he is in effect (re)creating the be-ing of the object. In poetic texts,[19] according to Ricoeur, such a practice of vehement affirmation contains "le moment extatique du langage" (313), the ex-tatic moment of language, when language is outside of itself, expressing a desire to efface itself, to vanish within the confines of the "l'être-dit," the "being-said."

## Ex-stasy

When Buckler describes the "primary forms" of Emerson, or thus simply affirms their existence, he creates simultaneously a state of joy. The apparition of a humble object, an animal, a form, is accompanied by an influx of light and power, a flash of consciousness, an encounter with the sublime. Emerson argues that a mark of wisdom is to "see the miraculous in the common" (*Nature* 92). Buckler is Emerson's wise man, his transcendentalist who believes "in inspiration, and in *ecstasy*" ("The Transcendentalist" 90, emphasis mine). In "The Over-soul," Emerson defines the term "Revelation" as "the announcements of the soul, its manifestations of its own nature," and argues that it is always accompanied by "the emotion of the sublime." Such an experience is essentially a "communion," an "influx of the Divine mind into our mind" (*English Traits* 145). He observes that the individual's reaction can vary from a mild emotion to "an exstasy [sic] and trance and prophetic inspiration" (145). That Romantic "shudder of awe and delight with which the individual soul always mingles with the universal soul" (146) imbues the production of many an artist working in the first half of the twentieth century, from the Group of Seven and Emily Carr to Bliss Carman, and up to even that technological virtuoso Glenn Gould,[20] and it provides the very groundwork of Buckler's texts.

Barbara Pell has pointed out that the structure of *The Mountain and the Valley* is a sequence that is composed "not of actions but of spots of time or epiphanic moments" (31). The boy protagonist indeed has the capacity to see the miraculous in the common, and thus transcend, be transported or "translated," fusing the individual with the universal, the prosaic with the sacred. When, during moments that by themselves would be satisfying, he thinks of the words of the Christmas play he is to act in, he feels *"doubly* translated," as if he "touched the very quick of the day" (58). David connects with the essence of being in the most ordinary actions that Buckler, in one of his frequent passages of inner focalization, enumerates in an accumulative, paratactic style, akin to a crescendo. Flashes of connectedness generate ecstasy

> when you hit the ball and then ran to the tree and back, with your breath all gone and your side all shouting, just before the ball got back too; or when the calf you were leading suddenly began to caper and then run like the wind, you couldn't stop him, you could barely hang onto the chain, and then the laughing struck you, and as you bounced along, your feet barely touching the ground, the laughter gaining in you in each step, you seemed to be lifted right out of the bright daylight still. (59)

These moments of epiphany or of "Revelation," as Emerson puts it, occur apparently out of nowhere in *Ox Bells and Fireflies*, illuminating the ordinariness of the day like "fireflies of what could only be called pure joy" (51). The older narrator compares such an epiphany to the ecstasy that transcendentalists and theosophists borrowed from Eastern religions:

> It was a kind of instant Zen, come by with no effort at all. Perhaps in the most humdrum hour it would strike you right out of the blue, and for the length of one dazzling pulsebeat lift you higher than a June of kites into that sky of skies where *the glass between inside and outside melts completely away.* (52, emphasis mine)

Buckler achieves the fusion of the internal and the external, consciousness and universe, a privileged timeless state of pure being in which, to borrow Emerson's terms once again, the "act of seeing and the thing seen, the seer and the spectacle, the subject and the object, are one" (*English Traits* 138). It is a world in which "outside-the-kitchen and inside-the-kitchen meet hands out, at the open door" (*Ox Bells* 31), in an overlapping foregrounded by personifications, homely metaphors, and convoluted compound words.

In *The Cruelest Month*, Buckler conceptualizes on such experiences of intense correspondence. In a conversation between the protagonists

Bruce and Sheila, the young woman makes a declaration that is reminiscent of David, in *The Mountain and the Valley*, finding the introspective writing of a Forster "more rapturously adventurous than any odyssey of action" (244). Sheila declares that "the only events that matter are the ones that take place inside you. And nine times out of ten when *they come over you* you're still as a telegraph pole" (133, emphasis mine). Then, in a shift to inner focalization, and through the filter of language and culture—a technique that I shall examine more closely in the next chapter—Buckler explores the nature and manner of these epiphanies:

> Real events weren't verbs at all, they were phrases. She thought of them as heralded by a little premonitory dazzle, like when you first turned the television set on, and then some striking picture of truth or feeling falling into place. The most eventful lives of all might well be those that had the most little phrase-dazzles like that in them, though not a muscle was moving.
> And what flashed them on? Hardly ever the rat-a-tat and the verbs. Some line on a page. Some glimpse. Some glance. Some echo in the mind. Some quality of stillness....The way this April sun demonstrated all geometry in its shadow patterns on this ground. (133-34)

The passage indicates that the catalyst resides in the senses, perhaps principally in vision, in a sensibility to shape and form. Among the primary forms cited by Emerson (the sky, the mountain, the tree, the animal) Buckler in *The Cruelest Month*, as in many a short story, chooses the deer as his vehicle of epiphany. Practically all the protagonists in the novel experience an almost mystical encounter with a deer. In Buckler's fiction, the figure of the deer often exemplifies divine order, an ultimate and perfect Design. At other times, the deer is a metaphor for the human condition, as when the writer evokes the wounded buck wandering in the forest, "sick and puzzled and bleeding in the dark."[21] In *The Cruelest Month*, a wild deer "standing watching you" is the incarnation of the perceiver perceived, the fusion of subject and object of the gaze. The omniscient narrator describes it oxymoronically as "the stillest, livingest thing there is" (264). Then, through the eyes of Sheila, we remark that the animal incarnates the fusion of all opposites: stasis/movement, the material/the ethereal, fantasy/reality, the ephemeral/the infinite. It is of the world and yet other-worldly.

> It's very *stillness* was *electric* with life, it was framed there in the morning's immaculacy with an *airiness* of such *un*earthly grace that it seemed *hardly corporeal*. It seemed like something her eyes had *drawn* on the *air*. It seemed as if the whole morning had been *arrested*, and *forever*, in its posture of *the moment;* like those people in a *fairy tale* at the moment the spell (or the curse) is cast. (264; emphases mine)

The deer is perfection incarnated. At the scent of the human beings, its head goes up "flawlessly," and it begins to run with an "exquisitely smooth translation of statue into motion" as if its feet do not quite touch the ground, and as "sure-pathed" and as "collisionless" as "the light." Finally, we learn that in "one last transcendental parabola," it "*vaulted* a windfall" and was gone. It is at that precise moment that Sheila has her "*vaulting* insight" (264, emphases mine), her moment of epiphany. Her "illumination" is described as being "of the rare kind that comes only when the mind has been conditioned just so to be triggered just so by the present spectacle: when something in that spectacle turns the tumblers of the heart's combination the one way in a million that will make it fly open" (264). Sheila, an unhappily married character who has decided altruistically to give up her lover Bruce and stay with the husband who needs her, suddenly realizes with absolute, cold clarity, the significance of a concept that is present in overt or covert form in all of Buckler's texts and that I shall explore in chapter 4. The apparition of the deer, form of natural perfection, triggers the awareness of a cultural concept presented as a universal truth, and as the path to serenity. She undergoes a transcendental experience that transports her beyond perception to "*ap*perception" (266). Sheila sees "in this sudden light, the charactered—rather than the caricatured—face of stoicism" and realizes "how little, how very little, happiness matter[s]" (264). She ceases to suffer, and in that moment, "without its being happiness at all," we are told that she "had never been so happy" (265). The perfect form of the deer is the vehicle that carries the dynamics of aporia.

Another protagonist, Kate, has already experienced the hyperclarity of an epiphany in all its blinding light, but not triggered by the glimpse or glance evoked by Sheila, but rather by "some echo in the mind" or "quality of stillness" (134) occurring after her father's death. Her vision is compared to the blinding clarity of a beam of light revolving in the darkness, or the way "a light-bulb filament seems to distend the room with sudden brilliance just before its extra charge extinguishes it" (75). Here too the epiphany is ultimately a unifying force: it creates a magical mathematical fusion between diametrically opposed concepts, transforming one event into infinity itself: "once for everything was enough. It was simple arithmetic. Once was only one more than never, subtracting. But *divide* never (or zero) into once and you found out how many times once contained it. The quotient was infinity" (75).

Ex-stasis is an illumination comparable to being struck by grace. It allows the subject to break beyond the surface of things, catapults him or her out of time and space into an "eternal and unaging present" (266) where the past joins the future in a neverending now. Such manipulation, even conquest, of Time is a recurrent strategy in Buckler's fiction, and is evocative of other modernist writers, such as Marcel Proust, who in his *A la Recherche du temps perdu* also used art to provide access to what is beyond Time and Space. In *The Mountain and the Valley*, David experiences a sudden "complete translation to another time," not a memory with an "echo quality" to it, but a "transfiguration":

> It is not a returning: you are there for the first time, immediately. No one has been away—nothing has changed—the time or the place or the faces. The years between have been shed. There is an original glow on the faces like on the objects of home. It is like a flash of immortality: nothing behind you is sealed, you can live it again. You can begin again. (289)

In the unpublished short story "Indian Summer," it is through a dream that the protagonist achieves the state Buckler is always striving for, the God-like straddling of past and future in which looking ahead is equivalent to looking back. In the character's dream he is once more a child surrounded by playmates, but they are not really any younger:

> We seemed to be talking about all the things that we knew were *going* to happen. You see, we knew what they were, because we were our own selves at the same time....But that

was the nicest part of the whole dream, knowing all the things that *had really gone, but still having them to look ahead to* as if we hadn't used up any of them.²² (second emphasis mine)

In *The Cruelest Month*, Bruce's glimpse of the deer dissolves and rearranges 'reality' in a fashion similar to the dream. His mind leaps backwards to the time in his childhood when he once saw such an animal, a "wild, secret, beautiful thing that not even the grown men of the place had ever set eye on" (267). He is projected into a golden age, a Garden, a shining Orphic society in which even the trees and fields are young, in which there

> was no ghost from the outmoded future then to cast its shadow on the present and corrode it like a machine. There was no consciousness in anyone or anything, not even in the rocks, of Time's outmoding its very self. All things lived on a plain of a replete and self-renewing now, which stayed as young to the adult as it did to the child. (266)

Ultimately, the state of "ex-stasy" allows one to fully participate in Merleau-Ponty's "chair," to lift the corner of Shelley's veil, to glance out of Plato's cave, to go beyond appearance and divine the essence, or what Buckler calls the *is-ness* of things, a concept that I shall examine within the framework of his aesthetic philosophy in chapter 5. Immediately preceding the apparition of the deer, Sheila notices with extreme clarity all the forms around her, which seem to be the physical manifestations of a divine order and design. On the ground beneath the "living growth" the narrator contrasts the "blasted remnants of other seasons" and specifies that in "both these *diagrams* of life and death was represented every *linear* or *curvilinear pattern* possible" (262; emphases mine). We witness the striving toward unity, toward ultimate fusion with the universal Be-ing, that remains forever, tantalizingly, just out of reach:

> She felt the exaction on her of each detail's being precisely as it was; an indescribable beckoning to her to know its essence through and through and so *erase its excommunicate otherness*, yet never yielding up that last punishing bit more than sight could quite devour. (262, emphasis mine)

Celebrating "each detail's being precisely as it" is and evoking its "indescribable beckoning...to know its essence" are the things that Buckler does best. He, like Emerson, sings that "wonderful congruity between man and the world" (*Nature* 84), and yet does not deny its "excommunicate otherness." This desire to erase the ineffaceable alterity of what is not the self, to overcome the dynamics of aporia and dissolve the many into the One, is what generates Buckler's writing. He blends the concepts of art proffered by Plotinus and Schopenhauer, for whom ecstasy is the process of identification with the absolute. For Plotinus, God emanates, and the individual, by contemplating the Divine, can achieve identification and fusion. For Schopenhauer, art is an intuition of the absolute, granting us access to Unity, as opposed to science, which grants us access only to "the phenomenon, its laws, its context and the resulting relations."[23] (108) While science can never reach a final goal, art, according to Schopenhauer, "is everywhere at its goal" (108). The philosopher's development of the observation that the true work of art "repeats or reproduces the eternal Ideas grasped through pure contemplation, the essential and abiding element in all the phenomena of the world" (108) would seem to be a precise description of Buckler's writing. It certainly is the groundwork for the virtual novel that his protagonist David means to write but that is always just outside his grasp. We can compare David's embryonic ideas for the novel with Schopenhauer's commentary on the ideal work of art:

> All the faces there were everywhere else in the world, at every time, waited for him to give the thought to exactly how each of them was. (What about the Englishman or Frenchman or the Micmac who might have stood on this very spot exactly how long ago?) There was the listening fact of the presence outside him of every eye, every lash, every smile-wrinkle of every cheek that had ever been; possible to be known, but unattended, because he had never seen them...And the frightening clarity...I could realize *the whole content of everything there is*, he thought, if they didn't swarm so. (*Mountain* 295-96, emphasis mine)

> For [the work of art] plucks the object of its contemplation out of the stream of the world's course, and holds it isolated before it. And this particular thing, which in that stream was a minute part, becomes for art, *a representative of the whole, an equivalent of the endless multitude in space and time.* So art

pauses at this particular thing; it stops the wheel of time, for art the relations vanish; only the essential, the Idea, is its object. (*Schopenhauer* 108)

We can see that for Buckler too, there is an absolute Unity, the *noumenon*, that is apprehendable when we go beyond our senses, beyond appearances, thanks to the power of imagination, that Schopenhauer acknowledged to be "an essential element of genius" (110). If it were not for the imagination, the philosopher remarks, the intellect of the genius "would be limited to the Ideas of the objects actually present to him personally, and dependent upon the chain of circumstances that brought these objects to him" (110). In this way, the artist's field of action would be drastically restricted; David would be able to apprehend only the faces that he himself had encountered. But if it is conceivable for him to apprehend "every smile-wrinkle of every cheek that had ever been," that has ever existed or will ever exist, it is thanks to the powers of the imagination, which extend his horizon, in the words of Schopenhauer, "far beyond the limits of his actual personal experience, and thus enable him to construct the rest of the picture out of the little that comes into his own actual apperception, and so to let almost all the possible scenes of life pass before him in his own consciousness" (110). The protagonist of *The Mountain and the Valley*, like its author, can indeed aspire to relate "the whole content of everything there is" (296).

Buckler's texts are evocative of Coleridge's synthesis of Kantian and Schopenhauerian concepts, notably in his concept of the secondary Imagination, which "struggles to idealize and to unify" and which is essentially "*vital*, even as all objects (*as* objects) are essentially fixed and dead" (Coleridge, Biographia 452, emphasis in original). Coleridge's Romantic idea finds itself at the heart of many other modernist writers, such as Proust, who also realized that art transports us to the other side of individuality, of the divide. Like David, who is often his mouthpiece, Buckler realizes that a single core of meaning underlies all things, that it is "manifest not differently but only in different aspects, in them all" (*Mountain* 298-299). The gaze of the writer, the work of art itself, makes up "the single beam of light" that is "enough to light all the shadows, by turning it from one to another" (299). But Buckler keeps an ironic distance from his protagonist, who, following a representation of a whole series of self-delusions,[24] confidently affirms that finding the single core of meaning is "so gloriously simple" (298), and who does not stop to "consider *how* he would find it" (299, the emphasis is, significantly, Buckler's).

Ultimately, Buckler's texts are the "line on a page," the "glimpse," the "glance," the "echo" that trigger in many a reader the flash of ecstasy that puts them also in communion with the cosmos and its divine origins, even if only for a blinding moment, as it did for Pamela Frye of McClelland and Stewart when she read *Window on the Sea*:

> The sentences, leaping out at me, set up such a singing in my head that it became a whole orchestra. It made me feel exactly the way I feel when, after months and months of dark grey city life, a sudden burst of sky or landscape, or even one tree or one flower, brings all my senses alive and prickling, and I am again at the beginning of the world.[25]

## Beyond Perception: Apperception

The philosophical elements that are so dominant in the epilogue of *The Mountain and the Valley*, but recur throughout all of Buckler's fictional work, are not only centred round the questions of perception or Imagination but also grounded in self-reflexivity. They can often be found in earlier non-fictional material. In an early and delightfully humorous essay on metaphysics, "So What and the Seven Paradoxes," which was not included in the selected prose and verse of *Whirligig*, Buckler playfully engages the reader in a reflection on the concepts of movement, change, epiphenomenalism, causation, continuity, self-determination, time, and space ("mere 'forms' of thinking"),[26] all paradoxes "of the first water, no matter how thin you slice it or how many metaphors you mix" (1). Encouraging the reader to participate in the process through the use of imperatives, rhetorical questions, and informal phatic interjections such as "stick with me," "attaboy," "yeah you win" or "it gets funny later," he gives us a guided tour of thinkers (philosophers but also writers) from Berkeley, Hume and Kant, to Joyce and Faulkner. Although he quotes his philosophy instructor as saying "It's very difficult to put the cosmic mystery into a proposition an undergraduate can remember," he himself succeeds rather well, particularly with the device of cacology—the deliberate over-use of the mixed (and dead) metaphor: "determination from behind, like a kick in the pants, becomes self-determination—which is a horse of a different color, if not the shoe on the other foot" (7).

Another humorous but philosophically profound piece, "By Guess or By God," was also ultimately cut from *Whirligig* because it seemed to Diane Swift, editor at McClelland and Stewart, to compete with the essay "Alienated" in the realm of donnish humour. Structured as a discussion between a student of philosophy called Phil and a student of cybernetics called Cy, it playfully juggles concepts of chance and design, appearance and reality, causality and free will: "how can anyone look at a lobster and not believe?"[27] There are more serious notes, as when the skeptic Cy foregrounds all the trivia, the mediocrity, the pettiness in the world to dismiss the idea of any transcendent planner or First Cause. He asks Phil to consider

> [n]ot the catastrophes, or the evils, or the villains on a godlike scale, mind you. Just the bunglers, the butterfingers, the chuckleheads, the galoots....Not death, but bunions. Mark you all that's straggling and incomplete; a row of rotted fence posts sprawling every which way, the carroway [*sic*] seed that *doesn't* sprout....Never mind rascality, but note what's merely fishy or fraudulent. Not the slum, but the puny nasturtiums growing inside an old auto tire beside a farmer's dingy porch. Consider everything that's not the real thing, but the shoddiest imitation—in dress or in character. All the "cheapnesses." (7)

In this overtly philosophical text, the startlingly grotesque zeugma yoking death and bunions, the hypnotic alliteration, the metaphorical dynamics using the particular to suggest the general, the concrete to evoke the abstract, are the same favourite devices that Buckler uses in his fiction, which, too, is heuristic. Several passages in these two pieces provide material for later fictional works. One example is how Buckler in *The Mountain and the Valley* reworks certain reflections, notably for David's altered microcosmic mode of perception in the Epilogue. In "So What and the Seven Paradoxes" Buckler had explored the impossibility of perceiving deviation from uniformity if the process is too slow or too fast for our mode of attention. *The Mountain and the Valley*'s final self-reflexive outpouring illustrates this concept. In this passage, a unit breaks down into subsequent subunits, which in turn are spliced *ad infinitum*: "the single thought seems to contain it all. But just as I move on to something else the thought breaks down like a stream forking in the sand. Then the forks fork. Then the forks' forks fork, like the chicken-wire pattern of atoms" (296). The movement is from the macro to the microscopic and through the infinite progression toward the infinitesimal, back to the cosmic:

> And "hand" is a word, and what is a word?...And "n" is a letter in the word, shaped exactly that way, and sounded by exactly that movement of the tongue, and in exactly how many other words? And behind the tiniest delta in the tiniest line in my father's cheek, and behind the smallest of the smallest arcs of movement of his arms, were implicit all the thoughts that led him here...exactly here...exactly then... (296)

The outpouring moves with remarkable originality from metalanguage to what we could call meta-thought. Although an attempt is made to structure thought into signifier and signified, to delimit it in space and confine it in time, it soon escapes control and proves to be "broader than space and faster than time" (297). The movement is one of simultaneous acceleration and deceleration, implosion and explosion, a vertiginous splicing of time and space, reality and virtuality:

> Suddenly there were all the voices of all things everywhere at all times as they *might* have been. If the wind had been exactly that infinitesimal different sometime....If somewhere some face had smiled a hair's breadth differently...If only one thought had shaped itself exactly that little way other than the way it did....Then all the rest of it....He heard the crushing screaming challenge of the infinite permutations of the possible...the billion raised to the billionth power...
> 
> He screamed, "Stop, stop..."
> 
> Then he thought: Myself screaming "Stop," Then he thought: Myself thinking of myself screaming "Stop," thinking of myself thinking of myself thinking of... (297)

This rushing process, this Chinese box spiral of meta-metas, is the fictional re-enactment of Phil's challenge to Cy in "By Guess or By God": "Do you think it is no miracle that a man can think about something and think about his *thinking* about it, *at the same time?*" (6), and of

Buckler's concluding paragraph on self-objectification in "So What and the Seven Paradoxes":

> How can the mind watch its own activity...that seems like a job for *two*. The eyes, for instance, see objects, but they can't see *themselves*. And how can the mind watch itself and, *at the same time—not later*, watch even it's [*sic*] own watching? That's no trick of words, it'll get you if you think about it. That is, think about how the mind can think about itself thinking about itself thinking about its own thinking....Gertrude, I believe you've got something there! (14)

Anticipating Merleau-Ponty's theoretical elaboration, Buckler argues that our gaze must be coupled with another gaze, a complementary one: ourselves seen from the outside, as another would see us, in the process of contemplating him or her. Buckler's writing is thus a continuous exploration, a body of metaphysical questions, an epistemological attempt to arrive at an understanding of the nature of society, of the human mind, of the cosmos, and of knowledge itself. Throughout all of his work, he strove toward an ultimate synthesis of the soul (unity of all our representations), the world (unity of all phenomena), and God (or First Cause). In a letter he wrote in 1939 to *Esquire*'s readers' column "The Sound and the Fury," Buckler had expressed contempt for writers of fiction who attempt to tackle philosophical issues. He argued that "someone should tell them that cosmic formulas are too complex, much too complex for them: and that you can't make a neat little story out of a theory of being, any more than you could make a ballet out of a differential calculus."[28] But in this chapter I have demonstrated how preoccupied Buckler himself was by such theories of being, by a desire to come to an understanding of the cosmos and of the nature of knowledge itself. If Buckler manages to take up the challenge and generate story out of a theory of being, it is doubtless through the hermeneutic dimension in his texts.

Buckler's phenomenological and ontological preoccupations are closely intermingled, and his writing explores the relationship of perception and apperception, language and being, language and the world (the subject of the next chapter). The metalinguistic extract from the epilogue of *The Mountain and the Valley* that we have just looked at notably anticipates Foucault's open dimension of

> un langage qui ne peut plus s'arrêter, parce que, jamais enclos dans une parole définitive, il n'énoncera sa vérité que dans un discours futur, tout entier consacré à dire ce qu'il aura dit; mais ce discours lui-même ne détient pas le pouvoir de s'arrêter sur soi, et ce qu'il dit, il l'enferme comme une promesse, léguée encore à un autre discours. (56)

Buckler, like Foucault, calls attention to the fact that the task of the commentary, by definition, is never completed, although it is turned wholly toward "la part énigmatique, murmurée, qui se cache dans le langage commenté" (56). Buckler perceives, as does Foucault, that the commentary engenders underneath the existing discourse another discourse that is more fundamental, more "first" ("comme 'plus premier'" (56)) which it sets out to restore.

We have glimpsed how closely language and the world are intertwined, how Buckler's texts tackle questions of consciousness and self-reflexivity to attempt to come to terms with the concept of perception and of Being itself. There is a gap between being and essence that Buckler explores. Faced with the dispersion in degree, quality, and hierarchy of the various beings we can apprehend—God, a table, a bucket, clearly cannot be put on the same plane—Buckler attempts to grasp Being in terms of Merleau-Ponty's "binder" or "flesh," the be-ing that unifies all objects or beings, in the very manner of the copula "to be," whose function is to link subject and predicate. In the struggle to make everything speak, to give a voice to every particle of existence, his narrators contemplate themselves in the act of contemplating, his protagonists describe themselves describing and think of themselves thinking. Perhaps we readers also end up looking at the eye of our own watching.

# The Word and the World

Je propose à chacun l'ouverture de trappes intérieures, un voyage dans l'épaisseur des choses, une invasion de qualités, une révolution ou une subversion comparable à celle qu'opère la charrue ou la pelle, lorsque, tout à coup et pour la première fois, sont mises à jour des millions de parcelles, de paillettes, de racines, de vers et de petites bêtes jusqu'alors enfouies. O ressources infinies de l'épaisseur des choses, *rendues* par les ressources infinies de l'épaisseur sémantique des mots!

—Francis Ponge,
"Introduction au galet," *Proêmes*

Michel Foucault has pointed out that humanity's original relationship to texts was identical to its relationship to things, consisting in both cases in perceiving, decoding, and interpreting visible marks or signs and their correspondences. A symbolic perception of the world persisted until the Renaissance and beyond: Nature was God's book, in which the signatures were hermeneutic points of departure. One read and interpreted the world through correspondences and resemblances between the high and the low, the spiritual and the material. Objects and places belonged to a pattern or design governed by unity and sympathy, relations between the part and the whole governed by analogy and proportion. The world was a text that could be read and decoded—it was pregnant with significance, the microcosm echoing the macrocosm, the visible surface reflecting the invisible just as time reflected or was the mobile image of eternity. Scientific and technological advances had not yet marginalized the symbolic and mythological conception of Antiquity. The secularization of society and the loss of the symbol of the Golden Age had not yet distanced the concept of Paradise from the archetype of the ideal *topos* or place or displaced it from the heart of the poetic imagination.

In a similar fashion, language before the ahistorical, mythical Babel was allegedly a perfectly transparent sign of things, which it resembled. After Babel, this transparency, this resemblance to things, was destroyed, and the languages that we speak today are rooted in this lost similitude, in the space left void (Foucault 47-51). Language no longer directly resembles the things it names. As Emile Benveniste points out, nothing signifies anything by itself or through any natural vocation, but through combination regulated by a strict code—the structure of the whole conferring significance or function on the parts (*Problèmes I* 23). The sign's lack of co-naturalness, remarks Hegel, is actually the source of the strength and richness of alphabetic language: the arbitrariness of the signifier liberates the imagination and allows arrangements not possible in a hieroglyphic language. But even if it no longer resembles the things it names, Foucault argues, language is not separated from the world. It continues to be a part of the space in which truth manifests itself, and its relationship with the world is as much that of analogy as that of signifying. Nevertheless, Benveniste remarks a serious difficulty that Saussure encountered but did not resolve: knowing if and how we get from the sign to "la parole" (*Cours de linguistique générale* 148, 172). Benveniste points out that the world of the sign is closed, that from the sign to the sentence there is no transition, that a hiatus separates them (*Problèmes II* 65). In his writing, Buckler seems to be trying to explore this relationship, to bridge the hiatus.

Buckler's texts would seem to be grounded in a vision of the world as text, a world in which signs circulate openly. There is a hermeneutic dimension in his work, a certain reordering of the world through *logos*. For Buckler—to use the terms of Foucault—the writer's knowledge involves making everything speak. It involves interpreting, superimposing the secondary discourse of commentary upon the visible marks, upon what Emerson called "the cipher of the world" (*Complete Essays* 279). It involves calling attention to the congruity, the correspondences to which town dwellers have become blind, as in the following passage combining personification and the blending of sense analogies:

> This morning, the windows of each house have their eyelids up....The hill beyond the houses talks softly to itself. (…) The hill talks to itself, and this one day in the year the morning talks *about* itself.
>
> I think…of people I have seen in town looking as if their faces were dragging themselves behind themselves. As if their bodies had gone out. How could they ever let themselves fall into that dreadful numbness, as if they didn't see what they heard or hear what they saw? (*Ox Bells* 32)

Resorting to metalinguistic metaphors, the narrating I of *Ox Bells* argues that city dwellers, too, have become disconnected from the cosmos, blind to correspondences:

> In the city you walk down the streets with their eyes put out, and noises without voice beat against each other without knowledge....Each face has its window to itself walled up, each with the small world behind it running like clockwork wound up and forgotten. They jostle each other, the eyes only a thing to steer them by. Headless subjects and predicates, no two ever joining to blood-stream a sentence. There is a bleaching yawn of distance between the closest things. (85)

But the narrator of *Ox Bells*, singing a paeon to a lost rural world in which each face is "written and readable in the same language as its neighbours'" (84), makes things speak. His relationship of sympathy with the universe is shattered only momentarily when death strikes the community. As I have illustrated in the preceding chapter with a passage from the typescript "Snow Apples," later published under the title "The Orchard," in which the evocation of the sister's death rendered the stones "deaf and dumb,"[1] only a momentous event like death can temporarily fracture the correspondences with Buckler's organic universe.

> There seems to be some sudden terrible question in the air. In this great stroke of silence from the dead that even the leaves hear, it shrieks to be answered.
>
> I am stunned. I go outside.
>
> I look at things. And look at them. But they don't tell me anything....
>
> They've retreated inside themselves, inside that ring of deafness, where they only talk to each other....I pick up a stone. I stare at it. It doesn't tell me anything....
>
> That night, we go to the dead man's house. Its windows do not speak. (*Ox Bells* 13)

In "The Orchard," the voice of an older narrator superimposes itself upon a childhood memory that he recounts, the diegetic events occurring in the past, told in the preterite, seeming to be mere pretexts for the narratorial voice unfolding in the present tense to luxuriate in commentary that is actually metaphysical speculation. In a moment of complete stasis in the narrative, the narrator establishes a relationship of complicity with the reader, confiding that

> [y]oung and old, we nearly always discover the nature of things by a chance illumination, touched off by what need be no more than a seemingly irrelevant trifle.
>
> Let your eye "happen" at the right moment on a moss-eaten shingle that has lost all but one of its nails to the winds of the years, and you will know all there is to know about melancholy. ("Orchard" 29)

The following extract from *Ox Bells and Fireflies* also illustrates how Buckler practises the technique he announces in the above passage from

"The Orchard." We can see how by juggling the abstract and the concrete, the particular and the general, synecdoche and metaphor, he fills with significance the most fleeting, at times trivial, elements or "trifles" that make up the spheres of both nature and culture:

> A calf's bangs. The Big Dipper. Huckleberry shine. A bluejay feather. The smell of oranges or pickling spice or britchen straps. An owl's eye. Looking down a deep hole. A snow crystal landing on the end of someone's nose. Seven 9's making 63. Everything being exactly what, when, and where it was at that very moment—stones being heavy, apples being round, water being cool. The touch of hand or sun or breeze. The taste of fern "meat." The sound of crickets winding their clocks. The fuzz on a bumblebee....Hundreds of things like these. ( 57)

Many reviewers have drawn attention to the way Buckler notices things, to the attention he pays to the smallest details in the world around him. Claude Bissell has remarked that in his prose, Buckler sought, first of all, for that glint of reality, the detail that illuminates, that makes you exclaim "That's how it really is!" ("His Prose"). The interweaving of language and the gaze, of seeing and saying, in this extract is illustrative of Buckler's recurrent strategy, similar to that of the modernist French poet Francis Ponge, of compiling, in the sense of the Greek *legein*, of bringing together into a whole, everything that has been seen and heard, that has been told by nature or by humans, through the language of the world or that of artists. "Connaître une bête, ou une plante, ou une chose quelconque de la terre, c'est recueillir toute l'épaisse couche des signes qui ont pu être déposés en elles ou sur elles," argues Foucault (55). Everything is *legenda*—things to read or decode. Nature is a fabric made up of signs, words, and marks, the world made up of stories, characters, forms, and discourse, as Buckler suggests to the reader repeatedly in *Ox Bells and Fireflies*. In an abundance of metalinguistic metaphors and similes, a technique we have remarked above in the extract on city dwellers from *Ox Bells*, it is through the lens of *langue*—language as system—and through the filter of print culture that he evokes (all emphases mine) "[e]ach object and all its *case inflexions*—the slope of a hill, the curve of the road, the up-and-downness of trees, the back-and-forthness of clapboards on the house" which "bask in being exactly themselves" (27). He evokes the ancient graves in the cemetery whose borders are "*traced* as if with some invisible *brush* of chapel light and chapel deafness," and which are "like *tablets* of inscrutability, *written* on the ground," asking "who would linger to *decipher* them, when the *inscription* the sun made on all the daisies and in all the green meadows of the blood was freshness everlasting?" (24). He refers to "the host of things that *spoke* from no '*text*' whatsoever, were mere *remarks* of themselves" (116). He describes a spring day flooded with the transforming force of sunshine:

> Bushes, vanished to only *initials* of themselves, are given back their total beings. Kingfishers bright as rings *draw* perfect parabolas on the air and sing of them. Clocks brighten at the thought of company, the bread knife awakens, and plates become *transitive*. (9)

Marigold seeds are "like little *commas* (as its blossoms are like *commas* in the solid *prose* of a summer afternoon)" (11), clouds during a funeral are "*black-capitaled* with the *word* 'never'" (17), the years an old couple has been together are "*lettered* on the air" (109).

For Buckler, just as for Emerson, words and deeds are in fact "quite indifferent modes of the divine energy" (Emerson, *English Traits* 170). Further on in this chapter, I shall demonstrate how Buckler embodies the definition of the writer that Emerson gives in his essay "The Poet," a definition that places artists among the ranks of heroes, even demiurges, and that equates writing and acting, word and deed (*English Traits* 169).[2] But never does Buckler forget that the writer is also "the Namer, or Language-maker," who names things "sometimes after their appearance, sometimes after their essence" (178). Buckler's constant striving for the right word corresponds to Emerson's injunction to put "eyes and a tongue into every dumb and inanimate object" (176), and to give to each thing "its *own* name and not another's" (178).

Buckler's texts revolve around the relationship between the word and the world. In the short story "Another Christmas," the author gives us access to a writer's innermost thoughts through the device of inner focalization. Using an embedding technique, the writer discourses when writing, and within his writing causes his protagonist, a writer, to discourse about writing. The voice of Steve, the writer-protagonist, blends and blurs with Buckler's voice, perceiving an untold story not only in the "big things," the "never-to-be-fathomed stuff of space and time, the human heart, the way the face is, the great gossamer-drifting mists of thought," but also "in all the little things too…the pebble and the snail's eye and the sleepy cat-thoughts and the worm's track you never saw and the billionth blade of grass" (*Rebellion* 31). The rhetorical device of polysyndeton—the extra repetition of the coordinating conjunction between each unit of the string of nouns—emphasizes the movement from the macro to the microscopic. In each smaller entity, there are "a million things" to tell, "more than you could ever tell in your whole lifetime" (31).

Buckler seems to sense that nothing can be understood without the medium of language. As Benveniste points out, language is the only proper instrument to describe, conceptualize, and interpret all of nature and all of experience. The word equals power: the power to act upon the world, to transform it, to make it one's own. This is because language represents the highest form of a faculty that is inherent to the human condition: the faculty to symbolize. The emergence of *Homo sapiens* from the animal kingdom is due above all to the faculty of symbolic representation, the common source of thought, language, and society (*Problèmes 2* 26-27). The writer-protagonist Steve is thus striving to reproduce and reorder reality through *logos*, just like David, the protagonist and aspiring writer of *The Mountain and the Valley*, who feels "the rush of communicativeness from everything he look[s] at," and then feels the need "to *possess* these things by describing them exactly in his mind" (201, emphasis mine). The equivalence between naming and possessing echoes Genesis, in which God has Adam name all the animals as a sign of his dominion over them. Through the inner focalization typographically signalled by parentheses, question marks, and suspension points the reader can trace the path toward the right word, the path to power: "(The water trickled in the ruts like?…like?…anxiety. *It was his now*.)" (*Mountain* 201, emphasis mine).

Although there are a million things to tell "and a million ways to tell every one of them…only one way for each of them [is] *right*" (*Rebellion* 32, emphasis mine). This throws light on the fear that underlies Buckler's texts, of not perceiving and recording everything exactly, the preoccupation with finding the perfectly appropriate expression, with combatting the "never-quite-exactness of the twinning of thing and word for it" for the multiplicity of things "clamour[ing] to be known exactly, and so possessed" (*Mountain* 201). David—here the writer's mouthpiece—reads the cipher of the universe in all its correspondences in "the glimpses provoked by the trick of a cloud pattern...or the blue dusklight seeming to come upward from the snow...or by any thing, face, thought, or feeling, which he seemed to see exactly, in an ephemeral instant" (232). But the multiplicity of the signs and the potential gap between the perception and the naming make the artist's task an awe/ful one: "There would be an awful challenge about each of these things, to name it. An accusing: as if it had been put there for him, and him alone, to see exactly and to record. As if in having neglected to perceive *every*thing exactly he had been guilty of making the object, as well as himself, incomplete" (233). The attempts he makes in his scribbler to record his perceptions seem at times "perfectly right" and are accompanied by the conviction that "if he wanted to, he could do as much for everything in the world." But then Buckler reports his dismayed realization that he can never witness the total picture in space and time, having missed certain "things gone by" and realized "all the things he would never *see*" and thus "know exactly." More than the dread of being able to find only words that are "inapproximate as a pattern built with crooked sticks," it is the "terror of failing [to see] even one particular" that paralyzes any attempt at "performance" (233).

It is here that Buckler places an ironic distance between himself and his protagonist, who yokes seeing and saying in too restrictive a framework. David does not make the distinction between the two forms of imagination that I discussed in the preceding chapter, articulated by Kant and then by Coleridge: the reproductive or primary imagination, the "prime Agent of human perception" (Coleridge, *Biographia* 452), and the creative or secondary imagination. While the former re-presents what we have stored away in our memory, the latter not only re-activates already existing basic images but reiterates, constructs, and represents in the sense of a performance. Buckler's structural irony posits that David is a failed artist because he fails to see that the imagination can mediate between life and conception. He can envisage only a mimetic presentation, and cannot see beyond or elaborate an aesthetic philosophy that involves a full representation or *mise en scène*.

In the novel's final chapter, David is visited in a series of epiphanic moments by the swarming images of

> [A]ll the faces there were everywhere else in the world, at every time, [that] waited for him to give the thought to exactly how each of them was. (What about the Englishman or the Frenchman or the Micmac who might have stood on this very spot exactly how long ago?) There was the listening fact of the presence outside him of every eye, every lash, every smile-wrinkle of every cheek that had ever been; possible to be known, but unattended, because he had never seen them. (296)

The realization does come to him that he need not have seen every "particular" (233) in order to "know how it is with everything" (298), and he experiences the fusion of word and world: "As he thought of telling these things exactly, all the voices came close about him....He went out into them until there was no inside left. He saw at last how you could *become* the thing you told" (298). In a sudden illumination, David realizes that the writer need not re-produce the myriad details that make up the total design:

> It wouldn't be necessary to take them one by one. That's where he'd been wrong. All he'd have to do...oh, it was so gloriously simple...was to find their single core of meaning. It was manifest not differently but only in different aspects, in them all. That would be enough. A single beam of light is enough to light all the shadows, by turning it from one to another. (298-99)

The search for the "single core of meaning" staged through the metaphor of light is strikingly similar to that of Buckler's other writer-protagonist, Steve. In "Another Christmas," as well, the artist's ambition is

> To find a single light that would come suddenly so that everything would fall into place as if you were looking at a picture that was only broken lines at first but as you looked at it, steadily, *suddenly all the broken lines flowed into a single image*, and the separate lines were gone and *everything was part of the same thing*. (*Rebellion* 32, emphases mine)

This view of telling, of representing, in which the author's voice blends with his protagonist's, resembles that of an Impressionist or post-Impressionist painter such as Emily Carr, whose 1935 entry in her painting journal describes in similar terms the canvas of *Fir Tree and Sky* that she was working on: "There is to be *one* sweeping movement through the whole air....The movement must *connect with each part*, taking great care with the articulation. A movement floating up. It is a study in movement, designed movement" (21). These remarkably similar outlooks seem to stem from a monist yearning for Unity, the search for the Plotinean One that lies behind the Many, for the fusion of the beholder and the object of vision reminiscent of Schopenhauer and Emerson. But according to our writer-protagonist Steve, the search is doomed to fail, and words in the end are but derisory: "you never found that single light...that single plan. No one ever did. So how could the little separate part you had told matter at all?" (*Rebellion* 32).

Buckler's other artist-protagonist, David, with whom he maintains an ironic distance, is not so lucid.[3] Even David's acknowledgement that he had been wrong is part of the structural irony, since his error is merely transformed. The markers of a too hastily formed evaluation in the inner focalization "*All* he'd have to do...*oh, it was so gloriously simple*" (*Mountain* 298) distance implied author and, thus, reader from the protagonist's ignoring or belittling the effort, even labour, needed to elaborate a full representation. The subsequent use of italics, parentheses, modalizing terms, and markers of evaluation call attention to the protagonist's perfunctory dismissal of the vital cultural dimension of thought, and criticize his eliding of process in favour of (vainglorious) product:

> He didn't consider *how* he would find it. (The words he'd put in the scribbler before now had never fallen smooth over the shape of the remembrance, or enclosed it all. But the minute he put the scribbler away the perfect ones seemed surely possible to be found the next time.) Nor how long it might take. (If you took a hundred years, then...he would live a hundred years.) He knew only that he would do it....It would make him the greatest writer in the whole world. (299)

Implicit as a countertext in both the short story and the novel I have been examining, as in Buckler's other works, is the inadequacy of the linguistic medium. The perfect word is never the one formed in the scribbler; it is always the virtual one, the next one, for next time.

Drawing the parallel between the two protagonists is useful in more ways than one. David is a writer only in his daydreams, which Buckler mocks by substituting the preterite, marker of "real" events, for the conditional, marker of the hypothetical: "(They had all read his book now. He felt that wave of pride and humbleness both, as they looked at him and thought: he understands everything...)" (299). The reader can be inclined to think that the shortcomings lie with the protagonist and not with language itself, that the problem resides in David's stopping short of performance. But his double, Steve, has actually become a writer. The setting of the story is a Christmas party celebrating his first novel, just published, that has received great critical acclaim and is already being termed a "bestseller" (*Rebellion* 34). The book, it is suggested, is his real Christmas present. Yet the publication of Steve's novel is ultimately insignificant. The book is a product of artifice devalorised by the implied author through the construction of an underlying countertext.[4] It is placed much lower on the scale of values than another present received at another Christmas long ago—the gift of his first pair of skates, gleaming and "clean like speed itself" (33). It is implied that a writer can never capture the bliss of revelation of that perfect movement of the "long clean sweep" when the body is one with the motion, the bliss of the immaterial possession inherent in that "first time you crossed over on the new skates and felt the cool wing-sure dip of it and knew that now you had it, really had it...," the bliss of knowing "it was *right*"[5] (33). Steve the child experiences in "real" life a transcendent experience that Steve the writer despairs of ever capturing in words. Although the protagonist sings a hymn to the world of words, a parallel universe in which the writer is an explorer, he never ceases to question their adequacy.

In fact, just as I have argued in the preceding chapter that the dynamics of aporia lie at the heart of Buckler's ontological concerns, I shall now attempt to demonstrate that the writer's stance on language is grounded in ambivalence and tension. On the one hand, Buckler celebrates nature and the bookless society of simple farmers and fishermen. Language is a sham, and the absence of books is declared no lack at all, for the only text that is worth reading and that does not lie is the cosmos. The author forces the reader to share his point of view through the devices of rhetorical questions, anaphora, and zeugma, yoking the metaphysical to the trivial:

what was the lack? When everyone had read with his nerve ends the only great writers—earth, sky, rock, and tree—(not *these* the petticoated little pen-men mooning about doubt and heartburn)—and been strengthened by them. When familiar faces held all the texts that mattered....When there were whole libraries in the eyes of someone you'd been through all the weathers with—the eyes which had themselves read the only utterances (of sun and storm) that are without deceit, and the only records that are printed without falsity (on field and kitchen) messages that make words the mere chips and whittlings of feeling entire. (*Ox Bells* 193-94)

Buckler's discourse either overtly or covertly devalorizes artists, and denigrates men whose hands have been *"womanized* by pen and paper" (*Window* 57), who have become *"petticoated* little pen-men" (*Ox Bells* 193, emphases mine). I have pointed out in chapter 2 the presence of value judgments underlying the pejorative lexicon censuring verbal skills as being sterile and effeminate. As a corollary, we find in his textual universe that it is "the most common things" that "flash out with the statement of all things that could not be said," and that "you yourself could never describe" (*Ox Bells* 194). What more dismissive remark about verbal skills could be imagined than that in "The First Born Son," when the inarticulate farmer who loves his land offers this assessment of city dwellers: "[w]hen they talked it was empty...none of them had anything to say that could not be said in words" (*Rebellion* 22). And in Rabelaisian fashion, Buckler equates oral virtuosity with anal virtuosity, declaring that being articulate ranks learned people with those who "can fart at will" (*Ox Bells* 277).

Ostensibly, then, his texts proclaim the supremacy of nature and deny the power and significance of culture and language. Yet on the other hand, the writer thinks and relates to the world through the filter of culture—more specifically, through the filter of *langue*, or language as system. The following extracts from *Ox Bells*, like those at the beginning of this chapter, demonstrate how Buckler perceives and apprehends the world through the structuring principle of grammar, and maps it out in metalinguistic, self-reflexive terms:

> loneliness writes its sleepless letter of a name slantwise across everything like a cancellation mark (299)

> The hawks left the quotation marks of their wings' landing around the mouse blood on the frozen crust (302)
>
> conversation [that] striped the air like the lines on blank foolscap (266)
>
> "The" points to something in particular. "And" connects two things that are different. In the city, so much is alike that only a few "the's" are found, no more than a handful of "and's" is needed to couple them. Here [in the village] the "the's" were numberless, the "and's" infinite. (212)

In the rest of this chapter, I shall first connect this tension—this attraction for and denigration of language—to the heritage left behind by Emerson. I shall then demonstrate how the relationship between the word and the world, involving the dynamics of aporia—establishing and maintaining a deliberate irresolution between two opposing stances—rather than of dialectic, in which contradictions are resolved, constitutes the central question of Buckler's second novel, *The Cruelest Month*. The insights of linguists such as Saussure and Benveniste will provide an analytical framework for my reading of the novel, which ultimately posits that all major human experiences exist only through language.

Because of the immediate dependence of language upon nature, those who are close to the land, who work with the earth, are in Emerson's opinion the true poets, wielding a savoury, "piquant" language that "all men relish" (*Nature* 37). The artist is not the European aesthete but the North American "strong-natured farmer or backwoodsman" (37). Buckler celebrates this savoury language in *Ox Bells*, calling attention to the people's sure sense of metaphor. In an encounter between an old farm woman and a reputed history scholar, for instance, the domestic analogy is all the more powerful for its homeliness. When the professor tells the woman that with her observant eye and sure sense of detail she should be the historian, she demurs, saying "I'd rather knit a sock than unravel one" (248).

The farm is the material embodiment of the natural cycle or chain of being in which we all have our place, in which all parts work for the whole (*Nature* 16). Moreover, in essays like "The American Scholar," Emerson specifically extols the sacredness of work, applauds the "dignity and necessity of labor to every citizen," specifying that "[t]here is virtue yet in the hoe and the spade, for learned as well as for unlearned hands" (*English Traits* 15). Emerson scoffs at the notion that the writer or scholar should be "unfit for any handiwork or public labour," and proclaims that "Action is with the scholar subordinate, but it is essential" for, without it, "thought can never ripen into truth" (12). Action is "the raw material out of which the intellect molds her splendid products" (13).

Coming from a rural, bookless society, Ernest Buckler must have found most comforting Emerson's exaltation of manual work, and most attractive his description of the strange process by which "experience is converted into thought, as a mulberry leaf is converted into satin" (13). We know only so much as we have lived, claims Emerson— the "pearls and rubies" of discourse emanate from our experience, and so for a true scholar every opportunity of action passed by is "a loss of power" (13). This stance consolidates and valorizes the choices of an author who declares himself a "farmer who writes, not a writer who farms."[6] Buckler's decision to abandon a career in Toronto and to return to the family farm is in accord with Emerson's glorification of the advantages that "the country life possesses for a powerful mind, over the artificial and curtailed life of cities" (*Nature* 39).[7] We shall see how the dialectic between city and country is a powerful catalyst in Buckler's texts, such as his novel *The Cruelest Month*, in which the country boy Bruce leaves medical school and comes back to the land, "the only place where exhaustion made you feel cleaner at night, not dirtier" as opposed to the "pencil men" or "think men" or even the athletes with their "toy muscles" to do "the only work that made you feel you were plugged into life's main artery" (136).

It is Emerson's notion of life—of work and action as so much "raw material" for the artist—that we find forcefully present in Buckler's writing, as well as the philosopher's perception of life in terms of language and culture. As Emerson puts it in "The American Scholar," life is "our dictionary," while work, in trade and manufacturing as well as in country labours, is a means of "mastering in all their facts a language by which to illustrate and embody our perceptions" (*English Traits* 13). Buckler aligns himself with Emerson when in an interview granted to Don Cameron he argues, with earthy metaphors (although the metaphors are tame compared to his remarks in his personal journal) that when "too many writers get together it gets to be a kind of masturbatory enterprise. They tend to rub themselves off against each other and they tend to talk too much. And once you've talked a thing out, you've had it" ("Interview" 5).

Buckler certainly aligns himself with Emerson's claim that life is "the quarry from whence we get tiles and cope-stones for the masonry of today" (13). In the interview with Cameron, he contrasts writers who are introspective, who are "looking at what they are doing all the time," (5-6) with "people who really live" (5), who "just act" (6). Buckler argues that the writer is always "schizophrenic"—both actor and spectator: "You have to be acting to get some substance; you also, at the same time, have to be a spectator, you have to observe people who just act simply" (8). Emerson's vivid quarry metaphor will find its echo in Buckler's texts, but with a wry twist when characters emphasize the role of spectator at the expense of that of actor, when they place more importance on art than on life. This occurs in both the short story "Another Christmas" and in *The Cruelest Month*. In the short story, Steve, the writer-protagonist re-creates for us the parallel universe of words that he builds. This parallel world is presented in spatial and architectural terms, and the writer is a demiurge, in the Gnostic sense of subordinate supernatural creator, springing from the Greek *demiourgos* or skilled workman. Buckler introduces an element of uneasy ambivalence when the artist ceases to be an actor or participant in the real world, and is reduced to the role of observer, using the world as mere building material. The real world fades because it has become "only something to tell" (*Rebellion* 31). Significantly, in the play *By Sun and Candlelight*, Buckler proclaims the writer to be a "*shadow*-merchant in the thistle-down of words," and in a holograph draft of "Muse in Overalls," the opening section, which was later edited out, proclaims that the writer "feels like a *shadow*-merchant, an *echo*-merchant (...) [and] the architecture of fiction particularly may seem like that of a *doll's house.*"[8] Even in Buckler's earliest unpublished material, such as the embryonic piece "No Matter Which People Are There," the young writer's artist persona complains in the original ending of "the emptiness of white paper," and the "kind of emptiness it started when he tried to put things down." A certain vampiristic quality is reinforced when he claims that what has taken him off his course in "the real world" is "this wandering in the mirror world alongside it, the ghost-world of words."[9] This ambivalence is fostered, albeit from a different angle, in *The Cruelest Month*. I shall examine further on how one of the characters, the writer Morse, feeds on others for story.

Buckler's texts certainly share with Emerson's a certain wariness, even contempt, for pure book-learning. Emerson warns his contemporaries not to attach the sacredness of the act of creation to the product itself, equating such a drift to the manner in which respect for a hero can be corrupted into worship of the statue. As a result, society ends up not with a thinking human being, but with a "bookworm" (*English Traits* 9). In the light essay "School and Me," published in *Maclean's* magazine, Buckler methodically deflates book-learning, humorously pointing out how formal education produces knee-jerk mechanisms instead of promoting true understanding. When he and his fellow schoolboys "got stuck on a problem," they "multiplied everything in sight by 4.86 or 3.1414. If that didn't help [they] had to give up" (44). Buckler's standpoint is analogous to that of Emerson, not only when the latter proclaims that the intellectual must serve society, but also when he proclaims that life is "the only way to learn grammar. Colleges and books only copy the language which the field and the workyard made" (*Traits* 14). The philosopher posits that life is superior to art, for when the artist "has exhausted his materials, when the fancy no longer paints...and books are a weariness, he has always the resource to *live*" (15).

Life and art, the world and the word, strive ceaselessly for preeminence in Buckler's works. The tension between nature and culture is nowhere more central to his textual system than in *The Cruelest Month*.[10] Examining this novel, which is characterized by an intense preoccupation with language and an acute awareness of itself as writing, will allow us to apprehend more clearly the confrontation of two opposing stances, involving a central structuring paradox and sustaining deliberate, indefinite irresolution. Janice Kulyk Keefer, in her critical reading of Maritime fiction, calls attention to this central paradox:

> The "human condition," for Buckler, was essentially a linguistic one. And since language both delights and deceives, destroys and preserves, unites and divides, it comes to be a particularly poisonous serpent in his fictive garden. If Buckler compares the writer's practice to the mowing, reaping, and bundling of what has "blossomed" during the day, he also compares it to the less attractive bodily functions—defecation, masturbation, vomiting, and the eruption of boils. ( 222-23)

A deep suspicion of language is accompanied by a fascination with its metalinguistic faculty, and a conviction that, ultimately, "[n]ous pensons un univers que notre langage a d'abord modelé" (Benveniste, *Problèmes 2* 65). All the while denigrating language, Buckler seems to acknowledge that without the help of signs, we would be incapable of distinguishing between two ideas in any clear and constant fashion. He aligns himself with Saussure, who has argued that without words to express them, our thoughts are but an amorphous mass, and that nothing is distinct before the apparition of language (*CLG*, 155). Consciousness and its articulation in Buckler's novel are inextricably intertwined, as in Saussure's famous analogy comparing language to a sheet of paper, thought being one side and sound the other (157). Just as you cannot cut one side of a sheet without cutting the other, even so it is impossible to separate sound from thought or thought from sound. It is this constant connection between the universe and its articulation that makes up the groundwork for *The Cruelest Month*.

The characters thrown together at Endlaw,[11] the idyllic residence of the protagonist, Paul Creed, are divided into two separate worlds. The highly educated, highly articulate characters inhabit a world of books, of words, of abstract language whose register is so sophisticated and complex that they talk like a book. Describing to the other guests the first time he saw Endlaw, Morse, the writer, typically waxes eloquent: "You feel as if you are stepping into the very domicile of peace. And yet—an odd acceleration. As if the natural drift of all things interpersonal develops here with the short-cut pace of shipboard or dream" (11-12). If they talk like books, it is because they edit their speech the way authors edit their writing, as the alert reader can tell from traces of enunciation that Buckler places judiciously in his text, such as in the following phrases:

> Morse rattled on, taking none of his *usual* pains to pre-edit the clinkers from his speech (16)
>
> He was rattling it off extempore, with none of his *usual* breaks to rewrite it first in his mind (283)
>
> *it was the first time* she'd ever heard him speak a sentence that was not in some way writing-talking (282)

> *For once* they strove for no "arrangements" of their speech,
> with gesture or inflection. Even Morse's key was C natural.
> (204) (emphases mine)

The deictics signal to the reader that this type of language is contrived, artificial. The characters who wield this language—for it is presented as a sort of sophisticated weapon, and the verbal jousts likened to "fencing with party manners" (100)—are placed in diametric opposition to the characters who are illiterate and inarticulate, whose register of language is ungrammatical, earthy, and even crude, but who are the salt of the earth. There is the simple country girl, Molly, who cannot follow into the world of books her young husband, Bruce, who has spanned the divide and entered medical school. In the doctor's waiting-room, Molly stares at the words on the magazine page "as if she were having to translate them" (105). She glances at Bruce's books "proudly, but as if they might be building a new feature into him that she could never touch or be touched by" (104). There is Paul's housekeeper, Letty, who can barely manage to decipher the months on the calendar, the days of the week, her own name, and that of her employer, as well as "the short words you lived by"; the "long unfamiliar words" give her a "lost feeling" (8). Letty has no high opinion of books or of intellectuals and their concepts. Echoing the equivalence between oral and anal virtuosity that we have noticed in *Ox Bells and Fireflies*, she considers that "all the readin' and writin' that was ever done ('mollyhawkin' things over,' she called it), wouldn't amount to a fart on the plains of Arabia" (10).

Language, or rather languages, in the Saussurean sense of signifying or semiological systems,[12] divide. In one world, we have characters like Letty who are verbally inarticulate, incompetent, but who communicate efficiently through other modes. Buckler coins an interesting adjective to inform us that Letty has "voiceful hands" (21), that she can talk to Paul only through the "language of her hands" (24). The author presents her interaction with the world in terms of another language, a physical one—Letty is "restless for the conversation of her hands with the house's clutter" (271). Letty herself acknowledges that it is terrible that hands can be "so congested with fluency and yet so powerless to lend one smidgen of it to your speech" (24).

In the other world we have the abstract domain of language as we know it, the most complex and widespread, as well as most arbitrary, of semiological systems.[13] Benveniste argues that language is the interpreter of all signifying systems, and that its pre-eminence is due to the fact that language alone is invested with a double significance, combining the two distinct modes of significance—the semiotic mode and the semantic mode (*Problèmes 2* 63). Semiotics (the sign) must be recognized—yes for *saber* or *sober*, but no for *siber* or *seber*—while semantics (discourse) must be understood. Two distinct faculties of the mind are involved in the difference between recognizing and understanding—the ability to perceive the equivalence of what has been encountered before and what is encountered now, and the ability to perceive the significance of a new enunciation, in a new context. Unlike other semiotic systems, language is not one dimensional. It contains both the significance of its signs and the significance of its enunciation. Because it can create a second level of enunciation, a metalinguistic level, in which it is possible to hold significant statements on significance, language encompasses and interprets all other systems (*Problèmes 2* 64-65).

*The Cruelest Month* presents us with characters who are not only comfortable in this realm of language, but who actually incarnate it. As opposed to those who have but eloquent hands, these are "the talking people" who can speak to Paul Creed "in his own tongue" (24). Letty, who "thought the sun rose and set" on Paul, is excluded, for the "talking people" were "his kind," and she "was not" (8). They have the power that only language can bestow—the power to act upon the world, to transform it, to reproduce and reorder it. The gap between the two worlds is represented in spatial and architectural terms: the analogy is a reference to contemporary western culture, but the choice of extended metalinguistic metaphor posits an ahistorical, archetypal exclusion from the Garden, the garden of *logos*:

> He lived in the country of those people who seemed to know exactly what the world was *saying*, anyway, and she could only stare at the world like a child at the fair. She could only catch its short simple sentences. That was the wall between them. A dreadful wall for love to have to recognize the height and thickness of. (24)

Language would seem to represent the positive end on the axis of values, and yet it is not that simple. The world of language is a specious one, deceptively attractive and constantly devalorised by various authorial devices. Critics have notably found fault with Buckler's dialogues, with their belaboured opacity, which they have attributed to a maladroitness of style. But the opacity and facetiousness of the characters who talk like books—Morse even seems to "put a bookmark in the conversation" (19)—is, at least partly, a deliberate strategy on the part of Buckler to disparage his characters. Their heavy-handed use of the rhetorical device of asteismus—refined, witty banter involving the contrived twisting of the meaning of one thing to signify another—cannot fail to irritate the reader. Furthermore, the author repeatedly intrudes to distance himself, to make his reprobation felt, and to call attention to the pretentiousness and superficiality of his pseudo-intellectual characters, as when he overtly declares: "*Glibness* was the thing with them that first summer. They *still* were confident that they could get on top of anything, with words" (20). The implicit futility of words, the illusory quality of the power language brings, is effectively suggested by the use of the shifter "still." When not directly intervening, Buckler endows his characters with a precious style that calls attention to their spuriousness. Their use of French terms, notably for an Anglo-Saxon readership would smack of the foreign, of ostentatious affectedness, of sophisticated and therefore suspect artifice: "'Heavens!' Kate had exclaimed at Endlaw. '*C'est merveilleux! Incroyable!*' Morse had promptly dubbed it the 'Home for Incroyables'" (8).

To make the distancing from these characters perfectly explicit, Buckler adds to the facetiousness the enunciatory declaration: "That's the way they talked then." He goes further than mere distancing. He condemns the world of language outright, either in overt authorial declarations that pile on pejorative terms, such as calling their exchange a "juggler's act of sophisticated conversation" (130)—pejorative in equating their use of language with a circus act, with sham, show, artifice, and triviality—or through the point of view of the other characters, by means of dialogue or inner focalization. By gaining access to Letty's thoughts, we learn that "[h]alf the trouble in the world come [sic] from printin' things" because it isn't "natural" (181). By gaining access to the thoughts of Morse, the writer, through a hypnotic style generated by parataxis and anacoluthon, giving us the impression of a stream of consciousness, we learn that the boy Morse used to inhabit the clean, beautiful, natural world of Minnesota forests, in which "the axe more beautiful like swimming naked than the gun is beautiful like

Christmas" (80). But he has been corrupted by the world of words; he has "lost his clean beautiful axe somewhere and all he has to cut a path with is the beat-up sickle he's twisted his tongue into" (80).

Buckler chooses to pronounce the real indictment of the people who incarnate language in the most direct terms and through direct speech, putting the words into the mouth of Letty:

> Talkin' ain't *livin'*. Workin's livin'. Makin' things and doin' things for people. They never made anything you could lay your hands on. Not as much as an axe handle or a loaf o' bread....If they'd ever had to scratch for a livin', maybe they'd have something to take their minds offa their*selves*. But talk, talk, talk. All they've ever done is wag the air around with their tongues. It's like they're jist feedin' off the *smell* of things. (25)

The key word is undoubtedly the verb feeding. It introduces the leitmotiv of anthropophagy that is interwoven throughout the textual fabric. The motif becomes explicit in the rest of Letty's speech: "when they get tired o' talkin', they're kinda like cannibals...then they start pawin' around in each other's feelin's...and eatin' offa *them*" (25). The idea that intellectuals are cannibals, or vampires, is best illustrated through the character of Buckler's alter ego, the writer Morse. We learn that, with almost no exceptions, he has no feeling for anyone or anything "except for the story in it" (256). Kate, the forty-year-old daughter of a widowed archaeology professor, has already been vampirized by her father, who sucked out her youth. She worries that her new fiancé, Morse, "has no use for anyone once he's wrung the story out of them" (256), that she might be discarded like a squeezed-out orange. Morse does feed on others for story, actually drawing Kate into a life-threatening grass fire in order to acquire material for his new book. On the other side of the coin, Paul, who has an ambivalent relationship to language, who has one foot in both worlds, who has both a "flesh look" and a "thought look" (10), learns that he has angina and suddenly realizes that inhabiting the world of language, substituting words for physical, human contact, has bled him dry, made of him an empty shell: "He saw what his life had been, a refusal to visit inside the house of anyone's spirit because if the visit were returned he must always speak to them from the doorway of his own. Books the flesh of it. Talk the touch...Nothing" (63).

After barely escaping from the grass fire with Letty, and following a severe attack of angina, Paul totally rejects the world of books and talk, aspiring only to share the rest of his life in simple harmony with Letty the earth mother, Letty of the "natural flesh, with none of the wisenesses and innuendo" (293) of the other women. When he addresses her in his habitual upper register of language, he even feels "a strange mortification at his own correct syntax, as if it were some foppish garment specious to a wonted ground of trust" (295). It is a curious paradox, that Buckler should choose such a precious, even affected lexicon to indict correct language. It is no anomaly, however, merely another manifestation of a central structural paradox, sustaining a dialectic throughout the novel.

Making extensive use throughout the novel of social antithesis—that figure of thought that opposes categories of tone, register, and language as well as manners or clothes—the author constantly puts linguistic competence at the negative pole of the articulate/inarticulate axis. The alleged spuriousness of the articulate is contrasted with the unpolished and therefore natural/genuine qualities of the inarticulate. But while denigrating the role of language, that ultimate artifice, Buckler paradoxically constructs a world view grounded solely on language. It is striking how the perspective of the implied author, as well as the points of view of the characters—even the inarticulate ones—are shaped by linguistic concepts. The narrator and his characters perceive the universe through language, think and relate to the world in terms of language. Janice Kulyk Keefer remarks that "Buckler, like some linguist's King Midas, cannot help turning everything he touches into words," and that he "carries his verbalizing of the world into grammar itself" (203). We have already seen how Letty, who is illiterate, nonetheless maps out the world in metalinguistic terms in a sequence of inner focalization signalled by italics: "He lived in the country of those people who seemed to know exactly what the world was *saying*....She could only catch its short simple *sentences*. That was the wall between them" (24, second emphasis mine). The point of view of the protagonist and the voice of the narrator overlap, to underline the fact that she lives outside a spatial universe ("country") defined by language. It is suggested in synesthetic terms fusing sight and sound that she can catch only glimpses of this world ("short simple sentences") through the high, thick "wall" of her illiteracy (24).

Similarly, Buckler presents in a paradoxical fashion another character who is uneasy in the world of words. We realize, partly through the slips in grammar that Rex makes, that he has married above his station: his wife Sheila, is a rich and cultivated young woman from Greenwich, Connecticut. Nevertheless, his attack of severe migraine is presented in metalinguistic terms. We are curiously invited by the inner focalization to accept that Rex, who is totally out of his depth in the other characters' sophisticated verbal jousts, should perceive the oncoming pain through language, as if only language could make it real: "The quintessential perfume of loneness and apprehension had been like a vapour so attenuated that even the naming of it with noun or the description of it with adjective would make it sound too falsely substantive. Now, as if under such pressure that it changed its state, it condensed into physical pain" (166). We remark that as the ache takes hold, it is not accompanied by *feelings* of despondency and dismay, but that it is actually caused by the *words* themselves, as if the name were equivalent to the thing: "A kind of smoke of ache flooded upward into his skull, as if from a vial where the words that used to mean nothing to him—bruise and discouragement, disappointment and stain, dreg and frustration and gone—...were all being brewed together" (166-67). If pain is made real by language, exists only through language, the same can be said of all the other major human experiences—love, loss, time, death, thought itself. When Bruce, a widower, falls in love with Sheila, his flesh begins "to write a kind of poetry" (211), and he envisages an idyllic future with her in proportional metaphorical terms that equate the love relationship with decoding and mapping. His lover would be someone to whom his name and his face would not be just a scrambled *hieroglyph*, but *reading*" (211, emphases mine). When Bruce realizes he cannot have the woman he loves, the awareness takes the shape of letters on a corner billboard. The printed road sign "GRANFORT—FOUNDED 1782" leads to a metonymical association—all those that were living then are now dead. Through the elliptical compression of words, Buckler accomplishes a complex yoking. In a striking metalinguistic passage, he fuses the absent face of the beloved together with grammatical terms, with the concrete, physical shapes of language as incarnated in the letters of the alphabet, and with the abstract concept of time:

> Dead....Gone....Live....Love....Lose.
> Ago....Ago....The memory of Sheila's face stamped the word "ago" across everything.
>
> And then there came the moment—one definite, particular moment—when her face stamped itself with the same three letters. (269)

The passing of time, the inexorable march from the realm of the open, the virtual, and the possible to that of the closed, the lapsed, the impossible, announces itself too through writing. In a haunting passage, Kate wonders when her dying father had first realized that time had slipped away from him, wonders whether it was upon awakening from a nap to "see the message of 'gone' and 'forever' waiting for him, written in the afternoon's particular cast as clearly as if it were written on a paper in his hand" (68).

The experience of death is presented in striking metalinguistic terms. Paul has gone to a Montreal hospital for tests and is shown the X-ray of his thrombosis—"the photograph of death" (176). The metaphor is extended on a double level, the photograph directing a message at him as both visual text and script. Paul waits to be alone in his room before beginning to "read the message through" (177). The object that transmits the message becomes diffused, multiple, all encompassing. Paul's own body and external world have fused into one giant blank surface covered with the writing of doom. Paul reads the message "[o]ff the walls and the floor and his hands and his feet. Engraved there in a script so remorselessly legible it was without grace whatsoever" (177). The writing is analyzed self-reflexively. The discourse on the discourse is initially presented from the point of view of Paul, but soon the narrator intervenes overtly, signalling his presence with parentheses to muse over the virtues and qualities of signifiers as acoustic images—even personifying them—seeming to argue that they are not so arbitrary as linguists would have it, that they are not entirely divorced from the signified: "He read the part where it had all the words in it starting with "n," the most remorseless of all letters, the one that infects every syllable it helps to form. (Take it out of "alone," and you still had "aloe." No and nothing and never" (177).

The narrator—his voice once more blending and blurring with the point of view of a protagonist—seems to be groping for ultimate meaning embodied by some sort of logical unifying system linking acoustic image (signifier) and concept (signified). In a parallel manner, his character is seeking to decipher the message, to possess it and to establish himself in control by putting a name to it, like the Biblical Adam with the beasts of the field. But the metaphysical message, depicted in metalinguistic terms—coloured emotively through personification—is elusive precisely because it is difficult to parse: "This was not a noun, with a noun's face. It was a faceless verb. He couldn't tell if it was transitive or intransitive. All he could grasp was its *ad*verbial shadow" (178). Concentrating, rejecting one verb after another as not quite right, Paul strives to reorder his world through *logos* (discourse and reason). An epiphany finally occurs, and the verb's name flashes across his vision "like a bulletin": and the "verb was 'notify'" (179). The discovery of the perfect word allows the character to make sense of the cosmos, to reduce it to a familiar scale. The universe seems to be controlled by a divine Force that makes its commands known through some sort of cosmic post office. You are "notified," you stand there "with the implacable registered letter in your hand," (179) the letter that terminates all hopes and excuses.

Buckler's novel is peopled by characters who are, of course, but marks on a page. But even as the author strives to give them depth, to allow them to reflect back to us certain qualities of the human soul, he makes constant analogies, extended metaphors, with the world of language from which they spring. One character endures "ungrammared agony" (163). Another's mind is a blackboard: "A diabolic sentence limned itself for an instant on the blackboard of her mind. 'I wish it had.' No. No. She rubbed it out in a panic" (222). A face is a text to be decoded and read: "Her face was so close, so open to him. On its tiny space was written in the face's inimitable shorthand everything in the world he would ask for" (201). People undergo metamorphoses and turn into nouns: "Yes, there were things about being a doctor's wife that....Did doctors work so constantly that after a while all its terrible poetry was lost on them? Were they apt to turn into the nouns of their calling, like lawyers or bankers or other professional men?" (213). When contemplating the mysteries of life and death and finitude, the point of reference is always the writing process, the labour of constructing meaning through language. When Paul is faced with his death sentence and cannot think, his mind traces over and over "its changeless content of the moment, the way you pencil a word over and over when the next one won't come" (272). Buckler's use here of the second person singular is significant, as it creates complicity with the receiver, who is invited to share in the world view grounded in the Word. It is significant that, although the author constantly questions the validity of linguistic structures, he never ceases to measure the world in linguistic units. Like his character Rex, who gains access to "the essence of the word 'unnamable'"(167) when the vial of pure pain seeps down through his head, Buckler too seems to be always on the verge of breaking out of Plato's shadowy cave and of discovering, through language, the heavenly prototype, the divine ideal or essence behind all things.

# Aesthetics and Ethics

The last two chapters have demonstrated how Buckler attempts through language to discover ειδος (eidos), the essence or form behind all things. I have shown how Buckler's philosophy is grounded in the neoplatonic concept that the beauty of the world is a reflection and projection of ideal Beauty, and that it involves apprehending the supernatural connections that exist between the object and the cosmos. In this chapter, I shall attempt to define Buckler's elaboration of an aesthetic philosophy based ultimately on Aristotelean and neoplatonic ontology and revolving around the interconnectedness of the good, the beautiful, the true, and the useful. I shall explore his commitment to transmit a vision of ultimate divine truth, to transport the reader to a dimension beyond prosaic reality through revelation of the good. While Buckler fosters love for beauty by re-creating it in language, his writing is rooted in a strong ethical vision, a quest for the universal moral law that lies at the heart of

---

Notes for chapter 5 are on pp. 244-45.

nature. The artist's power to create delight by re-creating and transmitting beauty is a moral power. After providing an analytical framework through a confrontation with texts that serve useful exegetical functions, I shall focus on how in Buckler's heuristic published and unpublished fiction, his unique celebration of domesticity, of the humble elements that make up our everyday world, is a celebration of the good. His texts, we shall see, orchestrate the social ties that bind the community together and keep its order, whether it be behavioural codes or institutions. Finally, I shall follow up with another chapter showing the dynamics of his aesthetics at work, in which I shall closely study some of the dominant leitmotifs in the textual fabric, notably the central topoi of Arcadia and death.

Like modernist writers from James Joyce to Francis Ponge, like thinkers from Aristotle to Aquinas—who were being reread during the international resurgence of interest in Renaissance studies in the twentieth century—Buckler pursues the quest for the essence or substance behind *res* and *verba*, thing and thought. As I mentioned in the previous chapters, his standpoint resembles Francis Ponge's equally didactic determination[1] to take up the challenge that *things* constitute for *language* (*La Rage* 55). Picasso likened Ponge's detailed descriptions, evocations, and compilations of objects to sculptures, declaring that Ponge's words were like chess pieces, small three-dimensional statues (Sollers 1). Like Ponge, who confessed to writing pages on a humble subject like a bird in the hope of finding the knot, the core, the essential quality of the bird,[2] Buckler seeks to put "the roseness back into the rose, even the weedness back into the weeds, the is-ness back into everything there is."[3] By naming the world and the things that compose it, these modernists with their ontological vehemence re-create them for us all.[4] By naming, the writer—to use Shelley's terms—"lifts the veil from the hidden beauty of the world." The writing "reproduces all that it represents" (*Defence* 1076), and allows us to know exactly "*world*ness and *life*ness itself" (*Ox Bells* 52).

Buckler's quest is strikingly reminiscent of that of Stephen Dedalus in Joyce's *Portrait of the Artist*. There are undeniable resemblances between Buckler's aesthetic practices and the aesthetic philosophy developed by Joyce's mouthpiece. Grounding his reflections in the writings of Plato, Aristotle, Aquinas, and Shelley on the artistic apprehension of beauty, truth, and the good, Stephen Dedalus expounds on the "*whatness* of a thing":

> The radiance of which [Aquinas] speaks is the scholastic *quidditas*, the *whatness* of a thing. This supreme quality is felt by the artist when the esthetic image is first conceived in his imagination. The mind in that mysterious instant Shelley likened beautifully to a fading coal. The instant wherein that supreme quality of beauty, the clear radiance of the esthetic image, is apprehended luminously by the mind which has been arrested by its *wholeness* and fascinated by its *harmony* is the luminous silent stasis of esthetic pleasure, a *spiritual* state very like to that cardiac condition which the Italian physiologist Luigi Galvani, using a phrase almost as beautiful as Shelley's, called the enchantment of the heart. (*Portrait* 193, emphases mine)

Stephen here focuses his exegetical remarks on *claritas* — the radiance or clarity of an aesthetically pleasing object. *Claritas* can signify "the artistic discovery and representation of the divine purpose in anything" (193), so suggestive of the ontological reflection of the Divine that Buckler discerns in every concrete thing. Stephen's key words, "wholeness" and "harmony," interconnect *claritas* with the other two qualities that Aquinas claimed were required for an object to be beautiful: *integritas* and *consonantia*. Joyce's protagonist has just explained the two concepts:

> the esthetic image is first luminously apprehended as self-bounded and selfcontained upon the immeasurable background of space or time which is not it. You apprehend it as *one* thing. You see it as one whole. You apprehend its wholeness. That is *integritas*....Then...you pass from point to point, led by its formal lines; you apprehend it as balanced part against part within its limits; you feel the rhythm of its structure. In other words the synthesis of immediate perception is followed by the analysis of apprehension. Having first felt that it is *one* thing you feel now that it is a *thing*. You apprehend it as complex, multiple, made up of its parts, the result of its parts and their sum, harmonius [sic]. That is *consonantia*. (192)

For Buckler, too, there is an absolute Unity that is apprehendable thanks to the powers of the imagination, and his artist personas can aspire to relate "the whole content of everything there is" (*Mountain* 296). The protagonists' search for wholeness, the "single core of meaning" (298), the "single light" that causes all "the separate lines" to flow into "a single image" (*Rebellion* 32), can be put into parallel with the author's compilations, the contiguity of the structures establishing relationships of analogy, if not of equivalence: a bringing together that "brims us whole," as Buckler terms it in *Ox Bells and Fireflies* (117). All of this generates a quality in Buckler's writing that Claude Bissell has termed "a transfiguring glow, as if everything, the world outside and the world inside, were aspects of one unifying vision" ("His Prose"). Buckler's aesthetic stance echoes as well the pleas for wholeness of Emerson, who argues that the role of the artist is precisely to give us a vision of the whole. In "The American Scholar," Emerson protests how the division of labour reduces people to "things," to functions, instead of whole human beings, and how the individual as a powerful, original unit is shattered by modern society, minutely "subdivided and peddled out...[and] spilled into drops" (*English Traits* 6). The role of the poet, then, is to repair this fracture and to give us a vision of the whole. It is the artist's "integrity of impression," writes Emerson in his essay "Nature," that "distinguishes the stick of timber of the wood-cutter, from the tree of the poet" (*Nature* 10).

Emerson's analogy is exactly what Buckler illustrates in the scene from *The Mountain and the Valley* referred to in chapter 3, in the confrontation between Steve the "wood-cutter" and David the "poet," between the material and the ideal, the part and the whole. For Steve, a tree is an object for his use, "a thing for the axe"; "a field is a field," something to be ploughed (238). In contrast, when David regarded the land, "it was if the outline of the frozen landscape *became* his consciousness: that inside and outside were not two things, but one—the bare shape of what his eyes saw" (281).

There is an interesting parallel with a passage from Emerson's essay:

> The charming landscape which I saw this morning is indubitably made up of some 20 or 30 farms. Miller owns this field, Locke that, and Manning the woodland beyond. But none of them owns the landscape. There is a property in the horizon which no man has but *"he whose eye can integrate all the parts, that is, the poet,"* (*Nature* 11, emphasis mine)

Clearly Steve would see the farms, the individual units of property, while David would see the landscape, the horizon in a holistic fashion, marrying matter and mind. The protagonist's "great white naked eye of self-consciousness" (281) embodies the poet's eye that integrates all the parts, that teaches us to look beyond the many and to see the One.

The word "teaches" is an apt term for Buckler's strategy, which has a strong didactic dimension, and which stems from a strong ethical vision that seeks to instruct as it delights. Emerson explains in his essay "Discipline" how "all things are moral" (*Nature* 51), linked to reflect and to obey a divine order. In chapter 3, I evoked Buckler's wondering description of a humble daisy, of how the precision and complexity of its patterns evokes a divine plan, a cosmic design in which "[e]ach speckling, or roundness, or pointedness, or wallpaper scrolling, or shading of color into color was as perfectly in pattern as if a draftsman's lifetime had gone into the making of it" (*Ox Bells* 106). Buckler's almost orgiastic descriptions of such humble objects, his atomization and focus on detail[5] detached from a whole, concur with Emerson's depiction of a nature so glorious with form, colour, and motion that "every globe in the remotest heaven, every change of vegetation from the first principle of growth in the eye of a leaf, to the tropical forest and ante-deluvian coal-mine, every animal function from the sponge up to Hercules, shall hint or thunder to men the laws of right and wrong" (*Nature* 51).

Each humble element carries an unceasing reference to an immaterial, eternal source, and is penetrated by an ethical character, submitted to a moral law.[6] The organicist belief in a unity of nature, found in Emerson and the Romantics as well as in certain modernists such as Joyce, resides in the persistence throughout the Middle Ages and the Renaissance of the idea of universal harmony, the conviction that even minor features of human life are associated with a greater system, that all aspects of existence are related, bound together, have a specific function, and share a community of purpose in one large ordered design that is a manifestation of the wisdom and goodness that created it.[7] Grounding their theory in Aristotelian ontology, the thinkers of the Middle Ages elaborated rigorous metaphysical notions on being, on the good and the beautiful, and on their reciprocal transmutation. As Umberto Eco points out, scholasticism, with its Christian dimension, constructed an enduring aesthetic world view that nevertheless resembled the *kalokagathìa* of the ancient Greeks: the fusion of *kalos kai agathos*—the beautiful and the good—the harmonious conjunction of material beauty and virtue (42). It differentiated between inner and outer beauty, between what is exterior and visible, and what is interior, equating moral beauty with *honestum*. The true, the good, and the beautiful are thus convertible and indissociable. Truth consists in the disposition of the form with respect to the interiority of the object, while beauty is the disposition of the form with respect to its exteriority (Eco 48). Five centuries later, we find rooted in the same aesthetic stance the famous lines from Keats's "Ode on a Grecian Urn": "Beauty is truth, truth beauty,— that is all/Ye know on earth, and all ye need to know" (lines 49-50).

A broad resurgence of interest in Renaissance studies was first propelled by people such as Joyce and C.S. Lewis (*The Allegory of Love, The Discarded Image*). The later work done in Canada by thinkers such as Whalley, Frye, and McLuhan was representative of this international backdrop, of this general interest in Aristotle, the Middle Ages, and the Renaissance. In publications such as his *Anatomy of Criticism, The Great Code,* or *The Secular Scripture,* Frye explored the patterns of thought and literary production handed down from Greek antiquity to the Middle Ages, Renaissance, and onwards. His analyses gave a prominent place to Aristotle, Aquinas, and Saint Augustine, as well as to writers such as Dante and Chaucer.[8] Whalley, whose teaching made use of a wide range of texts, including Renaissance ones, was an Aristotle scholar who translated *The Poetics*. McLuhan, fascinated by pre-print culture, promoted an understanding of the Renaissance as a period of revolution in communications, with *The Gutenberg Galaxy* and *Through the Vanishing Point*. Similarly, the writing of Buckler, a trained philosopher, is clearly permeated by concepts formulated centuries earlier by thinkers such as Saint Augustine and Thomas Aquinas, and stemming from the Aristotelian harmonious marriage of form (*morphê*) and matter (*hulé*), the Pythagorean mathematical conception of the beautiful, a metaphysical aesthetics of light, and of vision, and a notion of form as splendour, as the very source of pleasure. Buckler's desire for beauty, a beauty endowed with formal perfection, as we have seen in the preceding chapter, generates writing rooted in the fundamental principles of interconnectedness, and of unity in diversity. The device of chaotic enumeration also seen in the preceding chapter, to which he often resorts and which is fundamentally synecdochic, is but one illustration. In his request for a third Canada Council grant, Buckler had evoked his technique of "multum in parvo" as a sort of "shorthand," and likened it to a type of "pointillism,"⁹ In a later letter to his American publisher, Knopf, Buckler explained that the "pointillist, background-stippling bits" were meant to convey whole fields of implication. They were intended to "underline the omnipresence of the far in the near, the universal in the particular, the macrocosm in the microcosm, the duplicate rendering of every mood in some physical object or cast of nature, the translatability of the senses one into another, the inter-locking and cross-pollination of all things tangible or intangible."[10]

In Buckler's texts, the beauty perceived in the world, re-created and transmitted, is closely linked to the good. Its power to produce delight is a moral power, akin to the Aristotelean concept of pleasure generated by virtue in thought or deed. In the short story "The Quarrel," the family's greatest pleasure lies in walking through the garden exposed to "the full kiss of the sun; looking for any cast of ripening in the tomatoes, parting the secrecy of the cucumber vines to see if any fruit lay on the ground beneath, gauging the number of days before the corn would be really yellow" (*Rebellion* 42). But the sensuous bliss of this special Sunday leisure is destroyed when the parents quarrel and the "kitchen and the fields go dead" (41). The harmonious link with nature is severed by domestic disharmony, for the public and private spheres are inextricably intermeshed. The contrast between the child protagonist's "perfect August Sunday" and the Sunday that is "spoiled" (41) is quite Emersonian. For Emerson equates the effect that nature has on him to that of "a higher thought or a better emotion" coming over him when he has deemed he was "thinking justly, or doing right" (*Nature* 14). In the essay "Beauty," he stipulates that beauty is "the mark God sets upon virtue" (*Nature* 25). And the mark of the artist is a love of beauty that overflows. Artists have this love "in such excess, that, not content with admiring, they seek to embody it in new forms" (29).

Buckler is such an artist, fostering love for beauty by re-creating it in language and pursuing the good. We can better understand the lyrical, even sacred dimension of the farm in his texts. The description of Martha and Joseph on their knees gathering potatoes shrouds the couple in a holy, transcendent silence: "Soundless with distance, they looked as if they were praying" (*Mountain* 225). The potato field as church, as well as the equation of working and praying, echoes

Emerson's question: "What is a farm but a mute gospel? The chaff and the wheat, weeds and plants, blight, rain, insects, sun,—it is *a sacred emblem* from the first furrow of spring to the last stack which the snow of winter overtakes in the fields" (*Nature* 53). Buckler does not hesitate to make the connection perfectly explicit in *Ox Bells and Fireflies*, in the encounter I evoked in the preceding chapter between the old farm woman and the history scholar. At the professor's opening comment that farming must be "a well-nigh…holy…kind of life," Kate agrees and makes an astute metalinguistic remark: "Did you ever notice how little it would take to change 'acres' into 'sacred?'" (247).

Buckler's commitment to transmit a vision of ultimate, divine truth, to transport the reader to a dimension beyond prosaic reality through revelation of the good, resembles the vatic stance of the Romantics. In his approach to art as craft, it is true that Buckler divorces himself from writers such as Wordsworth and Shelley, who place emphasis on the role of inspiration. Their positions are in apparent contrast. In the passage from his manifesto *A Defence of Poetry* to which James Joyce's artist protagonist referred in the passage quoted earlier in this chapter, Shelley declares that writing is a mysterious power that cannot be exerted deliberately "according to the determination of the will," and that

> A man cannot say, "I will compose poetry." The greatest poet even cannot say it; for the mind in creation is as a fading coal, which some invisible influence, like an inconstant wind, awakens to transitory brightness; this power rises from within…and the conscious portions of our natures are unprophetic either of its approach or its departure. (1084)

Buckler distances himself from this romantic notion of the artist, who can in this way be seen as a passive agent, or even submissive receptacle, rather than as an actor in the full sense of the term. With the following insightful piece of advice, like his pre-Romantic predecessors, he foregrounds the importance of hard work: "Never wait for inspiration: there's no such thing. Inspiration is merely that little click something gives when the gap in the wall opens, the gap that only the battering ram of your sweat has prepared the crumbling of."[11]

But in spite of this divergence, Buckler shares many of the Romantics' tastes and ideals, such as the reference to natural objects, the self-revelation of the writer, the emphasis on emotion and personal experience rather than on authority, the belief in a supersensuous reality, and the quest for the sublime and transcendent. He particularly adheres to Shelley's notions concerning the social or functional role of the artist. Shelley notably stipulates that poets are

> not only the authors of language and of music, of the dance, and architecture, and statuary, and painting; they are the institutors of laws, and the founders of civil society, and the inventors of the arts of life, and the teachers, who draw into a certain propinquity with the beautiful and the true, that partial apprehension of the invisible world which is called religion. (*Defence* 1073)

He reminds us that artists "in the earlier epochs of the world" were called "legislators or prophets," for they are the ones who discover the laws according to which present things "ought to be ordered," and who also behold "the future in the present" (1073). Shelley argues that the imagination is the "great instrument of moral good," and goes on to explain how writing acts to "produce the moral improvement of man." It "awakens and enlarges the mind itself by rendering it the receptacle of a thousand unapprehended combinations of thought," and "strengthens the faculty which is the moral nature of man, in the same manner as exercise strengthens a limb" (1076).

Shelley's standpoint anticipates Emerson's claim in his essay "Idealism" that the only difference between a poet and a philosopher is that "the one proposes Beauty as his main end; the other Truth" and that the "true philosopher and the true poet are one; and a beauty, which is truth, and a truth, which is beauty, are the aim of both" (*Nature* 68-69). It anticipates in particular Emerson's doctrine of Use, and will be echoed by the strong ethical dimension to Buckler's art, his quest for what Emerson terms the "moral law" that "lies at the center of nature and radiates to the circumference" (*Nature* 53).

Buckler's aesthetic stance is centred around not only the classical concepts of beauty and truth, but also the concept of *aptum* or decorum. This doctrine from antiquity, transmitted from Cicero to Saint Augustine and then to all of scholasticism and onwards, distinguishes what is beautiful on its own from what is beautiful with respect to something else—in other words, beauty that is functional. Saint Augustine's *De Vera Religione* notably spread the idea that anything natural or artificial is beautiful only if it is useful, if it takes a step toward the invisible and the eternal. Emerson's essay "Commodity" (*English Traits*) can be seen as an extension of the medieval and Renaissance stance on the good, on the functional dimension of art and its association with craft. He insists on the fact that the arts too have a useful role to play in the network of society. Like the post office, book shop, or court house, the work of art too must advance a "farther good" (*Nature* 17). In other words, the writer, the artist, like the craftsman, must benefit others, must *serve*.

The interconnectedness of the beautiful and the functional is at the heart of Buckler's aesthetic standpoint. He follows Emerson's doctrine of Use, reminiscent of Locke's utilitarianism, that "a thing is good only so far as it serves, that a conspiring of parts and effects to the production of an end, is essential" (*Nature* 52). Art is craft in *Ox Bells and Fireflies*. In the chapter "A to Z," the character App is famed for his manly strength and skill. He is "powerful enough to throw a steer," can "split a deer's skull with a Mauser bullet at five hundred yards," and can "whet a scythe so that it sliced through the bluejoint like singing" (278-79). Yet App is also a "born storyteller" and an artist who transforms the functional into the beautiful through the judicious choice of raw material, a touch of fantasy, and loving detail: "He carved a clock face out of apple tree wood, with the twelve letters of his wife's name in place of numerals" (279). As for the carved toy that he builds for his children, its beauty stems significantly from the fact that the tiny elements actually work: "he built a miniature castle for his children, down to the tiny *workable* chains for the tiny *workable* drawbridge, inside a vinegar bottle" (279, emphases mine).

The description of the countrywoman Kate's talents in the chapter "A Woman" also emphasizes the interconnectedness of beauty and utility through the perfection of form and the vehicle of labour or craft. All of Kate's gestures and the products that result from them are equivalent because they are equally worthy of admiration whether they be stitching quilts "as neat on the underside as on the top" (245), laying shingles, freehanding a rug design "no one could fault," or stooking oat bundles into "pyramids that the fiercest winds couldn't tear apart" (246). Buckler emphasizes that his character "knew exactly the simple touch of decoration that would turn the barely useful thing into a thing of grace" (246). Similarly, in *The Mountain and the Valley*, Buckler sings the domestic creativity of the Canaan women, who transform poverty into beauty, by knowing that "just as you could feather-stitch Anna's petticoat with bright thread, though it was only flannelette, so you could pleat the curtains instead of letting them hang flat" (23). As a foil to the Canaans' domestic art, the author juxtaposes the allegorical description of their neighbour's kitchen:

> Rachel's kitchen was as bare as ever. The floor was clean, but without covering. The wooden lounge had a grey woods blanket spread over it, but no cushions. The chairs stood about the room, uncompromising as sentinels. The stove was like Martha's: a low square firebox, with the barrel-shaped oven rising on a long neck. But its animacy was annulled by the bleak square of zinc beneath it and the blindness of the front drafts. They were always closed so the wood wouldn't spend itself in excess. A slop pail held the dirty water. There was no sink. The clock stood nakedly on the mantelpiece. There were no envelopes tucked behind it. No basket of remnants (twists of yarn, short pencils, old buttons…) softened its relentless tick. It shared the shelf with a bottle of ink only. The bottle was still in its carton, a pen thrust rigidly upright beside it. There were no cupboards in the pantry. All the dishes could be seen from the kitchen, naked on the bare shelves. (203)

Rachel's kitchen is a synecdoche: the writer is displaying material, aesthetic, and spiritual poverty in all its baldness. The notion of destitution and deprivation is transmitted through an accumulation of negatives in various forms: determiners (no), conjunctions (but), adjectives (bare, bleak, naked), adverbs (not, nakedly), verb (annul), preposition (without), prefixes and suffixes (*un*compromising, relent*less*). The lack perceived is not that of money, but of beauty. This beauty can be generated by desire, fantasy, imagination, and, yes, work. The desirable home, source of comfort and serenity, is where the blueberries are made into fungy, not "just" stewed, where the lettuce is not left plain in the bowl but "fixed up" with potatoes, where the curtains have ruffles, the kitchen has mats on the floor (albeit made from recycled rags), and the front room is brightened with a jar of daisies—and what could be more accessible and humble than such contents and such a container? (49).

Buckler's aesthetic stance is clearly centred around the classical concepts whereby beauty is a step toward the invisible and the eternal, leading to an underlying truth. The function of beauty is to foster admiration and praise of a divine order. These aesthetic concepts imply a strong didactic element in art, which must involve a process of learning. The two functions of art—to instruct and to delight—are fundamentally interconnected, and the pleasure that art procures should be a useful one. Twentieth-century Renaissance scholars such as C.S. Lewis were calling attention to the doctrinal content or anagogical level of meaning that medieval and Renaissance literature contained, and the philosophical utility that the audiences and readers of those periods expected to find. Although this anagogical level of meaning was dispersed in the seventeenth and eighteenth centuries, certain Romantic poets, as we have begun to see, once more asserted, as did the nineteenth-century utilitarians, the connection between the beautiful and the useful, and underscored the didactic function of art.

Shelley's manifesto *A Defence of Poetry* is a culmination of the standpoint whereby art is a way of confronting ultimate questions, and whereby the artist is a seer whose function is to teach by giving delight. For Shelley, true utility is the production and assurance of pleasure in the highest sense, and those who produce and preserve this pleasure are the poets or "poetical philosophers" (1083). He argues that there are two kinds of pleasure, "one durable, universal, and permanent; the other transitory and particular" (1082-83), and that utility may express the means of producing the former or the latter. He specifies that "whatever strengthens and purifies the affections, enlarges the imagination, and adds spirit to sense, is useful" (1083), and that pleasure in its highest sense is often connected to sorrow, anguish and despair. He reminds us that the highest species of pleasure can take the form of the "delight of love and friendship, the ecstasy of the admiration of nature, the joy of the perception and still more of the creation of poetry," and that the "production and assurance of pleasure in this highest sense is true utility" (1083).

The concepts that Shelley cites are precisely the things that Buckler celebrates. The writer has inherited this substantial legacy of art that celebrates beauty all the while underscoring its didactic dimension. He puts into practice the notion that literature exists "to teach what is useful, to honour what deserves honour, to [make us] appreciate what is delightful" (Lewis 214). There is a strong ethical undercurrent in his works: transmitting the truth of his experience is his primary concern, and his mode of representation is chosen for its appropriateness and rhetorical effectiveness.

In Buckler's pencil manuscript notes on *Ox Bells and Fireflies*, the writer has organized a page of notes in columns of abstract concepts, senses, emotions, and virtues (reminiscent of medieval morality plays). Under the label "Create," he includes concepts such as wholeness, nearness, and straightness, along with knowledge, concord, and truth. Under the enigmatic heading "Verses," he lists memory and production, foresight and anticipation, oracle, health, hope, wonder, pride, as well as habit, goodness, benevolence, gratitude, forgiveness, right, respect, and unselfishness. Although some of the concepts listed belong to a religious or mystical vein, such as reward, heaven, revelation, and spell, many of them can be labelled the social glues that bind the community together and keep its order, whether it be behavioural codes or institutions: friendship, courtesy, love, marriage, and justice.

Similarly, a scribbler in which Buckler jotted down notes for his novel in progress, *The Cruelest Month*, contains pages entitled "Ideas and Touches," in which he reminds himself to "demolish" certain institutions, notions, categories of thought, including the eclectic items "Puritans, narrow-mindedness. Sex critics. Education...hypocrites, gossips, snobs, literature's stuffed shirts, turtle-necked and spiky-haired intellectuals." Under the title "Devices," he reminds himself to work into the dialogue of the novel, "each of the philosophical thoughts" listed in "Ideas and Touches." The list contains items such as "the bleakness of residual things," "a hair perhaps divides the false and true," "the nature of time: now is all," "the light (heightened tenderness) that knowledge of approaching death casts on things," "we all kill our sons," "the strange world chronic pain puts you in," "does personal happiness matter," "love the only answer to all things," "commensurability of all values."[12] As I have already shown in the preceding chapter, and shall develop further on, what generates the text, more overtly than in his other works, is philosophical and epistemological speculation on truth, time, suffering, death, happiness, the family, values—in other words, concepts that define the human condition and the study of which can throw light on an absolute reality.

The quest for the good is the principal generator of text in Buckler's writing. One of his earlier unpublished stories, "Would You Know It If You Fell Over It,"[13] is constructed quite like a traditional morality play. The protagonist, Karl, is Everyman in a quest for happiness. Certain autobiographical touches meant to confer verisimilitude do not, in fact, add depth to a story that is nothing other than a parable, an *exemplum*. The country boy Karl has always sought happiness in the abstract as the ultimate good. First he is convinced that it lies in education, knowledge, the life of the intellect. By the age of fifteen he has pushed himself to college entrance. The structural irony involving a naive protagonist, persuaded that "picking the biggest ([college] and leading the class and getting the best education" would be "the sure road to happiness" (1) will be echoed in later works such as *The Mountain and the Valley* and *The Cruelest Month*. In *The Mountain and the Valley*, the epilogue makes the irony explicit by telescoping with a daring use of the conditional tense David's series of delusions into one final, false—because retrospective—vision in which he looks ahead/back to grand achievements that will forever (never) happen(ed): "When he grew up he'd be the best fiddle player in the whole world.... He knew he'd be the most famous mathematician there ever was...suddenly he knew he'd be the most wonderful dancer that people had ever seen...he knew he'd be the only man who ever went every single place in the world and did everything in the whole world there was to do" (290-91). The irony is rendered more acute through the mingling of the noble and the trivial, and the hyperbolic crescendo of the superlatives toward the impossible unicity ("the *only* man") and the impossible totality ("*every single* place," "*every*thing," *whole* world"). Intertextuality signals to the alert reader a similar irony latent in *The Cruelest Month*, in the epiphany that sweeps over Bruce, the country boy who dropped out of medical school after the death of his young wife. The epiphany rings hollow not only because of the exaggerated, even exalted nature of the escalation that the detached narrator signals through italics and interjections, but also because it reiterates the recurrent/belied "he knew" of *The Mountain and the Valley*:

> then it was that his mind took its vaulting leap ahead. With the slip, like fingers into gloves, into a single socket of purpose, he knew as surely as he'd known his destiny, that April day so long ago, what he was going to do now. He would be a *children's* doctor—yes, yes, a children's *psychiatrist*. (268)

In the more overt narration of "Would You Know It If You Fell Over It?" by graduation, Karl has destroyed his health and suffers from daily migraines that "tear through his brain like stubborn leeches sucking his face and his life grey"[14] (1). His diploma, his accumulated knowledge, ring hollow. Happiness must lie in health. Karl imposes three years of isolation and rest on himself, but by the time he is entirely liberated from his migraines "the torture was so dim in his memory that he was not wildly thankful." The omniscient narrator intervenes directly in the internal focalization to stress that "[g]reat gifts are spoiled if they come by dribbles, piecemeal" (2). Karl has health but now regrets the time he has missed, the "stupid unmeaning waste." He concludes that happiness must be money, success, independence. Each time he "was sure, this time, that it had slipped its disguise, that his eyes were open to false mirages, that he knew what he sought and where to find it" (2). The structural irony signalled by the qualifier "this time," which draws attention to Karl's series of repeated delusions, as well as by the gradual perversion of the desirable good into "something always ahead, something you had to *buy*" (3, emphasis mine) is meant to bind the projected reader to the implied author's moral stance, to invite him or her to disapprove of the obviously misguided hero.

The irony gains in subtlety, shifts toward what Linda Hutcheon in *Splitting Images* terms Irony Self-deprecating. The protagonist turns to writing, determined that he will find happiness and fulfillment by "writing the tale of second sight, his uncanny penetration to the bleakness behind everything that human beings think rich and full" (3). But Karl's creativity is indeed Shelley's "fading coal," lacking the "click" of inspiration that even Buckler has acknowledged to be necessary. The protagonist embodies Shelley's declaration that "[a] man cannot say, 'I will compose poetry.'" Everything Karl wrote "was informed with economy of suggestion, every word fit, but there was missing some spirit, some sap that was present in clumsier writing, some likeness of things alive. They were like beautiful stripped corpses" (3). Buckler goes on to intensify his portrait of failure. He sends his hero back to the country village for sustenance and relief. But even life on the land is unsatisfying: Karl finds the country people uncommunicative and narrow, "shallow breathing shells," even "more shrunken receptacles of inspiration than the money-mad people he had left." They are, moreover, "inattentive to the beauty and fascination of the soil" (4). Disillusionment finally causes Karl, the prototype of David and Bruce, to move toward a form of wisdom favoured by the stoics and culminating in Schopenhauer's asceticism or negation of desire as the road to inner peace. Seeming to follow Schopenhauer's call to end the cycle of desire and suffering, to put an end to servitude, Karl learns to want less instead of more. Instead of satiation, he seeks "isolation from appetite," and begins "a stripping of desire, a wilful negation of the mosaic of character" (5). But just as Karl decides that all he needs to be happy is "a sufficiency of simple feeling, to see sights, to hear sounds and to feel" (5), in a twist of cosmic irony Buckler causes him to go blind. His description of the character's holding fast in his lightlessness to an image or two, "lest he lose even that," telling his mother that "he would be happy if he could just make out the shape of the window-pane" (5), is a more than sobering moral; it is a grim—even ferocious—lesson.

Forever fascinated by the issues of free will and fate, Buckler frequently places his characters in situations in which they must make a painful choice. Invariably, the choice involves a certain self-sacrifice in order to do right by someone else. In the story originally titled "Mary Redmond," published by *Chatelaine* in 1956 under the title "The Dream and the Triumph," and later included in the collection *The Rebellion of Young David*, a rural couple has raised their orphaned grandson and sent him to engineering college in the city, but when the grandfather dies suddenly, the young man Paul is sucked back to the farm. The story makes palpable the feelings of loss and loneliness[15] through homely objects and gestures, a touch of anthropomorphism, and a sure sense of detail. After the sudden death of her husband, Paul's grandmother Mary protests that she will manage. But the following inner focalization transmits the pain and bewilderment to the reader all the more poignantly through the use of the second person form of the pronoun:

> And have it no less still all afternoon than when you blew out the lamp and went to bed? Never cooking anything to be divided. To have your thoughts creep back into your mind from the touch of table and chair which need two faces in the room to have a face of their own? And sometimes to sit, after your needle was put away, and stare mindlessly at your own hands and feet? (*Rebellion* 69)

Paul's sense of obligation and guilt, of which the reader of passages such as the one above is brought to approve, makes him stay on at the farm to support his grandmother, but the education and career that he has sacrificed create "an area of constraint" between them that is "as tender and diffused as a blind boil" (70). Paul's regrets are expressed in a passage reminiscent of Henry James's short story "The Jolly Corner," whose protagonist Brydon is obsessed by and finally makes a supernatural encounter with the (better?) man/shadow he might have become if he had not gone away as a youth to live in Europe. Although his soft hands have toughened, "the shadow of Paul's city life still lingered in him, disconcerting him. What kind, what better kind, of someone else might he have been if he had stayed there?" (70). But Paul comes to learn and to love the good. He comes to place the values of solidarity and community, the values of the land that ensure a victory over time, above those of the city, "where you left no track, where almost everyone was servant to something, where the memory of you stopped with your breath" (80). When Paul takes his grandmother to the city for an expensive eye operation, he, like James's Brydon, expects to see everywhere "the torturing ghost of his other possible life" (80). Instead, he undergoes a "bloodless operation on his own vision" (80), one of the numerous epiphanies that are so recurrent in Buckler's texts. The grandmother's physical illumination, her return to sight, is accompanied by Paul's spiritual enlightenment:

> he longed to be back where you could see the paths your feet had made on the yielding earth. Where your only masters were sun and storm. Where in your neighbours' registry of deeds any little individuality you'd ever achieved was perpetually recorded. And where your little kingdom would always be known as "the Paul Redmond place" as long as the windows of your house still looked out on the spot where you lay. (80)

In many of Buckler's earlier short stories, the philosophical reflections are worked directly into the dialogue, in accordance with the strategy set out explicitly in his scribbler notes. "The Concerto," for example, like many of his earlier works, takes the form of almost exclusive dialogue, and reads like a play.[16] A thirty-year-old man, Dave, who has lost a finger and who can no longer play the piano, hears a young woman playing a concerto at a party. Mona is playing the one piano concerto he had never managed to learn, "the most difficult one of all" (65). The dialogue that ensues philosophizes on work, ambition, time, play, choice, and significance.

Dave essentially regrets not having worked hard enough at his music when he had the opportunity, and remarks to Mona bitterly,

> You see, there'd always be lots of time. It's a trick when you're young, this time business...there's no hurry, what can happen to you? You don't know that if there's anything you have to do, you'd better make sure of it right away. And no one ever tells you what it's like if ever the time's gone by. (65)

The story risks being reduced to a dramatized but simplistic form of moralizing, were it not for Buckler's exploration of choice and of the importance of play. Generally, people tend to perceive play as a gratuitous activity and to associate it with wasted time. They oppose play (the frivolous) with real life (the serious) and time well spent. The commonplace notion is that play is sterile, unproductive, useless. It creates nothing and produces no wealth. But among the social scientists who have studied and revalorized play, Johan Huizinga, (*Homo ludens*) and Roger Caillois (*Les Jeux et les hommes, le masque et le vertige*) have demonstrated how play is one of the main forces responsible for the development of culture within a civilization, and for the moral, intellectual, and physical development of the young.

Buckler seems to have divined this. His protagonist Dave chose to have fun and never became good enough to play the concerto, while Mona chose to work and missed out on the fun, for as she points out, "[t]here isn't time enough for both if you want to be really tops" (66). But she refuses to accept Dave's self-accusation that he wasted his youth on fun that was crazy and worthless, because "[w]hen it's gone there's nothing" (66). Buckler makes us see that both Mona's and Dave's forms of play are refuges with their own system of rights, privileges, and responsibilities. Caillois classifies play into four categories: *agôn* (or combat: play dominated by competition), *alea* (games of chance), *mimicry* (carnival, theatre), and *ilinx* (or vertigo). He places them on an axis containing two poles: *paidia* (involving uncontrolled fantasy, improvisation, impulse or drive), and *ludus* (involving discipline, constraints, a taste for the difficult, the pleasure of surmounting obstacles). Mona's long and hard-earned musical skill has evolved from a long combat that excluded dancing and having fun; it clearly belongs to the pole *ludus*, for it involves applying knowledge, intelligence, concentration, self-control, patience, and endurance. Dave's dancing, "chasing around," and doing "a lot of crazy things" (66) can be classified as vertigo, the physical exhilaration and organic or psychic disarray produced by jarring the senses voluptuously with strategies such as speed, movement, or danger (he lost his finger in the engine of an old boat that he gambled would take him to Newfoundland, while Mona never even "*thought* of doing anything that was dangerous to [her] fingers" (66)). His play is a form of *paidia*, involving elementary impulses, including the primary need for movement, linked with the basic desire to assert oneself, to be a force and a cause. While Mona's achievement is a creative, constructive victory over obstacles, imbued with the value of triumph, Dave's pursuit of sensation and pleasure is linked to the generally repressed but basic desire for disorder and destruction.

But Buckler questions the rigidity of values and relativizes judgments. Mona blurs the gap between the two poles when she tells Dave: "Don't ever make the mistake of thinking that fun is nothing because it's gone, or because it was crazy," insisting, "[t]here is only one time for fun like that. You had it then. And now it doesn't matter that the time's behind you." She adds that "it wouldn't matter a tinker's damn" to her if she never played a concerto again, and that "[y]ou have to accomplish a thing yourself to find out that it doesn't matter" (66). All the while relativizing the value of training and achievement, Mona pleads for a place for freedom, for unbridled fantasy. She suggests that they play the concerto together, Dave taking the bass, which is less complicated. When the music begins to come out clear and smooth, Dave realizes that being able to play the concerto no longer matters, but that this is because Mona's being able to do it suffices to content him. The term "concerto" means "together," we are told, and in a true couple, whatever the one has done, the other has not missed. The story, which rather patly ends with Dave asking Mona to dance/share his life, nevertheless questions our values on fundamental social issues such as work, play, creativity, merit, and worth.[17] It is grounded in an ethical stance that places great importance on the social dimension of human beings: we are stronger and more fulfilled when we share our assets, when we bond and create a synergetic community. Buckler's story exemplifies Emerson's maxim that the "axioms of physics translate the laws of ethics," according to which "the whole is greater than its part" (*Nature* 41).

Although Buckler himself never married, the whole greater than its parts in his works usually takes the shape of a married couple. The normative outlook that regulates his texts is grounded in the traditional notion of marriage as the ordering principle of society, the reflection of a divine order. Marriage is the generator of stability, which thinkers from antiquity to the Renaissance have argued to be the most desirable and accessible good. While the pleasures of passion and desire are transitory, and can lead to suffering and disorder, submitted as they are to the whims of fortune, marriage as a political and social institution is a means to conquer fortune. It ensures the perpetuation of the species, and the marriage contract with its vows of loyalty and fidelity builds a cohesive unit or microcommunity without which our society would, it is argued, disintegrate. Buckler, like his scholastic predecessors, regards political and social issues as moral problems, essentially revolving around the relationship between love and *probitas*, or moral virtue. At times prevailing in his work is the Socratic idea that Reason is the organ of morality, that morality is an affair of knowledge. The latent notion underlying his texts is the one handed on by Plato to the stoics: the existence of a natural law that implies that to see the good is to know it and to do it.

One of the major essays that the young Buckler wrote to obtain his MA was on "Aristotle's Psychology of Conduct," more specifically on Aristotle's notion of *akrasia* (*akrates* signifying "without force," or "powerless"). Even as a student Buckler was interested in "the actions of those who know what is right but who fail to act upon the good," who lack "strength of will."[18] Buckler's early short fiction often revolves around these notions of knowledge and will, alternative endings at times reinforcing the "moral." When the story "The Balance" was rejected for publication, Buckler suggested a different, "ironic" ending, whereby "the coercion of habit in the lonely man would be stronger even than the revelation."[19] Old Man Hennessey is a rigid, isolated old bachelor obsessed with the black scribbler in which he keeps his accounts down to the last cent. No one ever visits him, not even children on Hallowe'en. When young, he had let slip the opportunity to marry Ellen because he had decided not to speak till he had saved up $100. When Ellen's son dies in an accident, he realizes in a flash how he has excluded himself from sharing the pain but also the joy of the other members of the community, drawn together by the family roles that they share. His life has "dried up and fallen down...while the other men were talking with each other over their fences, or mending the hoe handles their children had broken, or looking in the catalogue with their women at the things they could never buy."[20] In his fury at his sterile isolation, he burns his precious scribbler. The final version of the story, published in *Ox Bells and Fireflies* as "Another Man," does contain the alternative ironic ending questioning the limits of free will, for the character (rechristened Syd) goes back to the store after the funeral to buy another black scribbler, condemned (by what?) to go on as before, relegated to the margins of society.

Another unpublished variation of the scenario, entitled "Snows of Christmas, Snows of Spring," contrives to get the estranged couple together again in the end. Buckler uses multiple focalization to transmit to the reader from the inside perspective of both man and woman how their celibacy marginalizes them from the community. The young woman Flo (not the mother of the child in this story, but the nurse who is called to the scene of the accident), contemplates what it means in her social environment to be a woman who never married, cast into a mould: "You get so you cast no shadow on anyone. And you parch....And you never have a child....A woman who never married. A woman who never lived."[21] Similarly, Glenn realizes the peripheral position of a bachelor: "You don't belong to anyone, he thought. I am not *like* anyone else in the place. They hardly separate me from the fields or the trees they look at....I am only a shape" (13). When the mother of the hurt child takes the father's arm, the thought dawns on Glenn, "A woman will never look at me like that. I will never know what a woman is like" (13). Flo casts no *shadow*, and Glenn is only a *shape*. The unmarried are ghosts relegated to the edges of society. They cannot *know* life. As indicated by the equivalence of *married* and *lived* established by the epanalepsis "a woman who never...a woman who never," they do not even exist. (Until, of course, they decide to get married in the end, at which point they realize they now have the status allowing them to visit anyone on equal footing, even on Christmas Eve, that hallowed evening reserved for intimate family and friends.)

In *The Cruelest Month*, the work that Buckler told his agent was a "novel of ideas,"[22] and that I examined in the preceding chapter, the writer proceeds in an inverse but parallel fashion. In this profoundly moral and didactic work, he does not allow his heroine, Sheila, to leave the husband she has come to despise. Rex retains her in the end through a suicide attempt that was botched in an ironic way, botched by its near success—he had not thought the rifle was loaded. Through Sheila's choice—albeit based on delusion—to adhere to her marital commitment and to give up her lover, Bruce, the author devalorizes adulterous passion, demonstrates the ephemeral, derisory, even subversive nature of any desire for personal gratification, and underscores the importance of stability and integrity:

> She saw that there would always come a Copernican revolution in your life, when with your weighing eye you saw that happiness, your happiness, was not the earth the sun revolved around—but no more than a tiny planet of no more lustre even to yourself than the planet of another's happiness. That there would always come a time when whosoever's gestures that were now the wands of love, and its bludgeons, would become no more than unaffecting mannerisms. Bruce's no less than Rex's. And that *the ones you'd known the longest were by far the most binding.*" (264-65, emphasis mine)

Many of Buckler's short stories offer a similar lesson, some of them in simple—even simplistic—allegorical form. In the unpublished manuscript "The Music Goes Round and Round,"[23] a broken cog almost wrecks a car's transmission, causing needless damage and expense that could have been avoided if the small problem had been seen to earlier. The mechanical breakdown is a metonymy, and the cog is a synecdoche of a small misunderstanding between husband and wife that is grinding through the gears of their marriage, wearing it down. Not trusting the reader to make the connection, the narrator spells out the parallel as it dawns on the husband, who resolves not to let the marriage go the way of the car.

In general, on the axis of adult sexual life, marriage and family represent the positive pole, while celibacy, the single life in its diverse forms, is the negative pole, a sort of vacuum. In "Nettles Into Orchids,"[24] a glamourous actress, Margot, comes back to her small town to triumph over a rival, Kate, whose husband, with whom they were both in love, has died. The story is almost entirely dialogue (like "The Concerto," it reads like a play), composed of verbal jousts that oppose two antithetical roles. I use the term "role" not in the theatrical sense but in the greimasian or narratological sense of a program, a narrative or social stereotype, rather like a semaphore, that makes the unfolding story easy to foresee. The two antithetical roles in the story are those of the career woman and the housewife. In the beginning, Margot seems to hold all the trump cards. Independent, adulated, wealthy, she moves in the higher artistic and public spheres of the metropolis, whereas Kate is limited to the narrow sphere of the backwoods, and the even smaller private sphere of the home, deprived— now that she is a widow—even of the man to whom she had devoted her whole existence. But the morality play runs along its course. The verbal jousts reveal that Margot is aging, that she has had no successful shows in years, and that she is alone, while Kate is the one who has the privilege of playing the only really important "role" that matters, the "real life part of a mother."[25] Life is greater than art, proclaims the text. Children are real, all the rest is illusion, and the triumph of the Wife and Mother rings devastatingly in Kate's challenge to Margot: "which would you rather have—a child of Peter's or that flossy cigarette lighter from a leading man whose name you can't even remember?" (6). The two characters are only types, not meant to be understood as individuals but only to be recognized as roles. They conform to a system of values and a certain vision of the world that link woman's function to reproduction. This reproduction is not merely of a biological nature, for if the nuclear family has such a highly charged ideological significance, even today with the advent of a new millennium, it is because it perpetuates a certain social order.

"Nettles into Orchids," relentlessly promoting a certain ethics, would lack subtlety were it not for a certain ambivalence introduced by an ending that is more of an opening outwards than it is a closure. Upon learning that Margot is an actress, the young son asks her to perform something for him, and Margot begins to recite "a splendid speech that begins like this. 'The quality of mercy is not strained...'" (9). We are told that Peter understood nothing whatsoever of the words, but "as he listened to that suddenly luminous voice his eyes shone; because even without understanding he could tell that he was in the presence of some kind of magic" (9). The synaesthesia and the repeated lexemes of light/illumination are not gratuitous. By giving due credit to the power of Shakespeare and the power of the interpreter, Buckler is proclaiming, like Schopenhauer, the power of words and art to help us contemplate the ultimate Idea, to transcend. For Schopenhauer claimed that we can put an end to servitude, to the cycle of desire and suffering, through Art—the disinterested contemplation of the Idea or immediate expression of the will—as we can through a certain asceticism, the negation of desire, to attain a state not unlike that of the Buddhist nirvana. These are the concepts that are also at the heart of *The Cruelest Month*, which, as we have seen, contains a profound ethical and aesthetic questioning, and which also contains the dynamics of aporia.

The "real life part of a mother" is all that really matters on an explicit level in "Nettles into Orchids." But there nonetheless exists a strong tension stemming from a countertext that maintains a deliberate irresolution. The countertext suggests, in accordance with Schopenhauer, that art is an intuition of the absolute, and that the true work of art "reproduces the eternal Ideas grasped through pure contemplation, the essential and abiding element in all the phenomena of the world" (Schopenhauer 108). The countertext also echoes Shelley's message whereby art "makes immortal all that is best and most beautiful in the world; it arrests the vanishing apparitions which haunt the interlunations of life, and veiling them, or in language or in form, sends them forth among mankind, bearing sweet news of kindred joy," redeeming "from decay the visitations of the divinity in man" (*Defence* 1085).

In these last two chapters, I have attempted to bring out the strategy of tension that infuses the writer's preoccupations with life and art. I have also shown how Buckler's stories—such as "Nettles into Orchids"—tend to consolidate the traditional foundations of social order, and to defuse the desires and dissatisfactions with one's lot that can cause unrest. The short story *The Doctor and the Patient*, for instance, has a limp plot, but it tackles issues that are also central to *The Cruelest Month*: being, desire, purpose, usefulness, free will, and destiny. The story drives the reader toward a moral rooted in stoicism. The moral is reinforced with a narrative twist,[26] and it proclaims that wanting to do something very badly is no guarantee that you would be good at it: "Maybe it's better to be doing what you can do, than what you want to. That you can do it so well, even when you think you should be doing something else, isn't that a pretty good sign that it's the proper thing for you?"[27] (66).

On the other hand, Buckler does not hesitate to challenge certain ingrained social prejudices. When he does so, however, it revolves around the central, paradoxical relationship between nature and culture, and seems to consolidate the former at the expense of the latter. As we have seen him aptly put it in "Muse in Overalls," "in any clash between a squash and a sonnet, the squash wins every time" (*Whirligig* 86). In one of Buckler's earlier short stories, "The Educated Couple," the domain of the squash triumphs morally, culturally, and socially. The story focuses on a village woman, Stella, whom everyone looks down on because she is illiterate. The community speculates as to why her educated husband had ever married her. When her husband has an accident and is sent away to hospital, the professor who employs Stella to clean house teaches her how to read and write, so that she can write to him. The story is a reflection on language and thought, for parallel to the learning of writing we find an awakening of consciousness, and the exploration of the human faculty to symbolize. The professor is stunned to hear the cleaning woman make metalinguistic remarks: "Ain't it funny," she said, "'furniture' is such a long word and 'love' is such a short one. You'd think it would be the other way around....Don't it give you a funny feeling to see the *shape* of thoughts you never even spoke out with your tongue before? It makes you feel like you ought to be more careful how you talk."[28] Although such metalinguistic reflections would not have been possible before Stella's acquaintance with print culture, Buckler seems to posit that one does not need a formal education to think deeply about the interaction between mental existence and cultural existence, and to perceive the arbitrariness of signifiers. He questions the way that society gauges the worth of an individual, by measuring the extent of their material or cultural baggage. We readers arrive at the moral of the story when the professor's new-found respect for Stella, and her integrity and perspicacity, proportionally increases his respect for her husband, who saw with his own eyes and did not let society impose its value judgments on him: "[h]e was an educated man not because he could read books, but because he knew that Stella wasn't *un*educated because she couldn't" (15).

Buckler's stories are essentially domestic, rarely extending beyond the garden or the street. Many of his short pieces revolve around the relationships between father and son, as attests Robert Chambers's grouping of stories under the heading "Fathers and Sons" in *The Rebellion of Young David*. Besides the parent/child relationships, the fictional universe can revolve around the relationships between spouses, lovers, or siblings, but it is always oriented towards the family and the community. If his texts are essentially homely (in the old-fashioned sense), it is because he associates the homely and the home with wholesomeness and with hope.

To conclude on a less serious note, should readers accuse Buckler of excessive moral earnestness, they have but to glance at a few of his satirical pieces to see that the writer does not set himself up as a judge of righteousness, but writes from the detached, benevolent, and frequently amused stance of the ironist, not hesitating to place himself among the targets of mockery. In the Ovid-like "Drink Now, Pay Later," he writes:

> Take two shots from the champagne bottle
> And suddenly you're wiser than Aristotle.
> Mix two more with bitters (mild)
> And suddenly you're wittier than Oscar Wilde.

The (very Canadian?) self-derision is quite cutting in the poem's concluding couplet:

> But when you face tomorrow *morning's* glass, alas,
> The thing you see reflected there is Balaam's ass.
> (*Whirligig* 62)

# Arcadia and Death

In the preceding chapter, I attempted to define Buckler's elaboration of an aesthetic philosophy based not only on ontological considerations but also on an ethical vision committed to transmitting ultimate truth and a perception of the divine order. In this chapter, I shall show the dynamics of his aesthetics at work in the central *topoi* that dominate his texts—Arcadia and death. A *topos*, a non-physical space offering common ground for agreement (Hunter), is a privileged place for the writer to strive for the *noumenon* or absolute supersensuous Unity, as well as to elaborate the didactic strategy I examined in the preceding chapter, allowing Buckler to instruct as he delights. In *Under Eastern Eyes*, Janice Kulyk Keefer has demonstrated that Arcadia is a *topos* of Maritime literature in general (16), and in "The Pastoral Vision of Ernest Buckler in *The Mountain and the Valley*," Alan Young has studied Buckler's first novel within the framework of Arcadia and the pastoral tradition. It is this very topic that made Knopf editor Angus Cameron agree to publish *Ox Bells and Fireflies* with such enthusiasm, calling it "the most evocative book of that lost world"[1] of a pastoral paradise, and, as I pointed out in chapter 2, caused Scribner's to reject the same manuscript for its nostalgic representation verging on the kitsch, even on "solid crème de marrons."[2] In his portrayals of a vanished idyllic agrarian community, Buckler nonetheless makes a point of protesting that "Nova Scotia is no Shangri-La" (*Window* 111). If, as he assured the Canada Council, *Ox Bells* is not just another wispily elegiac excursion into "the happy valley of childhood,"[3] it is through the pervasive presence of death, which for Buckler is a part of the fabric of life, a conundrum that knows all the conundrums yet never unriddles itself (*Ox Bells* 131). Consequently, after exploring the dynamics of the myth of Arcadia, I shall study the commonplace of death and, more precisely, the iconographical motif of *Et in Arcadia ego* in Buckler's heuristic prose. Finally, I shall end the chapter by examining some earlier fiction, focusing especially on an unpublished and undated piece that the young Buckler called a study in the misunderstood quiescence of the very old. I shall examine the transformations that this meditation on mortality underwent in the variants of the story, later to be incorporated into *Ox Bells and Fireflies* and *Window on the Sea*, and which reveal a shifting aesthetic and philosophical stance.

## Arcadia: Time, Myth, and Form

Arcadia, in arid, rocky central Greece, has come to represent a Golden Age of plenty, innocence, and bliss for those who believe in a gentle primitivism. The Arcadians lived in the domain of Pan, and were renowned for their musical talents. They were also famed for their moral sobriety, their illustrious lineage, and their rustic hospitality. But today we tend to forget that they were also notorious—we have only to read Juvenal, Philostratus, or Ovid—for their ignorance and poverty not only of body but of mind, and for a way of life resembling that of wild beasts, a life in which the arts played no part. Samuel Butler's little poem places him in a long line of poets that have satirized this nation that allegedly existed before the birth of Jupiter and the creation of the moon:

> The old Arcadians that could trace
> Their pedigree from race to race
> Before the moon, were once reputed
> Of all the Grecians the most stupid. (281)

But Virgil idealized the Arcadians. He emphasized their virtues, adding traits to Arcadia that it had never had: luxurious vegetation, eternal spring, endless leisure for voluptuousness and love. The Arcadia in his *Eclogues* to which he transposed the *Idylls* of Theocritus was a fictive place, and, as Erwin Panofsky points out, it is Virgil's imagination that gave birth to the concept of Arcadia as it is familiar to us today: a place of felicity, a Utopia, not in Thomas More's sense of *ou-topia* or "no place," but in the later sense of *eu-topia* or "good place."

During the Renaissance, Arcadia became a Utopia distant not so much in space as in time—a haven from an imperfect reality, from the present. Soon the nostalgic yearning for the inviolate peace and innocence of an ideal past, which until then, as Panofsky remarks, had been impersonal, took on the bitter, personal quality of an indictment of a real present.

This double dimension colours Buckler's fictional memoir, *Ox Bells and Fireflies*, just as the presence of the older narrator, the narrating "I" overlaps that of the younger protagonist, the narrated "I." His "novelistic non-fiction"[4] as well as much of his fiction, notably *The Mountain and the Valley*, adhere to a pastoral tradition that has been thriving in Europe with authors such as Jean Giono, with whose writing Buckler was well acquainted. Giono devoured Virgil, Melville, and Whitman as he was growing up in the wheat fields of France, and then in turn, adopted a sensual lyrical style to celebrate nature and the peasants' communion with the earth. Similarly, Buckler himself critiques for the *New York Times Book Review* a novel by Sara Lidman on Swedish rural life at the beginning of the century. His remarks on *The Rain Bird*, certain haymaking scenes of which, he claims, "recall Jean Giono's," could well apply to his own work:

> By precision use [sic] of the simplest language with the densest penumbra she articulates the texture of village life in the northern Sweden of 50 years ago to the very letter. Her book is also a stark line-engraving of the human heart....And in the evocation of a spellbound atmosphere wherein "signs" and fatalism haunt the land...her characters...are actual as breath.[5]

Then, closer to home, there are the pastoral works of W.O. Mitchell and of Gabrielle Roy. Roy's prairie landscapes and simple Manitoban people acquire a mythical dimension in *La Montagne secrète* and *La Route d'Altamont*, both so successful that they are immediately translated into English. Buckler reviews the translated novels, praising Roy for the persistence in *The Hidden Mountain* of "the haunting claims of light and trees and water (that 'sang the known and the unknown of life') to be given speech."[6] In *The Road Past Altamont*, like Buckler, Roy sings a lost but timeless world by, as Buckler puts it, "drawing on the parables of lake, prairie ('this reminder of the total enigma') and hills," and "takes the very pulse of wonder, love, aging, the dividends of solitude, the interweaving of generations, the way the anti-poles of past and future can split a spirit."[7]

Buckler (re)creates this lost world of simple, eternal values and places it within our reach by eliminating the separations both of space and time. Here is how *Ox Bells and Fireflies* begins: "I'll call the village 'Norstead,' the boy 'I.' They stand for many. The time is youth, when Time is young" (3). The narratorial voice imposes its power and authority immediately through the use of the auxiliary "will" (while in other chapters it does so by using imperatives that implicate the reader directly). It draws attention to the arbitrary—because purely authorial—choice of the first person pronoun, and emphasizes the synecdochic function of both the protagonist and his village. "*Je est un Autre*"[8]/"I is Another," Buckler is saying along with Rimbaud. He is in effect making a distinction, creating a certain distance between the creator-author and his creature-narrator, all the while blurring the distinction between speaker and receiver, reducing the distance between the narrator and us readers. The geographical location—the precision of the naming process annulled by the revelation of its arbitrary nature—and the individual identity of the boy are non-specific, totalizing, all-inclusive. If we belong to the "many," it is our story that we are about to read. It is our story, whatever our social class, nationality, regional appurtenance, or cultural background may be. For the "feather and stone of hope and foil are the same everywhere. The rooster's comb is the same color as the Cardinal's biretta" (*Ox Bells* 20).

The typographical distinction Buckler makes between "time" and "Time" blends and blurs the ahistorical and historical modes. The writer, all the while depicting a common generational experience, magnifies it to a mythical plane. Childhood is equated to the dawn of time, and since we were all young once, a leap in memory can project us back to this edenic world. Memory is the miracle that can "send the mind skimming back over the rails of time and space," and the heart can take us "straight back to the pulse of another time" and can "unlock 'ago' like the master key of dream" (21).

Claude Lévi-Strauss argues in his *Anthropologie structurale* that all myth refers to past events (before the creation of the world, or at the dawn of humanity—in any case, "a long time ago"). But the intrinsic value attributed to myth derives from the fact that these events, which allegedly occurred at some moment in time, form a permanent structure that refers simultaneously to the past, the present, and the future. Myth, like political ideology, actually has a double structure. It is both historical and ahistorical, as demonstrated by the reaction of the first-generation English Romantics to the French Revolution, both the event and promise of regeneration—best illustrated by Wordsworth's famous line "Bliss was it in that dawn to be alive" (*Prelude*, Book XI 108). In Buckler's idyllic community, time "was neither before you nor behind you: you were exactly opposite the present moment. It made a rushing sound that the sound of your consciousness was in total chorus with" (*Ox Bells* 103). Buckler's use of myth allows readers to connect with their own past, with relatives or ancestors removed in space and time, operating an anticipatory and prophetic fusion that attempts to make sense of both the old and the new, the better to confront the future.

The myth of Arcadia structures the perspective that the narrator gives us of his community, provides the framework for lyricism, a nostalgic yearning for a golden past, a complaint for a society that is timeless and yet a pale shadow of its former splendour: the story of Paradise Lost and perhaps, if readers take heed, of Paradise Regained.

The voice of the older narrator in *Ox Bells and Fireflies* overlaps the boy's point of view in a way that telescopes the old and the new, contrasts the traditional and the modern, the natural and the artificial, in a number of ways. Particularly significant is the use of the marker of food, part of what French critic Philippe Hamon calls a network of normative evaluation (118). Anthropologists and literary critics from Lévi-Strauss to Northrop Frye (*Anatomy* 118) have remarked that the domain of food is not only that of the appetite, of desire, of pleasure, but also the reflection of a society's structure and world vision. Let us take a look at Buckler's treatment of the signifier of food in the following passage from *Ox Bells and Fireflies:*

> Downstairs, the kitchen would beckon with the smell of food and the pulse of living. Cereals had not yet been blown from a gun, refined to all but predigestion, and packaged about some object of miniature weaponry. We breakfasted on oatmeal bubbling like lava, and on bread browned in a wire toaster held over the fire itself. The boiled eggs would be peeled with great caution from their shells. Their glistening perfection of geometry would be admired for a moment before we plunged our spoons into the golden yolks. That children should have to be coaxed to eat, as if food were something as distasteful as fractions, we'd have found completely baffling. (43)

Food, as well as mediating between domestic life and art, between the beautiful and the functional, is the marker that separates Then and Now. It associates the past with life (the explicit declaration of the notion reinforced by the personification of the kitchen), and associates the present with death and destruction. Today's food is adulterated beyond recognition, deformed, destroyed by modern technology which is likened to military arms. The refining process, the stripping of natural fibres and minerals, is likened to an act of war. The food is manufactured by a gun and is as devoid of life and nourishment as the miniature gun it is packaged with. Yesterday's food, on the other hand, has undergone only a slight transformation in accordance with the pattern described by Lévi-Strauss (*L'Origine*), in which cooking is the mediator between nature and culture. Lévi-Strauss's famous culinary triangle (*Le Cru et le cuit*) demonstrates the conjunctive and disjunctive relationships between the raw (the natural or non-elaborate), the cooked (elaboration in the form of cultural transformation), and the rotten (elaboration in the form of natural transformation). Buckler's boiling oatmeal, the toasted bread, have been only slightly elaborated by a grinding and a cooking process that, as with the boiled eggs, is done entirely with the natural elements of fire and water. The wholesome cooked breakfast of yesterday has the significant symbolic function of mediating between the subject and the physical world. The glistening perfection of form that fuses the functional and the beautiful (the aesthetic dimension highlighted in the passage by the use of alliteration), the golden yolks that are a metonymy of the Golden Age, attest to an ideal state of harmony and plenitude that is an indictment of a present that has exiled itself from the Garden. When food is distasteful, society is dys-functional.

Buckler repeatedly has recourse to the world of food to illustrate the breakdown, to cast over his Garden the shadow of exile perpetually to come and yet always having come, the day when *yet* becomes *already* and *with* becomes *without*:

> Not yet—not for a long time yet—the faintest premonition of that later gust which comes from the other objects when the brand of parting or of buried chances smokes inside you. You stop at the cluttered roadside lunchroom on the day when "with" has become "without" forever and it comes at you from the missing letter in the swinging metal sign. You step inside and it comes at you from the slush stains tracked into the floor. You go to the counter and it comes at you from the artificial flowers beside the yellowed cactus plant beside the bowl of stagnant water where the feet of two small turtles clutch stuporously for footholds on each other, not knowing each other from rocks. (*Ox Bells* 31)

The use of the second person pronoun projects us as readers into a sordid present that is all the better a foil for the shining haven he paints elsewhere. The sordidness overwhelms us with an inexorable quality generated by the use of epanalepsis ("and it comes at you" is repeated four times) combined with a series of parallel structures (you stop/you step inside/you go to the counter; the missing letter/the slush stains/the artifical flowers), and a final spiralling concatenation (beside the/beside the) evocative of a cinematic panning technique, that atomizes reality until it is reduced to the brutish body fragments of reptiles so cut off from their natural state that they cannot recognize their own kind.

In the two passages I have looked at, Buckler's temporal markings, as usual, are vague. He projects us back and forth from an undefined past to an indefinite present through shifts in aspect, and through adverbial phrases that, Janus-like, look both backwards and forwards: "Cereals had not yet been blown from a gun" (43); "Not yet—not for a long time yet" (31). We often do not quite know where we are in time, whether we are Then, or Now, or in some sort of liminal space between the two. The diegetic past is carried indifferently by the preterite, by the conditional signifying an iterative, or by the present tense; it meshes and mingles with the narratorial present, the present of discourse. But even when the narrative is firmly placed in the past, Buckler's temporality is cyclical, diurnal, or seasonal—it is winter, or the first of May, or Sunday, evening or morning—almost devoid of chronological references, evoking only a vague edenic past with an ahistorical lexicon. The narrator does introduce sporadic references to the historical landing of Champlain at neighbouring Port Royal, which is "hushed with history" (22), but it is to set up a dialectic between a derisory manmade clock time and the primeval timelessness of nature that endures. Listening to the tales of his grandmother, the boy narrator "could feel the earth give a sort of tremor when Champlain, bringing Time with him, set the first discoverer's foot on this whole timeless land" (22). In a symbiotic fusion with a personified land, the boy projects himself into a historical past and then beyond to a pre/a/historical time: he actually "heard the stroke of the first settler's ax on the first astonished trees, which would give him both his home and his heat," and "touched the first blade of grass that brought the first living smell where there had only been the closed forest breath of endlessness and secrecy" (23). But the past for the boy protagonist "was only reading," and whenever he "closed its book, everything was always and forever Now" (23), a Now that shares the timelessness of the dark trees "whispering together their primeval messages" (23).

This eternal present is one of felicity, fraternity, peace, and plenty:

> A kind of muted resonance echoes in our bodies from the steady note of plenty that comes from the potato bins; from the carrots buried in sawdust to keep them firm; from the heads of cabbage laid out side by side along the big cellar beams. We own ourselves completely. Everything around us seems to be the fruit of us. (36)

These are our original rustic Arcadians, who derive satisfaction from nothing more than a store of humble vegetables and the knowledge that they are their own masters. But like Virgil, Buckler embellishes his Arcadia. His Arcadians are in perfect communion with a bounteous Nature and with one another. The following description of harvest time, with its Romantic imagery illustrates how the fruits of the earth are true riches to rival the coffers of emperors:

> The heavy squash glisten like gnobby green bone. I break them off their labyrinth of vines and the stupored pumpkin moons off theirs and make mounds of them. They too will be left outside a few days more to soak up the very last of the sun. I squint my eyes. They look like piles of emeralds and gold. (34)

We have already seen in chapter 5 how in *The Mountain and the Valley* Martha and Joseph Canaan are the new Adam and Eve, attaining oneness in the Garden through mutual undertakings. When they are "on their knees, picking up potatoes in the acre field" they look "as if they were praying" (125). In *Ox Bells and Fireflies* too, work is a form of prayer, a communion with the divine; it is equated with plenitude and perfect harmony with one's fellows. The narrator's description of how the family lovingly gathers the potatoes together is imbued with a sacred dimension strikingly reminiscent of the oneiric fusion of the Canaans, who move "without images, melting through each other like the configuration of clouds" (*Mountain* 126):

> The three of us kneel together beside the rows. We assemble the scatterment of them into round heaping basketsful. The cleaned stretch behind us as we work our way along is like hours lived out to the full. The feeling of home is stronger in us than at any other moment of the year. (*Ox Bells* 34)

The church-like quality is extended to include the family meal that follows the end of the harvest day, a meal evocative of a religious service even without the explicit religious lexicon and imagery (host, religion, creed, altar, mystery):

> The supper food this night is warm and supperly as never before. The teapot sits like a gentle sovereign at my mother's elbow. The dishes are like smiling accomplices on a pleasure about to be sprung on someone. Appetite shimmers. The meat and the bread and the tea are like the host of some affable religion whose only creed is the denial of sternness. The table is the altar of kinship between the stove warmth and the lamplight. The plainest of mysteries; facelight, knits its shield above the table and around us. (35)

In one among many long litanies that mingle elements in a dialectic fashion, Buckler evokes the air that smells of sunlight, of wild roses, and of apples (the domain of the natural) but also of the cloth over rising bread, and the hair of children (the domain of the cultural) (27). The stone walls on which the wild roses grow symbolize the harmonious fusion between the two domains: the wall is an artificial construction, but the building material is entirely natural. The boy narrator of *Ox Bells and Fireflies* himself embodies this fusion, reminiscent of the wholeness of humanity before the Fall, as we can witness from the following passage, steeped in neo-Platonism:

> I open my shirt and let the sun touch my chest. I listen to the brook and there is not a cavity of any kind within me. I fit into myself like the brook to the bank.
>
> I listen to the brook, and my own flesh and I are such snug and laughing brothers that I know we are forever mingled with the sun's pulse (or the wind's or the rain's) and forever unconquerable. (12)

The same vein of neo-Platonism generates the *topos* of Arcadia in *The Mountain and the Valley*, in which the idyll consists of a multitude of intermediaries from the spheres of both nature and culture, and belonging to both historical and ahistorical modes—placed in deliberate alternation—that allow David to encounter a life force:

> cold water reaching to the roots of his tongue when thirst in the haymow was like meal in his mouth…the touch of the crisp dollar bill he had changed his dented pennies for at the bank in town…the light on the water curling white over the dam when his line first came alive with the dark, secret sweep of the trout…the cut clover breathing through his open window just before summer sleep…the sound of his father's sleighbells the night of the day he'd sent for the fountainpen…the date of the Battle of Flodden looked up tremblingly in the book and found to be exactly the same as the one he'd put down, uncertainly, in the examination…the doctor coming out of the room and saying that Anna would be all right…his own name in printed letters on the envelope from the city…the moment in the dream when he climbed to the top of the mountain and looked down. (81-82)

Far from the shattered units of modern society that Emerson declares to have been "subdivided and peddled out" or "spilled into drops" that "cannot be gathered" (*English Traits* 6), the inhabitants of Buckler's Arcadia live in a harmony and one-ness that completes the "perfection" of the world. The hymn the writer sings is an illustration of Emerson's Unity in Variety, for currency, mail-order catalogues, and school marks interconnect with the purity of the natural elements of water and light, and the organic activities of breath and sleep, to create a perfect whole. Similarly, in *Ox Bells and Fireflies*, when the parents of the boy narrator sow seeds in the field together, "something about their nearness fills up that little hollow in the perfect day put there by the day's very perfection" (29). Even the mother's knitting is metaphorical: when she knits a mitten for the father, she "knits [the family] closer still" (37). When he tries it on so that she can check where the narrowing of the thumb should start, it creates "one of those moments when he and she seem so mingled together that even sight can scarcely separate them" (37).

Wholeness in Buckler's texts is expressed particularly in terms of family bonds. The Canaans create a paradise for one another through small attentions. Bliss is a series of small gestures: it is the box Joseph places in a sunny spot for Martha to sit on the day she cuts the seed potatoes for him to drop; it is the "touch on his hands of the dry mittens which she'd warmed on the oven door and brought to him when he came into the yard with the second load of wood, when the pair he'd started with were clammy and cold" (*Mountain* 219); it is the boy David, touched by his sister's vulnerability, letting her catch him in a game of hide and seek; it is the children's trying to guess one another's Christmas presents, making each guess deliberately small, so "there'd be no chance that the other would be hurt by knowing that his present was less than the vision of it" (63). But happiness is also service beyond the family, shared task, and the granting of favours large and small: in *The Mountain and the Valley* all the men coming to help shoe the bad ox, or the women coming to a quilting; or, in *Ox Bells and Fireflies*, the neighbours helping to rake in the clover before a storm, or coming over in the middle of the night to help tend a sick child. Wholeness is thus also conceived in terms of extrafamilial bonding, of belonging to a larger community or unit. We see the men take leave of one another in *The Mountain and the Valley* so haltingly it was "like a rope fraying apart" or the women sitting with their needles "like one person over the tea" (57).

The wholeness is nonetheless not perfect, and the solidarity of the community not without flaws. At the Christmas concert in *The Mountain and the Valley*, the seating arrangements attest to the way the other women ostracize Bess, the mother of Effie, and exclude her from the circle of the community: "No woman her own age was sitting near her—they had located where she was sitting their first glance through the door, then sat somewhere else" (79). This moral inflexibility towards a neighbour suspected with being too "free" with men, is one of the harsher traits of the original Arcadians, the darker side of virtue, of moral sobriety. Buckler's Norsteaders treat sex like the healthful, natural thing that it is, "a blend of comedy and sheet lightning" (*Ox Bells* 170). Reminiscent of Ovid and his keen awareness of the ridiculous,[9] Buckler is never solemn about sexual love. He and his protagonists believe that sex is "the funniest thing in the world" (*Ox Bells* 169). In accordance with classical precedents, passion is not romanticized. Indeed, what could be less romantic than Buckler's mocking description of people "with their mouths together like guppies,' sprawled in the pose of grasshoppers" (169)? Consequently, in his idyllic community, responsibility and fidelity are the rule. Should a "slip" occur, the wedding followed at once, and once "couples were paired off they stayed that way" (*Ox Bells* 171). Any threat to this social order, like Bess, is dealt with accordingly.

Buckler's rural protagonists, like the original Arcadians, live in chronic poverty in a subsistence economy that technology seems to have forgotten. At first glance, certain intrusions of trivial details from mundane modern life nonetheless seem to clash with the lyricism of the pastoral descriptions of the farm or Garden, which belong to the elegiac mode. Yet a closer look reveals that the microcosmic paradise resists even the assaults of bathos. When the Canaan family kill their pig, they send to Anna, their daughter who has moved to the city, a package of tenderloin slices individually wrapped in waxed paper from cornflakes boxes. The pork, the paper recycled from factory food packaging, are manifestations of the lowly rather than the sublime, the prosaic rather than the poetic, our animal functions rather than our spiritual aspirations. But they are nevertheless true myth at work. As in the legend of Prometheus and the sacrificial bull, food is once more the basis of cultural identity and social cohesion, generating understanding when shared. The meat serves to dissolve distance and to reunite the absent daughter with her family through double pleasure—their pleasure in anticipating her pleasure in their remembrance of her.

As a counterpart to the material impoverishment of the region, the miniature paradise in Buckler's texts is a paradise of the senses. In this, Buckler's stance is reminiscent of Jean Giono's. In his first novels, published from 1928 to 1930, making up the *Trilogie de Pan*,[10] Giono exalted the powers of sensation, claiming that they were instruments to penetrate the world. In chapter 3, I have shown how in *The Mountain and the Valley*, pleasure is the deliciousness of a hot stick of wood in a cold bed, the smell of Christmas fruitcakes lying on inverted pans, the touch of chocolate-shaped chestnuts evoking "the smoothness of all the days that were gone" (54). A veritable paradise is constructed through a synergetic relationship established between the different modes of sensation of taste, touch, and sight.

But what makes the novel remarkable is the fact that this Arcadia is carefully assembled through form, not matter, through anticipation and expectancy, not use or possession. We have seen how the senses generate pleasure, how blissfully David inhales the smell of the Christmas fruitcases. But the pleasure he takes in the aroma is a sufficient one, a complete one. Similarly, just taking a nut out of the bag and rolling it in his palm is total bliss. It is not the material object itself, but the promise it holds out that is delicious. The ecstasy of anticipation is depicted as not only totally fulfilling, but almost excessive: "Then he leaned over and smelled the bag of oranges. He didn't touch it. He closed his eyes and smelled it only. The sharp, sweet, reminding, fulfilling smell of the oranges was so incarnate of tomorrow it was delight almost to sinfulness" (61). Perceiving touch as being too physical, David prefers the impalpable, ethereal quality of smell. The happiness of anticipation is such that David goes beyond even this immateriality. In a lyrical hymn to the magic of Christmas Eve, the memory alone of smell and touch contributes to generating complete bliss:

> And when Martha held the match to the lamp wick, all at once the yellow lamplight soft-shadowed their faces…like a flood and gathered the room all in from outside the windows. It touched the tree and the hemlock with the great red bell with the flaw no one could even notice, like a soft breath added to the beating of the room's heart: went out and came back with a kind of smile. The smell of the tree grew sud-

> denly and the memory of the smell of the oranges and the feel of the nuts. In that instant, suddenly, ecstatically, burstingly, buoyantly, enclosingly, sharply, safely, stingingly, watchfully, batedly, mountingly, softly, ever so softly, it was Christmas Eve. (65)

The hypnotic quality of the prose, with its prayer-like litany of adverbs, is but the beginning of a long paeon to virtuality. If Christmas Eve is magic, it is precisely because it announces the advent of Christmas Day. If Christmas morning is magic, it is precisely because of the metaphorical quality of its dawn—the dawn of hope, a privileged moment of stasis turned toward the contemplation of a future that is perfect because of its very virtuality. The text systematically emphasizes the deliciousness of anticipation over that of event:

> He and Anna *waited*, shivering in the hall, for Chris....They went down the stairs, shivering more than cold had ever made them shiver. They went past the dining room where the *wonder waited*, into the kitchen. Chris glanced into the dining room as he passed, but David whispered to Anna, "*Don't look.*" Neither of them turned a head...
>
> These were like moments *out of time* altogether, because they were up and *going to* do something splendid, but the lamp was *still* lit, the day *hadn't really begun.*
>
> For a minute *no one moved*. This was the tree of *hope:* the yellow globes of oranges hanging on the boughs, the perfectly scalloped garlands of popcorn, the white tents of handkerchiefs on the green limbs, and secretly between the branches, nearer the trunk, the mesmeric presents themselves. They knew so surely that everything they wanted *would be* there, they *could wait*. (67, emphases mine)

The wonders of waiting are such that the actual acquisition of object, the actual occurrence of event, is not only an anti-climax, but the tarnishing of the Ideal, the first step toward corruption. As the virtual becomes the actualised, as essence yields to materiality, as David breaks the first nut and breaks the skin of the first orange, feeling "the first incarnate taste of its sharp juice," we can note the death of the marvellous and the intrusion of the trivial and the mundane: "The tree was *delivered now of its mysteries* and *the plain having* began. The lamp *grew pale* in the beginning sunlight. Martha remembered *breakfast*, and

Joseph remembered the rest of his *chores"* (69, emphases mine). As with the new sneakers "with the black rubber soles so shining he could hardly bear to take the first step on the ground" (58), possession and use degrade what was perfect. When David actually puts on his brand-new jacket, he is dismayed at the process of deterioration:

> Little wrinkles were already showing at the crook of his elbows. He walked on, with his arms held straight at his sides. When they went into the house, he took the jacket off and folded it again the way it had been on the tree. It didn't seem to him that he could ever take it for everyday and have the sharp creases of the sleeves become round and sloppy. (72)

Similarly, when he takes up the precious new book he got for Christmas, David reads with "an ecstatic caution, as if even reading might soil its pages" (75). The perfect book, as with all other objects of desire, is the untouched book, the unread book. It is not the book itself but the Idea of the book that prevails. In the same way, the occurrence of event pales in comparison with the idea of it. When first granted permission to climb the mountain with his father, the young David, excited and feverish, ironically tries to put off the final moment of ascension in order to savour the moment of anticipation as long as possible. "He almost wished there was some way he could save it. The second time was never as good." (28)

Nature holds out her perfection in the admirable design of her humblest elements, and as I have demonstrated in chapter 3, Buckler celebrates Form as the very essence of reality, posited in an immobile eternity. I have evoked the description in *Ox Bells and Fireflies* of the lowly daisy, which "was as perfectly in pattern as if a draftsman's lifetime had gone into the making of it" (106). It is echoed by other representative descriptions evoking a perfect divine order, such as the following hymn to natural geometrical design:

> Beech leaves, students of the sun, expand their just-discovered shapes millimeter by millimeter, keeping the tiny leaf with all its serrated points always in *perfect scale* with the *map* of the finished one held before them in the hands of the warmth—and the leaves of the cherry tree, quickest learners of all, knowing *exactly* in each rim cell when *completeness* has been reached, stop there and bask in their accomplished goal like *theorems*. (210, emphases mine)

Buckler's Arcadia is a privileged space where one seeks and can attain this perfection of form. In chapter 3, I touched on the quest for perfect lines, forms, and patterns that is intricately woven throughout the fabric of Buckler's texts, from the beautifully straight lines of the plow in "The Bars and the Bridge" to the perfect pattern of the walnuts in the fudge in "The Christmas That Faced Both Ways." The exactness of the forms of things in Buckler's edenic universe is a sign of human participation in the perfect order and regularity of an immutable cosmos. In *The Mountain and the Valley*, David's father, Joseph, is admirable because he can find and even generate this perfection:

> When he cut the alder for a fishing pole, he searched and searched until he spotted *the perfectly straight* one you couldn't see yourself. When he made the whistle, he didn't do it practically, like a job. He did it so carefully and *so perfectly* as you wanted it that you wondered how it was possible. (27, emphases mine)

In a similar fashion, the father in the short story "Penny in the Dust" "could tap the alder bark with his jackknife *just exactly* hard enough so it wouldn't split but so it would twist free from the notched wood, to make a whistle" (*Rebellion* 6, emphasis mine). Similarly the son in "The Rebellion of Young David" wants his father to tell him when to pull on the fishing line, "just right *when*," and praises him for throwing him balls "*just* right…just *right*" (*Rebellion* 8-9; the emphases are significantly Buckler's). The boy narrator of *Ox Bells and Fireflies* seems to feel that his father is touched by some special sort of grace because he pilots the team of oxen with "matchless skill between the rocks and stumps" (51) and guides the plow "so skillfully that the wave of earth the plow tumbles onto the potatoes covers each of them to *exactly* the same depth" (30, Buckler's emphasis). The boy attains a state of ecstatic exaltation from the exactitude or perfection of the movement: "from every detail of everything I look at comes the sudden exclamation of its *falling* exultantly *into place* with me" (30, emphasis mine). Switching to second person narration to implicate the addressee further in the pleasure of perfection, the older narrator of *Ox Bells and Fireflies* makes us not only participate in, but actually become the agents of, a world of perfect equilibrium:

> Your muscles had the knack of what they were doing built into them like a recitation. They pleasured themselves in

> steering the share *just right* to curl over the first ribbon of greensward without a break, in giving the reins looped about your neck *just the right tug* to keep the horse's path *straight as a ruler*....On the return path, they pleasured themselves still more in rolling the second sod *so precisely* edge to edge with the first that neither would topple the other back into the furrow. (90, emphases mine)

Precision of gesture seems to translate the fusion of mind and matter, thought and thing, that Buckler finds so attractive. The "breathing space" between the narrator's thoughts is likened to the spaces between the trees. The work of cutting down a tree, of swinging the axe against the tree *"precisely* where the eye said the first wedge-angled blows must be struck" is a "miracle of translation, quicker than thought, quicker than light" (*Ox Bells* 93, emphasis mine) between brain, hands, and world.

The chapter "A to Z" composed of vignettes of various Norsteaders who have never gone to school, is a long litany of their natural talents, insisting heavily on precision of gesture. App, who can skate *"perfect* figure eights" (280), is famous for his exquisite craftsmanship: "He could cut a rafter *precisely the right length* by eye alone" (279, emphasis mine). With only a hand drill, Stella's husband cut slabs of granite rock from his quarry with "the skill of a diamond cutter" (285). Carrie, the dressmaker, "used no pattern, and when she poised her scissors for the first bold cut into a length of Shantung the customer would gasp, but she never made a miss" (288). Jake "could spot the hidden mechanics of an object with one glance." We learn that a log "so big that no three men could load it on to the sleds he could load alone, knowing *to an inch* where to lever the skids, where the peavy, where the chain." He taught the men where to elbow a stovepipe "so it would draw best; even how to balance a weathervane *just right"* (282-83). Hugh could call a bull moose across the bog "to within a rod of where he was hidden" (285), Zeb could judge a beef's weight "almost to the pound" (291). When sowing, he strode *"as evenly* as if he was following a marker, the seed fanning out from his hand *so evenly* that when it came up there was never a thick patch or a thin" (291, emphases mine).

Buckler's paeon to precision of gesture is perhaps most remarkable in *The Mountain and the Valley*, in the cutting up of the pig, an act not many writers have sung before,[11] and that here is invested with a lyrical beauty:

> They took out the flap of spareribs next. She kept steady tension on it while Joseph nicked it from the fat beneath. Then she indicated the contour of the ham with a quick circle of her finger. Joseph followed the circle *exactly* with his knife. He separated the ham from the body *precisely* at the glistening hip socket....He didn't know exactly how she wanted it done until she told him; but after she'd told him, he did it more *exactly* that way than she could have done it herself. She knew *just* the smooth boundary she wanted on the ham, but if she had taken the knife herself it would have come out haggled and botched. (206-207, emphases mine)

We witness a magic moment when essence takes on form, a form as perfect as the Idea behind it, whereas the forms of our world are habitually "haggled and botched."

This perfection is fragile. In the short story "The Quarrel," the August Sunday was to have been "twice as wonderful as ever before"—once more thanks to the bliss of virtuality, for the day "had in it the looking ahead to a tomorrow more wonderful than any day" the boy narrator has ever known, as on the Monday the family is to go to the exhibition in Annapolis. The day does open with a special sheen on it, "so perfect that even the consciousness of its perfection sprang into [the narrator's] mind" (*Rebellion* 44). But when his parents quarrel, the whole day bursts and tumbles around him: "They had broken it like glass, and no matter how perfectly you fitted the pieces together again, you'd know that the mending was there" (45). Buckler's protagonists have such a thirst for absolute perfection, such rage when form or matter fall short of the Idea of it, that they prefer to follow an all-or-nothing scorched-earth policy. Overlapping the point of view of the young narrated I, the voice of the older narrator introduces through a value judgment a note of compromise and resigned detachment, when he confesses: "I was such a foolish child that when a thing which was to have been perfect was spoiled the least bit, it was spoiled entirely. If I as much as scratched the paint on my new wagon I wanted to take the axe and smash the whole thing to bits" (*Rebellion* 45).

Buckler's Arcadia is a fragile one, but all the lovelier and more precious for the flaws that ultimately make it accessible, that make this ideal past a virtual reality, within our reach. For contrary to Scribner's disparaging dismissal of Buckler's "solid crème de marron," the writer himself puts us on guard against the power of memory which can be "harping, misleading, and treacherously sentimental" (*Ox Bells* 21). At the beginning of his fictional memoir, he acknowledges that memory often "conjures all sorts of things into a vanished way of life that were never there to begin with" (21), and he criticizes the "misty-eyed" minds of writers who dive back into their country childhoods and "come up with a jam jar of candied guff about Crokinole sprees and taffy pulls that were, in fact, mild horrors" (21). No, not for Buckler the "crème de marron" or the "candied guff." The world that he conjures up derives its beauty and its comfort from its very ordinariness: newly-fallen snow, a storm door that closes tight after the warped sill has been replaced, the sound of crickets, the smell of supper, sunlight striking through the parlour window, the colour of cornflowers, a child's first ice skates, rainbows and rhubarb. If these things shine with a special light, it is because Buckler somehow succeeds in carrying us to the very essence of things, so that we, like his protagonists, can "know exactly what *trout*ness [is]. And *brook*ness. And *leaf*ness. And, yes, *world*ness and *life*ness itself."[12]

At the same time, Buckler's Arcadia is not an Eden in which the human, nourished by a bountiful Nature, is free from the necessity of work. On the contrary, the writer does not conceal the gruelling labour required to earn one's bread, the endless repetition of tasks completed only to be begun again. The fragrant hay being hauled, for instance, turns "from feathery to leaden" in the sun's light that begins to "harden and smart" and becomes "remorseless" (*Ox Bells* 99-100). Similarly, the writer discloses the intrusion of pain and discomfort, the indifference or even hostility of the elements. Through polysyndeton, a recurrent rhetorical device that I shall examine in the final chapter, he stresses the fact that

> the ground hornets stung you when you mowed into their papyrus nest. And the rocks scraped you. And the bushes scratched you. And the rain turned the peak of your cap into pulp. And the snow water grayed the toes of your larrigans. And the sun and the wind scored your skin. (103)

In the same way, he does not gloss over the shortcomings of this world's inhabitants. Their faces can be "as scraggly as turnip knurls or as handsome as apples"; their talk can be "a dull rosary of empty shells they ticked off like parrotry or like a flash of eyelight that showed the whole blood-mesh of feeling behind it" (*Ox Bells* 20). In Buckler's edenic communities there are "some odd ones, some sorry figures, some cruelty" (264), as we have already seen in terms of Bess in *The Mountain and the Valley*. Buckler does not pretend that all country people lead lives we should aspire to. On the contrary, his alliterative description of the spiritual and intellectual poverty of the inhabitants of many other villages echoes the satires of the primitive Arcadians:[13] "Their senses were deaf as adders to the voice of the eternal around them; their spirits the width of rulers and the depth of thimbles; their hearts so pocked with pettiness, so cramped with caution, that they never set a foot ahead until they'd peeked first" (265). Buckler does not pretend that every Norsteader "was a blood ruby, or holy with that holiness of the unperjurable that bread baked by a wood fire has, or gold" (264). His Arcadia is not one-dimensional; his protagonists "might be a thing and its contrary at the same time" (20). The dual dimensions do not struggle against each other, but are interconnected in a liminal space, an interzone or space between two worlds, a "realm of pure possibility whence novel configurations of ideas and relations may arise"[14] that is not either/or but both/and. His textual universe corresponds to Ricoeur's definition of *muthos* as not only a mimetic rearrangement of human actions, but also a composition that elevates, that both restitutes what is essential and displaces it toward the highest or noblest sphere (57).

This tension between *mimesis*, restitution, or reality, and *muthos*, invention, and elevation is at the heart of Buckler's construction of Arcadia. The myriad of details making up his building material, their interconnectedness and teleological tension are what anchors his world in the material and in the transcendent. His pastoral Nova Scotian paradise belongs to, yet transcends, history: in it, myth and immediacy coexist. Like Genesis, it evokes a mythical past with all of eternity in front of it. And as I shall demonstrate in the following section, the bridge between time and eternity, myth and reality, can be found in the daily occurrences of death and the immediate human rituals surrounding it. These rituals, even in Buckler's Arcadia, are the only means to approach the "great sabled presence" that comes "over the rim of Never" and takes "back in its closed hand the breath of someone its hand [will] never open on again," striking "the stillness of stillnesses" (*Ox Bells* 130-31) in us all.

## Death, or *Et in Arcadia Ego*

"Et in Arcadia ego" is a Latin phrase popularized by paintings by Guercino, Poussin, and Joshua Reynolds between 1590 and 1769, originally depicting two Arcadian shepherds contemplating a huge skull being ravaged by a fly and a mouse (popular iconographical emblems of decomposition and time devouring all). Modern European readers have inherited a tendency to put the sentence in the mouth of the person who has died, and to interpret it as meaning "I, too, lived (or was born) in Arcadia." The phrase has in this way come to evoke a retrospective vision of insurpassable happiness, once savoured but irrecoverably lost, living on only in memory. It evokes a past happiness that has been shattered by death for the speaker, but that is still intact for the viewer or reader. But Guercino's skull is a death's head, the iconographical representation of Death itself—a talking Death's head was a widespread motif in art and literature right up to the seventeenth century. Consequently, it is not a dead person but Death personified who is speaking. With the "ego" referring to death, and the adverb "et" qualifying "Arcadia," the accurate meaning of the expression is "Death exists in Arcadia, too" or "Death exists even in Arcadia." The phrase is a *memento mori*, a warning that signals a present happiness that is undermined by death, a world in which in the midst of youth, beauty, and felicity, death can strike, and awaits us all. The original iconographical document is not elegiac, but didactic and moralizing, reminding the viewer of the ephemeral nature of all pleasures and the dangers of heedlessness.

Poussin, who was an avid reader of Virgil, and whose principles of classicism impelled him to reject the use of bizarre, grotesque, or macabre—in other words, baroque—elements, modified Guercino's composition and totally broke with the medieval moralizing tradition. His painting with its modified context, transformed the interpretation of the literary formula on the continent (but not in Great Britain, due to the direct influence of Guercino on Joshua Reynolds). There is no terrifying spectacle, no dramatic confrontation with Death. His Arcadians are not threatened by an implacable future; they are merely meditating on a past of pure beauty, and contemplating the concept of mortality. The moral lesson has been replaced by an elegiac sentiment.

It is productive to ask what place death holds in Buckler's pastoral paradise. Andrew Wainwright in "Fern Hill Revisited: Isolation and Death in *The Mountain and the Valley*," observes that it seems to be a most prominent and immediate one in Buckler's first novel. We can most certainly extend the observation to his other works. Janice Kulyk Keefer has pointed out in *Under Eastern Eyes* that "'the great sabled presence' of Death enters on the opening page" of *Ox Bells and Fireflies* (199). Indeed, after the very short first paragraph of *Ox Bells* (not) naming the narrator and the village and giving them a universal dimension, the second paragraph begins: "I was ten and I had never seen a dead person" (3). There are innumerable references to death in *Ox Bells*, references woven and intermeshed throughout the text. Some of the references are made covertly, as in the following enunciation of the older, wiser narrator when he recounts a childhood dream: "I don't feel the cold. I look at my father's solid face as the horse slows down to a walk, and there is no shadow then on anyone or anything of their not lasting forever" (8). In the declaration "there is no shadow then," the retrospection introduced by the adverb "then" ironically serves to add a shadow, understood to be ineluctable. It adds the shadow of death and loss to a freeze-frame depicting an idyll of light and splendour. The shadow generates a gentle contemplative mood, and encourages the reader to meditate on mortality, but does not take a particle away from the perfect beauty and felicity of the moment ("then"). As in Poussin's canvas, we are in the presence of an ideal past, which we can contemplate with nostalgia. The elegiac function becomes more overt, evoking regret for an innocence and happiness that, although now lost, can be reclaimed intact through memory. We can note how the use of the second person pronoun in the following discursive aside invites the reader to transcend the imperfect present, flawed by aging, loss, and grief, to find again this perfect past, untouched by pain or care:

> The day itself has all day long to model its dayness under the eave of Time.
>
> (There is no shadow on it—no shadow at all of any day to come when there may be no one you love left to turn the corner of the house and break the envelope of loneliness that encases every object in the room. Like a bird's nest full of snow.) (26-27)

It is in the same nostalgic vein contrasting a flawed present ("now," "still") with a glorious past ("once") that Buckler introduces the *ubi sunt* motif:

> People came from miles around to see the huge boulder that with the bare grip of his arms [Grandfather Wentworth] had heaved on top of the stone wall at the edge of the barley field. If you work your way through the thicket of second-growth hemlock the field has now become you can still see it there—but *where is* the strength in the muscles that once overcame it? (25 emphasis mine)

Even more, when the narratorial voice—this time under the guise of the second person pronoun for more powerful universality—recounts tending the graves in the cemetery with his wife, death is equated with peace and contentment; it is romanticized, idealized the better to foster a contemplative mood. We are in the presence of Death without teeth or claws:

> These were the ancestral graves. Their dead had been dead so long that all the challenge had been sifted out of their silence. And the grave-statement here merely gentled the air, engraved it (and you) with such contentment it was like an unseen fleece cushioning the edges of the breeze. (110)

Yet this classical approach is more the exception than the rule in Buckler's texts. His writing is shot through with references to death in the original macabre fashion, presenting death in all its physicality and sensuality. Death is sometimes grotesque, often terrifying, but always inexorable. In the short story "The Rebellion of Young David," when Art goes off to repair the fences with his small son David, they come across the skeleton of a horse he had buried, and that dogs have dug up. The "chalky grimace of its jaws" that stare "whitely in the bright sun" (*Rebellion* 11) is David's first dramatic confrontation with Death, and he looks at it "with a sudden quietness beyond mere attention; as if something invisible were threatening to come too close" (11).

Death comes to the old, of course, and Buckler movingly evokes the apprehension of those sliding down into its jaws, about to be swallowed irrevocably: "The old stare out at the small lakes of hard blue ice the wind has scoured bare in the fields. They sigh twice-deep for faces gone, then, with a third and deeper sigh, fasten what grip they can again upon their living blood" (*Ox Bells* 205). But Death awaits us all, young and old, not just at the twilight of the day or of our lives but also, as we have seen with the little boy David, in the bright sunlight of day. It waits patiently, lurking in the wrinkle that the child narrator notices for the first time on his young mother's face when the neighbour's coffin is being slid into the ground. Or it strikes unexpectedly and in varied, often violent, and even imaginative ways. In *The Mountain and the Valley*, a great number of characters are killed by accidents, war, drowning, leukemia, heart failure, or grief. In one short episode when the small David and Anna are musing over the tombstones, they find out how all those representatives of past generations died violent, painful, sordid, sudden, or lingering but always varied deaths, indoors or outdoors, from causes big or small. The free direct speech and parallelisms provide graphic, almost loving, details as to the diverse ways one can be snatched by Death. The individuals enumerated are actually *exempla*, from the woman who lost her reason and held her wrists against the saw at the mill, to the others who died "of consumption and black diptheria (three to a family) and scratches that didn't heal":

> This one died because the doctor was drunk and didn't scald the handsaw he took his crushed leg off with, and that one had to be laid out under an apple tree because her tissues were so swollen with fluid they dripped constantly. These three Elcorn brothers were always kept home so they wouldn't catch anything; but they all died within a week, of some strange disease that no one else who took food and helped at the house while they were sick ever came down with.
>
> And some of them died in bed suddenly of age or childbirth; and some of them suddenly outdoors, from the stroke of an axe or the falling of a tree, or the terror of a horse. And Barney Starratt there died because he didn't rest on the big rock in the centre of the lake, as his companions did, the Sunday morning they both started to swim across. (92)

In *Ox Bells and Fireflies*, too, death is a daily occurrence: one neighbour falls off the barn roof and breaks his neck; another is killed by a bolt of lightning that strikes the pitchfork he is carrying. A third is fatally thrown from his wagon when his colt bolts; a fourth drowns in the lake, while yet another punctures his ankle with his iceskate, develops gangrene, and dies.

War sweeps away the young. There are striking juxtapositions of life going on in all its dailiness while on the other side of the ocean life is draining out of boys gone across to fight. In the following extract from *Ox Bells*, we note the poignancy built by the contrast between the homely, concrete, and prosaic details, the humble objects (slats, bracket, kitchen wall, ironed clothes), the transitive verbs describing the mother's activities, and the intransitive verb "bleeds" that introduces the poetic synecdoche and conceit evoking her son's dying:

> A woman, pulling the slats out lengthwise from their bracket on the kitchen wall to air the ironing on (while the son with the strawberry birthmark on his left shoulder who'd come in from the hayfield that day to pump himself a drink, saying he'd decided to enlist, bleeds the drop that is next to the last drop that is round with all forgetting, at Vimy). (202)

War kills in ironic, indirect ways as well. Death can strike during leave from service, as it does for the young soldier who goes to see Scotland, the home of his ancestors. War has taken him out of his familiar surroundings and thrown him into a modern urban culture that kills: "The first night, not knowing, he blew out the gaslight in the hotel bedroom, as you would a lamp. In the morning he was dead" (*Ox Bells* 286).

The lesson Buckler teaches has the most impact when it involves the death of children. In the moralizing fashion of medieval and Renaissance artists, he reminds us brutally of the ephemeral nature of life and of pleasure. In one of the frequent litanies in *Ox Bells and Fireflies* evoking objects both ordinary and full of wonder, Buckler slips in the death of a child in such a casual way as to trigger shock in the unsuspecting reader. He lulls us with a short description of a homely scene, that of a man watching his "boy child" eat bread and marvelling at the silver in his "girl child's hair" (214). Then, sandwiched in between a series of binary structures that piece together the picture of life, like a colourful and sensual mosaic, the jarring reality of death intrudes. Following two paragraphs each made up of a single sentence fragment, whose parallel structure and alliteration induce a soothing, even hypnotic effect, Buckler strikes with a *memento mori* whose violence is enhanced by the intermingling of and contrast between visceral sound and unbroken silence:

> Grindstones and curtain stretchers.
>
> Goldthread and pleurisy root.
>
> Buttercups the children hold under each other's chins to see who likes butter best—and the wafered sunflower seed, thin as the host, that the child draws into his windpipe, choking to death on it, while his mother, her eyes screeching, strikes him the blows between the shoulders that his screeching eyes will never understand. (214-15)

Buckler's text depicts a world of day-old kittens drowned in a pail and of ornamented coffins for children who die almost as casually. From an idly opened album of faded snapshots springs the face of a child who did not come home for supper one night long ago because he had drowned in the millpond. A woman picking blueberries comes across the rusted tin cup once used by a small son who died of meningitis. In yet another passage that reconstructs the world through evocations that try to encompass all of human activity, Buckler intermingles life and death, demonstrating that the two are inseparable through the coordinator 'and,' the parallelism of the objects, and the universality of the impersonal second person pronoun. After evoking the touch of chestnuts and of the breeze, he goes on to mention in an equivalent fashion that generates pathos, the touch "[o]f the chisel you fashioned the wheel hub of your child's cart with when health sang in you without a faulty note, and of the stones you filled the well with after he'd been drowned in it" (231).

The didactic dimension is underscored by countless grotesque elements. We can note how in a passage like the following one devoted to the colours that make up our existence, Buckler intermingles the human and the animal, the senses of sight, touch, and taste, the innocence and the violence of playground chants, solid and liquid, playing and killing, Sunday clothes and messy gore, growth and promise, destruction and death:

> The Turkey red of the summer dawn and the Chinese white of the frozen cheek. The Indian yellow of the wind-wild flames and the hen's-foot yellow of the dead hand. "Grasshopper, grasshopper, grasshopper gray / Give me some

molasses or I'll kill you today." The Persian blue of the child's hair ribbon and the plums of purple blood where the wounded deer pants in the thicket. (218)

In a similar (con)fusion, we learn that the man who makes all the child coffins carves the lambs on the sides of them "with the same knife he used when he came to cut the calves" (24). A child's death is as much a part of life as the castration of cattle, or, to put it in another way, mutilation and death in various forms, animal and human, are all part of one grand design. Death is merely another entrance or exit, as Buckler suggests in a list of objects grouped together by shape, in which we come across the "rectangles of door and grave" (232). The same interconnectedness is suggested in the "contrapuntal prose"[15] of *Window on the Sea*, the collection of prose sketches and photographs that attempts to create a subtle interaction between text and visual image. Among the pictures that link up with narrative or expository fragments is a photograph of a battered mailbox next to a run-down picket fence separating the property from the tombstones and crosses of the adjacent graveyard. The contiguity of the objects establishes an equivalence. Many pages later, a prose fragment didactically renders the connection explicit. In Nova Scotia, "starker than anywhere else, are the reminders of how inexorably one's address shifts from the letter to the tombstone" (96). In *Ox Bells and Fireflies*, through another list of objects, Buckler elaborates on the resonances and echoes contained in the objects themselves. He suggests that our detritus is an accumulation of little deaths, from broken tool handles and old boots that leak, to the "lettering of the months and the numbering of the days on the calendar of the year that was past" (115). The extent to which death is an integral part of life can be transmitted by a striking zeugma (reinforced by alliteration) that trivializes death all the while reminding us of its ineluctability: Buckler evokes the conches that can be "blown like trumpets for *dinnertime* or *death*" (204, emphasis mine). It can be transmitted by the grotesque mingling of incongruous elements: "puddle scum" textually contiguous to ripening "oxheart cherries," or "the stilt-legged flies fastened on the dead mouse beside the clump of violets in the cowpath" (114).

Buckler's technique of associating heterogeneous elements, of exploding the customary and the banal, includes mixing the serious and the comic, even with respect to Death, which, as he reminds us, also has "its comic lore" (130). Buckler's characters have a habit of turning things "inside out" with a "jester's irreverence"—a habit known as "makin speeches"—and one of the stories that are passed on, in the playful and ahistorical mode beginning with "[o]nce upon a death years ago," recounts the struggles of an undertaker with a lisp in dressing a huge old patriarch: "As he strove with the skimpy underpants provided him he was heard (all the way downstairs) muttering to himself: 'Theeth drawth wuth never built for theeth ballth!'" (130).

Buckler's strategy finds its roots in a centuries-old comic popular culture, which Mikhaïl Bakhtin traces back not only to the Renaissance and Middle Ages, but all the way back to antiquity. Central to this popular comic culture is the carnival, situated in the interzone between art and life, blurring any distinctions between performer and spectator, based on the principle of laughter and total (joyous) liberty, and unfettered by any rules of decorum (Bakhtin 7). We cannot know if the tale is pure fantasy or if it is grounded in "reality"—whether it be a fictional reality or a reality anchored in the writer's experience. The undertaker has unwittingly become a performer, and so, too, has the dead man. The focus on the body of the dead man, in particular on his sexual organs, the irreverent remark made in familiar, even crude language, all joyously break the rules of decorum of a society that in multiple ways—including the use of euphemisms—tends to deny death. Buckler's funeral preparations foreground the regenerative force of laughter. They are reminiscent of the funerals in ancient Rome during which, as Bakhtin reminds us, the deceased was simultaneously wept and ridiculed, just as the conqueror during his Triumph was both celebrated and derided (6). Buckler's evocation of the dead man's testicles is a deliberate recourse to the life of the belly, a term popularized by Bakhtin to describe the activities of the lower part of the body (copulation, gestation, ingestion, digestion, defecation). It is one of the carnival's strategies of grotesque realism, which seeks to deflate the sublime, to drag life back down to its basest material clay.

The life of the belly stripped of the dimension of laughter is underscored by the closing page of *Ox Bells and Fireflies*. In an enumeration that explodes any tendencies toward edulcoration, accumulating image after image of the grim facts of existence, Buckler insists upon the brutish brevity of life in all its violence and sordidness, a world of predation, of blood and slaughtered innocence and decrepitude, of excrement and urine and slime:

> The hawks left the quotation marks of their wings' landing around the mouse blood on the frozen crust. The bag of day-old kittens in the pail drowned with their eyes shut. The leak in the hen pen slimed the droppings on the sodden straw. And old men with a milky film over their pupils tapped their way querulously with their canes to the outhouse they had once swapped the roaring jokes about with the neighbour who was helping them build it, their thin streams now missing the hole. (302)

But if the low(er) body, the earth, rather than the head, the high, the cosmic, signifies the reversal of the lofty, the presence of the tomb, it also signifies a new beginning. Alongside the killing of mice and kittens and the aging of men, the rabbits run "in the calm clear moonlight" and the children dream "of brooks and swings" (302). And what could seem profane in the humorous undertaker scene is in reality the recognition of the duality of the world. It is the carnivalesque coming together of the profane and the sacred, as in the rites of former societies that would mix celebration and mockery of the divine—for the serious and comic aspects of divinity, of the world, and of the human race were all equally sacred (Bakhtin 6). Buckler takes pains to point out that although Death has its comic lore, Death itself is never mocked, and that "[w]hen its great sabled presence came over the rim of Never and took back in its closed hand the breath of someone its hand would never open on again, it struck that stillness of stillnesses inside everyone" (131).

Panofsky points out how Guercino's formula "Et in Arcadia ego" evolved to the point where Fragonard, a precursor of Romanticism, accomplished a complete reversal with his allegorical drawing *La Tombe*. The two dead Cupid-like lovers who embrace in the broken sarcophagus surrounded by flying smaller Cupids seem to indicate that Guercino's saying "Even in Arcadia Death exists" has given way to the elegiac "Even in Death Arcadia can exist" (Panofsky 302). Panofsky also remarks how the two almost opposing views of the formula, one sinister and melancholic, the other soothing, were often synthesized by the Romantics. Buckler seems to place himself in such a tradition. We have only to look at a passage from *Ox Bells and Fireflies* in which the narrator, from his child's perspective, describes moments when he attains a total oneness with the universe. Using the second person pronoun, which allows him to go beyond speaking of his own self, and which on a first level is meant to implicate the reader and to fuse narrator and receiver, Buckler assures us of the continuing existence of Arcadia even when Death rears its head. You can be in perfect communion with everything around you even when "the black horses drew the black-tasseled hearse so slowly through the August afternoon and suddenly you knew what doomsday was—though not with any shrinking of the heart, because it would never be for you or for anyone you loved" (53). The scene is fraught with tension between the two interpretations of "Et in Arcadia ego." We have the contemplative meditation on the concept of mortality but in a context of unbroken happiness ("not with any shrinking," "it would never be"). But this is mingled with a *memento mori*, that is all the more dramatic for the structural irony that makes out as if to deny it. The more the childish point of view is convinced that the self and its loved ones are somehow exempt, the more Buckler forces us to distance ourselves from the child's point of view, and the larger the shadow of death looms over us. The writer, like Hemingway, whom he professes to admire, is reminding us for whom the bell tolls.

## Studies in Death

Death is a pervasive presence in Buckler's writing, often the very core of the textual fabric, as the following close studies attempt to demonstrate. One of his unpublished short stories, "Thanks for Listening," is the troubling, haunting song of a young man of twenty who has fought in the war and who turns up in the snapshots taken of soldiers in various locations of the Normandy landing. The story was eventually worked into *The Mountain and the Valley* as an embedded story that the protagonist writes but ends up throwing into the fire when part of it is accidentally read by his brother-in-law, who unlike him is able-bodied and involved in the war effort. Although the recycled embedded narrative acquires the added exegetic layering of narratorial comment— we as readers accompanying each stage of the writer-protagonist's creative process—the story actually loses rather than gains in complexity. The hermeneutic dimension of the original story has been sacrificed[16] along with the rhetoric of dialectic implicating the receiver.

The oneiric dimension in the original story generated by the first person narrator's words to an unidentified addressee is immediately disturbing. He explains that if people never guess those faces on the photographs are his, it is because "the flesh looks different when the blood is on the outside."[17] The disturbing quality is enhanced when the speaker seems to transgress the laws of time and exchanges young flesh for old: "I know you didn't recognize me the time our ship was struck and I was the doctor, because I was much older than I am now" (3). The reader is further disoriented when the identity of the addressee becomes defined only to become warped as well. Phatic interjections and question tags like "*You* believe I know how it was, don't you, Joe?" posit that the speaker is confiding in another man who has shared his experience. But a shift in tense in the next sentence transmits a jarring shock: "There was no picture the morning Joe died" (4). The narratee is dead, and yet since the discourse continues, an undefined addressee slips into the vacuum to receive the testimony. As the narration continues the receiver slowly takes on the contours of an attentive wife or sweetheart, only to be annulled in turn and replaced by an implicit listener. Anticipating the postmodern tendency to blend and blur printed text and photographic image, Buckler explores the inadequacy of both iconographical and linguistic media to express the inexpressible, but suggests that the verb may achieve a fuller representation: "I don't think there was anything a picture would have shown....I saw all the hearing and the seeing and the touching go out of him like a breeze that dies in the air quicker than running"[18] (4).

From the jarring realization that the narratee has died, the reader is projected toward the even more disorienting realization that the narrator, too, has died. The discursive voice goes on to describe the morning death came to him couched in the sound of time: "I had more time than Joe, and there had been pain and there was no pain at all now, but I knew. You can tell when you are young and you've never heard the sound the minutes make before, louder than the guns" (5).

Buckler explores death from the inside, and adds twist upon twist. The end of the story first discloses that the narrator is the incarnation of all dead young soldiers, then makes the final disclosure that he is an invalid who has never left his chair, who watched "all the Joes" (6) marching by his window. Like the dead, he has been to the other side of pain, and is not allowed to "forget like the others" and "come back" (6).

If a story like "Thanks for Listening" stages the pain and death that can strike the young, among Buckler's other early, undated works can be found a hybrid piece entitled "The End Came Quietly At...," which in a letter of submission the young writer called "a study in the enormously misunderstood quiescence of the very old."[19] Like the later *Ox Bells and Fireflies* and *Window on the Sea*, it is a cross between essay and fiction, prose and poetry, structured mosaic-like with contrapuntal bits and fragments. The agency shifts back and forth from that of the dying old man reminiscing and philosophizing in a lyrical fashion until his consciousness fades—"[s]o much of living is a preface and so much of it a brown leaf. So empty is its January and so shrivelled its December"—to the intermittent refrain-like voices of his family and friends

> How gracefully he has grown old, they said
>
> He is patient and happy again, they said, like a child
>
> How gracefully he has grown old, they said.
>
> Life for him, is a gentle motion
>
> The memories of the old, they said, are dim caricatures...
>
> He is smiling, they said

—until the final "My God, he is dead."[20]

This text seems to be an embryo of the later unpublished short story "The Snowman," which in turn will become the chapter "Man and Snowman" in *Window on the Sea*. It is significant then that in the very earliest text, Buckler breaks with the narratorial pattern of dual internal focalization at the very end. Until the concluding sentence, the point of view of "they," albeit in the third person plural, is effectively an internal one. But in the final sentence, an objective, external narratorial point of view intrudes: "But they found they had no tears." By its very neutrality—contrasting with the grandiloquence of the lyrical reflections of the old man—it brings home to the reader the bald fact that the dead are all too soon forgotten, that mourning is put away almost as soon as it is begun.

It is interesting to gauge the quantity of sentiment(ality) that Buckler adds to or strips from his three variations of the story, for the comparison reveals the tension that exists once again between the two interpretations of "Et in Arcadia ego." Buckler seems to move from the dramatic *memento mori* technique to an edulcorated, almost sanitized meditation on mortality in a context of unbroken happiness. "The Snowman" is a typescript written under the pseudonym of Owen Swift, which the young Buckler often adopted. The story is undated and difficult to situate in time. It is classified in the Thomas Fisher Rare Book Library archives along with other stories that were published as early as 1957 ("The Ring," eventually published under the title "Cleft Rock, with Spring" in the *Atlantic Advocate*) and as late as 1978 ("Snow Apples" finally published under the title of "The Orchard" in the *Review*). Many clues would indicate that several decades separate "The Snowman" and "Man and Snowman." The first is the presence of a simple object: the slate. In "The Snowman," when the old man has lost the ability to speak, Buckler mentions that they "put a slate beside his good hand."[21] In the later "Man and Snowman" version, Buckler feels the need to add, between parentheses, "(An old one of his own he thought it must be, for children had not used slates these many years.)" (*Window* 49).

The fleshed-out narrative "The Snowman," which begins *in medias res* with the sentence that sends us skilfully to a pre-text, "There had never been any pain," is the simple, moving story of an old man who, after a stroke, is gradually being cut off from family and community. Through his bedroom window, he sees his grandchildren building a snowman, using as material, apart from the mineral, inanimate snow and coals, the homely belongings of pipe and hat, so personal and yet so de-personalized, from which the old man is now cut off. As the snowman takes shape, the grandfather, too, builds. He thinks back to, and essentially reconstructs, his past life in blocks of time, in chunks of five and ten years, similar to the skips and leaps in children's counting when they are blindfolded. The flashbacks, in counterpoint to the sequences in which the family talks about him, are designed in impressionistic touches, with Buckler's self-termed pointillist technique. The following extract illustrates how through the devices of polysyndeton and chaotic enumeration, the writer re-creates the five- to ten-year-old child's universe in all its simplicity, in all its integrity of the senses, of spatial and temporal perception: "It was running…and bread…and mittens…and sleep…and moss…and minnows…and breezes…and suppertime…and dandelions…and rock tops…and tree forks…and hills...and hollows...and sunburn...and somersaults...and hours and hours and hours and hours..." (5). In the final published version of "Man and Snowman," we can already detect a shift away from this simplicity, with the addition of artificially poetic elements: "and breezes...and bobsleds...and rock tops...and tree forks...and dreams of thrones (seen on the coloured pages of the Bible with pictures in it)...and mornings (each one with prizes and surprises in it)...and hills..." (*Window* 52). These elements are rather forced, as in the internal rhyme prizes/surprises. Certain elements are even jarringly pompous, such as the clause and phrase placed between parentheses that break the soothing hypnotic rhythm of the original polysyndeton. Even the replacement of the comforting term "suppertime" with the concession made to alliteration (breezes/bobsleds) illustrates a newly contrived approach.

The simple, natural grasp of the dawn and progression of life has been replaced by a stiffer, more academic approach. The shift in the approach to death is the faithful corollary. In the earlier manuscript, there are hymns to life and love transmitted through the old man's recollections. We readers recover the magical sensation of straddling the earth that we can paradoxically have when we are small, as when during ploughing the little boy is lifted onto the horse's back: "all at once it was as if his heart let loose a flight of birds. He felt so high above the earth that he could tell where the sky began. The roll of the horse's muscles under his legs seemed like a mightiness of his own, the roll of the turning sod like a song"[22] (5). But at the same time there are constant reminders that decrepitude and death are a natural part of life. Buckler spares us none of the ugliness, either physical or moral.

The writer makes the physical decline tangible by insisting on the natural processes of waste and elimination: the "chair" for defecating that his son's wife brings, the bottle for urine that he spills in the bed, the diapers that the daughter-in-law eventually puts on him, the disgust that she expresses at having to clean the old man's teeth. Simultaneously, there is a long slide downwards into solitude and indifference, as the inexorable process of neglect sets in. Buckler reconstructs each stage faithfully. At first the whole family comes to the old man's bedroom every evening to tell him all that happened that day, down to the last detail. But "gradually the tales got sparser, then dried up almost altogether. Gradually, not to bother them, he ceased to write any questions on the slate. Now all he wrote was 'yes' or 'no'" (1). His son does not bother to tell him when a friend asks about him. When asked to go up and see if his grandfather needs anything, little Paul says "Awww, can't Lennie go? I go *all* the time"(6). The father/grandfather has been reduced to a shell, a burdensome, discardable package, as attests the fact that they have discarded his name: "[m]ore often than not, they spoke of him only as 'he'" (8). The family's feelings for him have been reduced to a sense of obligation (the son agrees to clean his father's teeth, for "[s]omeone *has to*" (8)), disgust (the wife opens his window to "air that *funny* smell out of the room" (11, emphases mine)), and self-interest (the son and daughter-in-law get him to will them all his property "while he can still sign" (8); the wife notes that he seems to be failing, in a voice "suddenly gentled with—was it twice-tenderness because it was half-wish?" (10)).

The ache of loss and grief, the elegiac yearning for a loved one who is gone is present in the text, but on another level. It is ironically the old man who idealizes another, who grieves for his long-dead wife, remembering "the beating his heart took from the skulls of everything he looked at that her hands would never touch again or her eyes ever see. Each leaf, each stone, each blade of grass had printed on it, each in its own alphabet, the one word 'gone'" (9). When Death strikes, it robs him not only of a loved one, but also of wholeness. It breaks up his relationship of harmony and interconnectedness with the universe: "[h]e saw the gaping socket of unrelatedness inside him, now that she was forever out of sight" (9). Death is terrifying, overwhelming. And it waits for us all inexorably, as Buckler emphasizes in the sequence that follows, in which the daughter-in-law is supervising the spelling homework of her son Paul, who stops her at the word "transient" to ask what it means.

This early story is thus essentially of a moral nature. All life is "transient," and in describing the beauty of life, the writer does not gloss over the horror of death. Death is in Arcadia, too. The later edulcorated version, "Man and Snowman," on the contrary, systematically removes the sting of Death through the double technique of elision and addition. Buckler edits out the diapers. He cuts out the teeth-cleaning episode. He causes the funny smell to vanish: the daughter-in-law opens the window merely to "air the room out" (*Window* 62). He excises the daughter-in-law's half-wish. He transforms the selfish reluctance of the boy to go and see his grandfather into docile acquiescence: "Downstairs, the wife said, 'Mark, go up and see if your grandfather wants anything.' 'All right,' Mark said. 'But he never does'" (53). In fact, Buckler goes even further in the reversal of the relationship with the grandfather and makes it an idyllic one in which, rather than avoiding him, the grandsons love him and seek him out. The son muses to his wife about the children's behaviour: "if they've made something in school...or anything...the first thing they get into the house they run up to show him. Before they even take their coats off. I never have to ask them to." (55). In another important reversal, it is the old man himself who initiates his withdrawal from society, to discourage his family's visits: "But gradually, a proud man, he came to discourage this demand on them. Gradually, not to bother them, he ceased to write any questions on the slate" (49-50). Buckler reverses the will episode as well. It is the old man who writes "deed" on the slate to let his son know he wanted to "make the place over to [him] while he could still sign" (55).

Parallel to the strategy of elisions and inversions, Buckler elsewhere extends the text. Not trusting the readers to draw their own conclusions, the voice of the omniscient narrator explicitly declares that the family "felt none of that burdensome recoil so often touched off by sickness in the old" and that they "tended him as involvedly as if he was nineteen" (49). At other times, less intrusively, he limits himself to the role of mere external observer and lays careful clues allowing his readers to deduce the sincerity and warmth of the family's love, as when the son reminisces over what a reassuring figure his father had always been to children: "*His eyes went suddenly still.* 'I only ever seen him cry but the once. It was one day he didn't have the money to take me to the circus in town.' *His eyes came back as breath does after a sigh*" (55, emphases mine). Buckler also adds references to a thousand small attentions, in dialogue that, like the following statement by the wife, is not so much an exchange between the interlocutors as a vehicle to transmit to the reader the quality of the care being given: "Yesterday when I took the broth up to him I told him I'd made it from the two partridge you'd shot for him in that wild apple tree at the edge of the burntland" (55).

Much of this material is overtly sentimental. The son shedding a tear over the father's once crying about having to deprive his son of the circus even endows the text with the *crème de marron* quality Buckler had been criticized for in the past. The older Buckler has moved toward the classical stance toward Death: inviting a serene meditation on mortality in an elegiac mood at times verging on the saccharine. But he has not entirely edited out the tension underlying the text, carrying the warning that all present happiness is undermined. The perfectly cyclical structure (in the morning the snowman has dissolved in the rain and the grandfather is found dead) emphasizes the natural end that comes to all things in a grand universal design. The old man dies trying to storm the image of his seventieth birthday,[23] to recapture and savour the final section of his life, but comes up again and again against a wall beyond which he cannot penetrate. We learn after his death that he was trying unwittingly to recall the future, to penetrate what had never been, for he had not yet reached that birthday. Buckler reminds us in a dramatic fashion of our limits, warns us in a series of remarkable conceits that we too one day, like the old man coming to terms with his existence and daring to venture to possess time, will meet up with "a wall blanker than smoke, a nowhere louder than silence, a stare whiter than zeroes" (63).

# 7

## The Rhetorical Phenomenon: Occupying the Interspace Where Subject and Object Are Joined by Language

When the young Buckler was discovering literature and beginning to write, the formalistic innovations of modernists such as Joyce, Eliot, Woolf, Stein, Mansfield, Forster, and Faulkner were at their height. Certain writers such as Ezra Pound, Hemingway, and the early Faulkner, were part of a movement promoting cultural nationalism that advocated a break with European stylistic decorum. They grounded their writing in the literary rendering of spoken American English, thus generating an effect of simplicity and repetition, even a certain liturgical monotony. Yet other writers, notably Gertrude Stein who subsequently influenced Sherwood Anderson and the older Faulkner, were fascinated with the mechanisms of language. They used multitudinous rhetorical functions,[1] and delighted in calling attention to the artifices of the writer's craft. Buckler's daring use of rhetorical devices, of startling imagery, places his works firmly within this modernist tendency. His

---

Notes for chapter 7 are on pp. 247-48.

sophisticated writing contains highly figurative and metaphorical language even in dialogue, as do the Faulkner works he so admired. As Janice Kulyk Keefer has pointed out, his true narrative voice is "not artless or folksy, but contrived, convoluted" (204).

Claude Bissell has commented Buckler's adventurousness in exploring language, and Alan Young, in his Preface to *Ox Bells and Fireflies*, pays hommage to Buckler's "daring and innovative search for metaphors and verbal effects that will express precisely the complexity of ideas and feelings that he wishes to communicate" (xvi). Yet little attention has been paid to Buckler's intense preoccupation with language. Except for the landmark book *Under Eastern Eyes* by Janice Kulyk Keefer and essays by Laurie Ricou, "David Canaan and Buckler's Style in *The Mountain and the Valley*," and D.J. Dooley, "Style and Communication in *The Mountain and the Valley*," Buckler's protean language with its plethora of conceits and artificially convoluted innovations has rarely been studied in depth, and has often engendered incomprehension and irritation in readers and critics alike. His tendency to present simple ideas in a brilliant but abstruse way—what French rhetors call *phoebus*—would be termed *bomphilogia* by anglophone critics, who foreground the device's dimension of boastfulness rather than that of brilliance.[2] Warren Tallman asserts with respect to the writing in *The Mountain and the Valley* that Buckler "has no compositional key except maximum intensity" and that "[s]entence after sentence is forced to a descriptive pitch which makes the novel exceptionally wearing to read" (14). Gerald Noonan criticizes the "overwrought verbiage" that engenders the novel's "structural and interpretative disharmony" (68). Andrew T. Seaman acknowledges Buckler's "poet's trick of transposing what is in the mind into figures of speech," resulting in an "intensity of emotional experience" exceeding anything done by his fellow Atlantic writer Charles Bruce. He remarks that as a result, whole sections of Buckler's prose become extended prose poems. But he finds the effect "not always desirable," arguing that while this is "perfectly appropriate in his pastoral idyll, *Ox Bells and Fireflies*," it "slows the pace of the already ruminative *The Mountain and the Valley* to a near standstill at times" (30). Janice Kulyk Keefer acknowledges that his prose is "at times superbly charged," but deplores its "tortuous quality," and points out that he "often tumbles into mere preciousness, or that he develops certain tiresome verbal twitches." She argues that the "verbal binges on which Buckler goes, his wildcatting with words, are not necessary risks taken in an inventive and experimental context so much as a frenzied whistling in the dark" (204). David Dooley is offended by Buckler's "overwriting" (672), by his "over-use of assonance and alliteration," declaring furthermore that the writer "uses paradox in too precious a way." All the while admitting the "suggestive parallel" of Faulkner and his "stylistic excesses," he claims that Buckler "is a writer who is trying too hard to secure his effects, whose style calls too much attention to itself" (671). Lawrence Mathews attacks Buckler most virulently, in a witty article that cleverly classifies CanLit critics into three categories. Although he chastises them for "their inability or unwillingness to come to grips with the problem of language" (4), Mathews flippantly dismisses serious studies that do exist, such as Laurie Ricou's analysis, calling it Ricou's "get-stoned-on-it theory of style."[3] Mathews calls *The Mountain and the Valley* "badly-written" (2), "ineptly-written" (14), "boring" (6), and "of no significant merit" (15), yet never backs up his subjective value judgments with any serious textual analysis, challenging critics instead to refute *him* and to demonstrate what Alan Young called Buckler's "triumphant successes" (Preface, *Ox Bells* 20). To take up the challenge, it can be useful to reconsider Dooley's assertion that Buckler's style "calls too much attention to itself."

The laws of rhetoric define three levels of style, ranging from simple to high or sublime. Buckler's frequent recourse to what Claude Bissell in his introduction to the New Canadian Library edition of *The Mountain and the Valley* calls his "high metaphysical style" (x), which Bissell likens to that of Melville, Faulkner, Wolfe and Bellow, is undoubtedly what many critics have found irritating. In his introduction, Bissell defends the "complexity" of Buckler's prose as stemming from a "reaching out of the mind and the sensitivities in many directions in order to encompass the full impact of an idea or a situation" (xi). Yet Bissell, too, deplores what he sees as the writer's occasional "vexatious obscurity." The criticism that follows reveals the gap responsible for the incomprehension: the gap between Buckler's aesthetic stance and that of a large part of his readership. Bissell maintains that "[t]here are times when one feels that the search for the word has become an end in itself; the novelist has lost touch with the event, which *must*, after all, be the essential unit of the work of fiction" (xi, emphasis mine). But must it really? As I have mentioned in my introduction, Buckler himself is aware of his inclination toward *cacophony* and *tautophony*,[4] admitting that he has a tendency to write "too fancy" and to get "too parenthetical,"[5] and that his prose consists of "all sorts of adjectives and adverbs tousling around with their hair flying."[6] But in opposition to Bissell's (and Seaman's) stance on the importance of "event," he professes no interest in verbs or plot: "I think that insides are much more important...*and* interesting...than outsides. That action...is far less important than its motivation." If Buckler frustrates a certain readership in search of 'event,' it is because he writes in the Forster style that his protagonist describes in *The Mountain and the Valley* as having "more to do with the shadow of thought and feeling which actions cast than with the actions themselves." Like David who finds the novel "by someone called Forster" an encounter with "absolute truth" that is "more rapturously adventurous than any odyssey of action" (*Mountain* 244), Buckler seeks the interior, the intangible, the abstract in word and thing.[7]

We have seen in the preceding chapters how Buckler is interested simultaneously in language and in the world. His writing is grounded in phenomenological and ontological concerns, and there is a strong hermeneutic dimension in his texts, which strain toward a metaphysical unifying system. Both dimensions of Buckler's work, linguistic and philosophical, are rooted in aporia. The reader is constantly confronted with an underlying cohesive yet irreconcilable tension between the Multiple and the neoplatonic prototype of the One, reminiscent of Emerson's "Unity in Variety" (*Nature* 55). We have seen how through the power of the word, echoing other modernist writers such as Joyce or Ponge, Buckler seeks the essence behind *res* and *verba*, thing and thought. In moments of illumination, his protagonists "touch the very meaning of the thing itself that the word for it had always stood in front of" (*Ox Bells* 124). Or they search for the "single core of meaning" (*Mountain* 298) underlying all things, the

> single light that would come suddenly so that everything would fall into place as if you were looking at a picture that was only broken lines at first but as you looked at it, steadily, suddenly all the broken lines flowed into a single image, and the separate lines were gone and everything was part of the same thing. (*Rebellion* 32)

Buckler's prose both stages the attractive force of the *noumenon* or absolute supersensuous Unity, and constitutes the means of attaining it.

> The voices [of the things he saw] became suddenly infinite....
>
> They sounded and rushed in his head until it seemed as if he must go out *into* these things. He must *be* a tree and a stone and a shadow and a crystal of snow and a thread of moss and the veining of a leaf. (*Mountain* 292, Buckler's emphases)

Through the device of enumeration, part of the rhetorical strategy of amplification, reinforced by polysyndeton, a rhetorical figure of accumulation, in this case the extra repetition of the coordinator "and," Buckler emphasizes the endless multiplicity and variety of the things in the universe that speak, waiting to be known and accounted for. The being that binds the speaker to the things around him manifests itself in the word, in telling. The voices that call from the outside find an echo in the protagonist's telling from the inside, until outside and inside blend and merge to form the One: "as he thought of telling these things exactly, all the voices came close about him....He went out into them until there was no inside left. He saw at last how you could *become* the thing you told" (*Mountain* 298, Buckler's emphasis). Countless passages in his first novel reflect, through the thoughts of the focalizer David, the philosophical approach of the author that structures his aesthetics and consequently his style. The following extract illustrates well the ontological stance underlying Buckler's recurrent device of synaesthesia or sense analogy: "Everything seemed to be an aspect of something else. There seemed to be a thread of similarity running through the whole world. A shape could be like a sound; a feeling like a shape; a smell the shadow of a touch...His senses seemed to run together" (*Mountain* 287).

The dynamics of Buckler's style, the plasticity of his language, with its stylistic acrobatics and outrageous combinations, are placed under the sign of paradox and aporia: the strategy of simultaneous conjunction and disjunction. On the one hand, we find the "thread of similarity," the "single core of meaning," the "single light" causing all the broken lines to flow into a "single image" that we have seen above. On the other hand, there is an accumulative ramifying movement branching outward in an exponential fashion attempting to encompass the "crushing screaming challenge of the infinite permutations of the possible...the billion raised to the billionth power" (*Mountain* 297). The ramifying movement is best orchestrated in Buckler's first novel by the thought process of the would-be artist striving to include everything clamouring to be told. David's idea "frond[s] suddenly like a million-capillaried chart of the bloodstream" (260). In a later phenomenological, epistemological sequence, the "single thought" that "seems to contain it all" "breaks down like a stream forking in the sand. Then the forks fork. Then the forks' forks fork, like the chicken-wire pattern of atoms" (296). The forks' forks' forking (the fronding effect foregrounded by the rhetorical device of polyptoton—the juxtaposition of words belonging to the same lexeme—which is further emphasized by the subsequent alliterative "frenzied forking" (297)), echoes the branch branching in the fusion of planetary, plant, and river metaphors that Laurie Ricou (690) focuses on when analyzing how Buckler jolts the reader from one frame of reference to another: "the obbligato of ache in his head chimed with the quiet feeding orbits of his thoughts (each one branching immediately, until he was totally encased in their comfortable delta)" (228). The delta metaphor concretizes Buckler's fusion of the micro and the macro, inside and outside, the mind and the universe, thought and thing. The branching off of David's thought evokes both blood and water, the capillaried blood/stream of the body or the streams and rivers of the world. The rhetorical device of parenthesis, a figure of enunciation interrupting the flow of a statement and carrying the function of substitution or deviation, one that Buckler uses recurrently in his texts, not only reproduces but also marks situationally and visually on the page the (so far) abstract ramifying process.

This final chapter is devoted to studying Buckler's rhetorical techniques. The analysis cannot fail to be productive in terms of this writer who is a trained philosopher, for rhetoric is not only the complex art of discourse but also the art of judicious thinking, linked by the ancient Greeks with logic and with philosophy. As Bernard Dupriez points out in his introduction to *Gradus*, everything relating to the speech act is rhetorical, and "the rhetorical phenomenon occupies the interspace where subject and object are joined by language" (xviii). This interspace and the conjunctive role of language is a central preoccupation in Buckler's texts, which self-reflexively portray each day as being "a train of quotes from the letter writing between sense and object" (*Ox Bells* 115). I shall focus on the diverse rhetorical strategies of fusion that channel Buckler's striving to encompass all and move toward the One. A study of Buckler's recurrent rhetorical devices discloses the fundamental dynamics of his writing, which involve creating simultaneously, yet paradoxically, a web of ramifications that generate an expanding cross-network of analogies. This "interlocking or cross-pollination of all things, tangible or intangible"[8] coexists with and corresponds to an inverse movement from the Many to the One. These tropes and rhetorical schemes elaborate, even constitute, the central question in Buckler's work, which is that of aporia.

They are part of an aesthetic theory that is inseparable from his conception of the universe, both of which resemble those of the German critic Friedrich Schlegel, theoretician of the early Romantic movement. Pleading in favour of an exuberant creativity that will be found in Buckler, Schlegel argued in his *Dialogue on Poetry* that the ontological chaos of the universe was a fertile abundance or *Fülle*, source of beauty and creativity, and he defined the essence of reality as not matter or *being*, but as an infinite *becoming*. His perception of metaphysics, as "alternating between chaos and system, chaos preparing for a system and then new chaos" (qtd. in Mellor 8) corresponds to Buckler's philosophy and aesthetics, and the global rhetorical strategy that they catalyze. I shall demonstrate that weaving throughout the fabric of all his texts is the affirmation of an irreconcilable tension between "chaos and system," a dynamics of disorder, displacement, disarticulation—in other words, disjunction, and yet a simultaneous dialectic or conjunctive striving toward synthetic resolution or unity, to be found in the devices—to name but a few—of simile, metaphor, analogy, conceit, synaesthesia, paronomasia, epanalepsis, enumeration, paradox, zeugma, hypallage, or simply the elaboration of convoluted compound words.

Buckler recurrently resorts to figures centred round accumulation, such as seriation, chaotic enumeration, concatenation, polysyndeton, metabole, or epanalepsis. What Laurie Ricou judiciously calls Buckler's "incremental style" (688), his "aesthetic of getting-it-all-in" (685), which he asserts is based on "lists or catalogues" (687), is in fact based on accumulation, a combination or juxtaposition of terms similar in nature or function, or merely having the same final sound. Seriation is heavily used by Joyce in *Ulysses*, as in the following piling up of onomatopoeic gerunds reinforced by a ternary structure of nouns and the device of polysyndeton: "a trampling, cackling, roaring, lowing, bleating, bellowing, rumbling, grunting, champing, chewing, of sheep and pigs and heavyhooved kine" (242). The device is by definition open-ended, raising the possibility that it can continue *ad infinitum*. It is exactly this notion that there is always something left to be said or to be clarified, an element overlooked or imprecise, a dimension unsuspected or unexplored, that is contained in Buckler's recourse to seriation, as in the (in)famous list of adverbs in *The Mountain and the Valley:* "In that instant suddenly, ecstatically, burstingly, buoyantly, enclosingly, sharply, safely, stingingly, watchfully, batedly, mountingly, softly, ever so softly, it was Christmas Eve" (65). Many readers and critics are exasperated by the seemingly endless list, which fulfills so well its function of suspension (delaying the presentation of information). Their exasperation is often exacerbated by the additional presence of neologisms such as "burstingly." Before proceeding to study the various other devices of augmentation, it is appropriate to point out here that the device of neologism so recurrent in Buckler's seriation is part of the outrageous baroquism practised by writers such as Joyce, Faulkner, Gertrude Stein, and Sherwood Anderson, their search for surprising, unusual, even curious ideas, figures, and words. The technique is actually toned down in *The Mountain and the Valley*, when compared to certain passages from "Excerpts from a Life," the young Buckler's first attempts at a novel. The following passage, representing the first sexual encounter of the young David and Effie, was not included in *The Mountain and the Valley*. Particularly extravagant is the neologistic, pleonastic transformation of the adverbs "now" and "never" into the shape of the cotextual regular adverbs or mangled adjectival present participles: "Together, David and Effie explored each for the first time, the great mirage. Warmly, fearfully, sweetly, softly, nowly, neverly, shamefully, forgivingly, tenderly, rendingly, shiveringly, laughingly, tautly, harshly, rushingly, paralyzingly, wringingly, tiredly."[9]

Buckler produces neologisms by derivation from existing structures, by compounding, by blending or amalgamating, or even by inventing or coining words. He does so on a lesser scale than Faulkner[10] or Joyce, whose *Finnegans Wake* is one extended neologism, but his neologisms serve the same function: that of stretching or bending language to create new concepts or to acknowledge concepts that the language (*langue* as system) can express only periphrastically. Buckler's neologisms encountered resistance from John Rackliffe, his McClelland and Stewart editor,[11] who expressed concern about the writer's use of "gallic present participles" such as "fascinant" or "utterant" in the manuscript of *The Cruelest Month*—afraid that some readers might be "put off" and argue that "such words are not in the dictionary and are therefore illegan [sic] and hadn't oughta [sic] happen." Rackliffe proffers another possible objection about the "coinages," arguing that they might be considered to be an "affectation" and therefore "a possible distraction, weakness, an impurity."[12] Buckler answers that the words seem to him to be "righter than another" but that if they smack of "affectation or preciosity"[13] he will be content to substitute. If these neologisms distract the reader, though, it is because they are meant to do so. They carry disorder and call attention to the creative power of linguistic and ontological flux. Neological compounds or artifically compounded words (not always hyphenated) strike the reader most particularly with their inventiveness, and testify most strongly to the writer's creative imagination. New visions are presented of pain that can "ache-eat" one's brain away (*Cruelest Month* 168), of the "flesh-dumb, vein-blind weight" of the male sexual organ and of its "eyeless olderness" (*Mountain* 98), of "glint-leoparding" (*Ox Bells* 116) or the play of light and shadow on ground and running water, of a woman with "voiceful hands" (*Cruelest Month* 21), of a man's "fist-mindedness," or of "face-light" giving as much comfort as lamplight *(Ox Bells* 119, 35). The almost forced fusion is similar in process to that of the metaphor, or rather of that more intricate and far-fetched image, the conceit, which, as we shall see, connects totally heterogeneous elements.

Other editorial objections besides those on neologisms concerned the device of seriation itself, more particularly the technique of chaotic enumeration, a disorderly accumulation of terms that are not of the same nature. Right down to the titles of the chapters, *Ox Bells and Fireflies* notably is rife with what Buckler calls the "bare recital of selected details"[14] that sketch a lost idyllic world: "There were cradle hills and sleigh bells. Rainbows and rhubarb. Catkins and robin hop. Locust eyes and chain lightning. Tombstone moss and lilies of the valley. Summertime and suppertime" (302). The writer piles up such poetic, musical elements in an enumeration that overlaps with the rhetorical technique of celebration. But he celebrates commonplace, pedestrian objects as well: "Kraut knives and brace bits. Earwigs and compasses.

Linchpins and patchwork holders" (215). Excessive or superfluous enumeration is a form of baroquism and can lead to the disorderly (and Joycean) extreme of verbigeration, or the production of text without meaning. Angus Cameron, Buckler's editor at Knopf, points out that the device might seem a "substitute for incorporating some of the impressions more fully," and argues that when these sequences are overused, they "destroy the illusion of identification: they become noticeable as devices."[15] In his answer, Buckler offers to let Angus Cameron cut out what he judges to be "instances of overkill," but he justifies what he calls the "pointillist, background-stippling bits," denying that they were haphazard or that they were an imitation of "the 'new' French writing"; he argues in what is a condensed version of his supplementary answers to the Author's Questionnaire on *Ox Bells and Fireflies*:

> I weighed every word with the greatest *selective* care. (Even the simple noun couplings were *handpicked* either for *contrast or parallel*.) Each bit was supposed to be a succinct "text," as it were, which would instantly convey...whole fields of implication. They were intended to underline the omnipresence of the far in the near, the universal in the particular, the macrocosm in the microcosm, the duplicate rendering of every mood in some physical object or cast of nature, the translatability of the senses one into another, the inter-locking and cross-pollination of all things tangible or intangible.[16]

What Buckler's argument makes explicit is that even in his (seemingly) chaotic enumeration there is an ordering principle. In the following extract from *The Cruelest Month*, we can perceive in the apparent disorder of the components, linked by the hypnotic use of polysyndeton, an underlying unity or perspective that transforms in a Schlegelian way "chaos" into "system":

> A kind of smoke of ache flooded into his skull, as if from a vial where the words that used to mean nothing to him—bruise and discouragement, disappointment and stain, dreg and frustration and gone—and the taste of brass and the sound in seashells and the touch on rope—were all being brewed together. And the content of one vial, so pure it was almost an odour again, was poured over the top of his head and seeped down through it: the essence of the word "unnamable." (166-67)

In this yoking of abstract, concrete, sensory, affective, and intellectual elements, the writer captures in an impressionistic, self-avowedly "pointillist" manner the very essence of pain that language cannot describe: the "unnamable." In a book studying fellow modernist Katherine Mansfield, whose phenomenological and subjective textual approach presents similarities with Buckler's, and more specifically in the chapter entitled "Some Basic Aesthetics of Literary Impressionism," Julia Van Gunsteren remarks that the

> Literary Impressionists, like the Impressionists in painting, focused on perception. They attempted to formulate reality by breaking it into momentary fragments, selected intuitively and subjectively. They relied on sensory (ap)perceptions, used clusters of images and rendered their emotions in a "slice of life" picture of some everyday, ordinary experience.

She argues that the "confused colliding of sensations, impressions and experiences" (55) of these literary impressionists are produced by" [l]ittle touches...placed side by side" and generated through the prevalence of accumulation and concatenation. The analogy is certainly apt for Buckler. In his little pointillist brush-strokes, his clusters of humble images, can be found at times links of a logical, causal, or temporal nature, such as "Of grandfather's hands when you were ten and grandson's hands when you were seventy" (*Ox Bells* 232). But very often the thread is of a sensory nature—smells, tastes, or shapes: "The perpendiculars of bulrush and crane leg. The triangles of deer track and trowel. Pears and wombs. Scrota and walnut shells. Cloud-shaped rocks and rock-shaped clouds. The rectangles of door and grave (...)" (232). Or the thread can consist in sounds, either of the things—

> The whisper of the scythes in the tall marsh grass after the rain, and the cracked voice of hinges.
>
> The murmur of acres and the peal of children.
>
> The ringing tap of the hammer on the wheel rim and the flump of groin against groin. (220-21)

or of the words themselves, such as in the paronomasia "Rain and rein" (232). The sounds that link can even be the sounds of silence: "of the heartbeat that itself can't hear; of pain" (226). The yoking that Buckler provides by a striking use of colours is reinforced by figures based on the additional resemblance of sound as well as by synaesthesia:

> The Turkey red of the summer dawn and the Chinese white of the frozen cheek. The Indian yellow of the wind-wild flames and the hen's foot yellow of the dead hand....The Persian blue of the child's hair ribbon and the plums of purple blood where the wounded deer pants in the thicket. (218)

Some sort of ordering principle can be found even in Buckler's most seemingly chaotic enumerations. His hypnotic litanies[17] are actually a form of enumeration that Fontanier in the early nineteenth century christened "conglobation,"[18] and accumulate in apparent disorder the components of a situation of which we grasp the unity or perspective. Conglobatio consequently obeys the laws of enumeration, which, unlike the strategy of accumulation (an open-ended combination of terms similar in nature, function, or sound), is a type of amplification. It switches viewpoints but, in spite of the seemingly contradictory components, has a purpose in view, a common general idea. By going back to an extract from *The Cruelest Month*, we can remark Buckler's distinctive use of the device—his tendency to place a grammatical odd man out in the final position of his series to mark the satisfyingly conjunctive closure, implying that all possibilities have been envisaged. In the extract the pattern set up by the three binaries of nouns is notably broken by the adjunction of the past participle: "bruise and discouragement, disappointment and stain, dreg and frustration and gone" (166). Even the series that are not explicitly closed constitute a definition of collective entities, which Buckler himself defines as "the inter-locking and cross-pollination of all things tangible or intangible"[19]: "A calf's bangs. The Big Dipper. Huckleberry shine. A bluejay feather. The smell of oranges or pickling spice or britchen straps. An owl's eye. Looking down a deep hole. A snow crystal landing on someone's nose. Seven 9's making 63" (*Ox Bells* 57). The author's questionnaire that he filled in and sent to Knopf, his publisher, provides exegetical remarks with respect to such lists of the natural and cultural components of the universe:

> I've tried to underline the omnipresence of the far in the near (maps of Tasmania on the cow's brockled sides); the universal in the particular (all geometry in the owl's eye); the

> macrocosm in the microcosm (whole galaxies in a pasture of wildflowers); the duplicate rendering of every mood in some physical object or cast of nature (all sadness in the swinging of an unhinged November gate).

The "infinite clusters of varying determinants of behaviour in the infinite variants of weather or season, the translatability of the senses one into another"[21] can also be illustrated by the following allegorical scene in two phases from *The Mountain and the Valley,* staging individual creatures that are actually *exempla* of the process of hunting and feeding, flight and pursuit, prey and predator, sound and silence, in other words, life and death:

> As the light retreated, the silence sprang up with the same shivering stain the light had had. The feeding silence of the bluejay's dark sweep across the road...the partridge whirr...the straight flight of the dark crow against the deepening sky...the caution of the deer mincing out toward the orchard's edge...the caution of the hunter's foot on the dry leaf. And then the silence of the moment when the first faint urine smell of rotted leaves came from the earth, and the memory-smell of apples lain too long on the ground, and the sudden camphor-breath that came from any shade stepped into, the moment the gun barrel first felt cooler than the gun's stock on the palm. The breath-suspending silence of the gun sight in the second of perfect steadiness, and then the spreading silence of the gun's bark, and then the silence of the bird not flying away. (119)

Buckler is skilful with enumeration, which linguists such as Roman Jakobson see as the exposure of the paradigm, outside the function of communication, noteworthy for its capacity to display in a small space (Dupriez). We have seen it at work in Buckler's texts in the inventories aspiring to exhaustivity. What we have here, enhanced with three coined compounds and refrain-like epanalepsis (the binaries "caution," "and then"; the ternary "silence") is partial enumeration serving as an *exemplum*. The enumeration (bluejay, partridge, crow, deer, hunter) carries out a metonymic strategy similar to that of *antonomasia*, serving to connect the abstract and the concrete, the general and the particular, and producing relationships of inclusion. The exemplum generates what the rhetorician Henri Morier calls the "*noema*," the theme or moral. It has a quasi-allegorical function, concretizing an underlying truth. Although none of the terms taken individually is a symbol in itself, the passage taken globally functions structurally like a simile or extended comparison, and is meant to be interpreted symbolically. Elsewhere, the recurrence of exemplary figures leads to the creation of structuring motifs, such as the emblem we have seen in *The Cruelest Month* of the deer, vehicle of epiphany, figure exemplifying perfect design or divine order.

The epanalepsis serving here to highlight the accumulation of analogical elements and the underlying theme, is also a recurrent device in Buckler's texts, generating a dynamic pattern, imposing form and impulse, linking heterogeneous, even antithetical elements. A glance at some other extracts will demonstrate how the repetition fits into Buckler's strategy of "ontological vehemence," to use Ricoeur's term once more. In the epilogue of *The Mountain and the Valley*, David's final climb up the mountain is accompanied by another progression, a progression in two stages organized around the description of the trees according to their appurtenance to two distinct species and the individual variants within each. We can note exactly the same strategies, the same techniques in both sequences, which involve amplification through an open-ended enumeration implying infinite abundance and diversity, and the cohesive structural framework produced by various forms of repetition linking and bonding the heterogeneous components into a whole. The first sequence corresponds to the beginning of David's ascent, and describes the tree growth at the base of the mountain:

> The black-green sweep of the spruces' lower limbs like an inhalation sustained immobile in the chest of the tree...the yellow-green of the hemlock branches, twig-laced in a snow crystal pattern, like a breath outward...the lemon-green murmurous-needled pine overturned by the wind, its ragged anchor of roots and earth like the shape of the thunder of its own falling....And, beneath the trees, was the other, inch-boundaried, earth-clinging forest: the brown-green moss and the mayflower runners and botany-book topknots; the grey-green, antlered lichens. And here was a stump that had once been green, but now was white as bone; and there was a grey rock, heavy with its own unshapeliness. It had never had any touch of green at all, nor ever would... (286)

We note the accumulative effect of the piling up of noun clauses, of the open-ended use of polysyndeton (an abundant use of "and"), of intricate neological compounds that evoke diverse notions and senses. The simile, "like a breath outward," and the imagery, "twig-laced," "snow crystal," and "antlered" are disjunctive and ramifying. The objects evoked are inherently metaphorical—intricate yet forming a whole. They re/present visually what is happening on the page and in the mind. They are objective correlatives, configurations of emotion, symbols or emblems of Buckler's philosophical and aesthetic stance of unity in diversity. We note the unifying framework provided by the series of similes, and by parallel structures such as "here was...there was," or the double occurrence of synaesthesia (the shape of thunder, the weight of shape). But it is the slightly varied concatenation of colours that remarkably provides a cohesive progression from dark to ever lighter shades of green, and carries a hint of time travel that blurs our perception of reality. The progressive paleness of the shades of green leads to a "once" green that is "now" white (proleptically announcing David's shroud of snow), and the erasure in turn gives way to a total absence of green—total and final because the quality is doubly projected into the dimension of time, encompassing both past ("had never had") and future ("nor ever would").

Buckler continues to paint his profoundly metaphorical vision as his protagonist continues his vertical ascent. Two pages further, the second sequence set up in parallel to the first corresponds to a spatial progression that proves to be metaphorical: the protagonist is drawing near to the summit.

> The hardwood, unlike the spruces, stood singly and separate: the gaunt grey-bare maples with half shells of fungus along their sides; the slim white-bare birches with kidney-shaped dappling of brown on their curling yellow-line bark; the shining-bare silver poplars; and the heavy-bare lizard-barked beeches. The cold yellow sun and the thin cold air hung and breathed in the spaces between them, like a great centrifugal eddy of lightness. Their limbless trunks broke into a twist of searching branches as they reached higher against the sky. They were as still as their own laced shadows in the soundless air. There was no green here at all. (288)

The description moves along a systematic enumeration of hardwood, from maples to birches, poplars, and beeches. This progression is accompanied by the linking concatenation of neological, synaesthetic, epanaleptic hyphenated compounds qualifying the trees: "grey-bare," "white-bare," "shining-bare," "heavy-bare." This in turn is accompanied by the epiphora 'with...with', the mirror effect of the additional compounds "kidney-shaped...lizard-barked," and the repetition of the suffixes of absence ("limbless," "soundless"). This second sequence is imbued with echoes from the first: twig-laced branches/laced shadows; inhalation, breath/breathed) but the "lower limbs" of the trees at the bottom of the mountain are inversely mirrored by their counterparts at the top of the mountain with their "searching branches" reaching "higher against the sky." The progressive erasure of green in the first sequence leads to the pure absence of green in the second, expressed with the flat yet totalizing "no green at all." The hypnotic parachesis of the description (mingling alliteration, assonance, and consonance) leads to the concatenation in the sublime style of the sequence of anamnesis that follows, the "complete translation to another time" (289), when David leaps back into the past. By generating a hypnotic mood verging on that of ecstasy, the repetition serves to re/create the magic of that long-lost day when the mountain was originally to be conquered:

> [H]e saw how wonderful his father's face was for *not* knowing (as he himself did) what a splendid thing he was doing as he adjusted the strap lengths of his pack...and his mother's for not knowing what mystery she dealt in as she packed the food...and his grandmother's for not knowing his legs could never get tired...and Chris's for not knowing how wonderful he was because he was going too...and Anna's because (all at once he thought he was going to cry) she had to stay home. (290)

The concatenation "for not knowing" not only connects the enumerated members of the family and the succession of their varied activities, but also highlights the essence of Being contained in the most ordinary of actions and points to the transcendental supersensuous Unity that only the artist—even an aborted one—in a flash of consciousness can perceive.

David's ultimate "translation" before death is analeptic and cyclical, echoing the child David's capacity to transcend, to be transported or "translated." In one of the idyllic early chapters of the novel, the boy is thinking of the words of the Christmas play in which he has a part. In this contemplative, rambling sequence spanning five pages and hence too long to quote here, repetition in all its forms is central in fusing the individual with the universal, and the prosaic with the sacred. The sequence begins with "the words were something no one else had" (55), a sentence that is reactivated in the middle of the sequence with "The words were a kind of refuge, when the moment was bare" (57). This in turn is reactivated by the double symploce (combining anaphora and epiphora) "He thought of the words too, when the moment was already brimming" (57), and "He'd think of the words in the play then, to make the moment really spill over" (58). The passage explodes outward in frenzied disarticulation, branching from unit to unit of the components of his universe, from the closest family members to the collective community, with all the human activities that their days encompass. But the thread of anaphora weaves in and out of the passage, knitting it into a cohesive whole. There is the principal framing series of "He thought of them *when*..." and the variant "He thought of them, *with*...," modulating finally to "He'd think of them then" with its insistence on frequency. There is the minor framed series within the primary series of the *when*s: "when the men dropped in," "they'd sit, they'd stroll, they'd slide their hands, they'd turn their backs, they'd take their leave." This minor framed series of anaphora introduced by "when the men dropped in," metonymically shifts to "or when the women came," leading to an open-ended series: "Or when....Or when" (57). The thought of the words in moments that simultaneously epitomize the ordinary and transcend it, generates ecstasy. We witness the moment when subject and object are joined by language, when David is "translated" (58). Words are presented in all their physicality: they "went through him shiveringly, like cold or heat." Thus begins another major series of anaphora: "They weren't like any other excitement" (58) is followed by an inventory of possible correspondences and rejected analogies: "Not like....Nor like" (59). This in turn shifts to another series of anaphora: "They were more like....They were still more like...," modulating to a variant of epanadiplosis: "Or when...or with." The intricate play with various forms of unifying repetition seeking to trace and channel a network of connections opens onto an open-ended questioning evoking the awesome fragility of life and mystery of death and the mystical: "Or were they most of all....Or were they most of all...?" The initial question/suggestion connects sleep and death, and the final one connects words with the divine, by evoking the human-designated day and ceremonial that in so many of Buckler's short stories symbolizes suprareality or the sacred: "Or were they most of all like Christmas itself?"

Just as enumeration "corrects" the chaotic dimension of accumulation, so too does the device of concatenation run counter-current to the dynamics of disorder and displacement in Buckler's texts. It has a synthesizing function suggesting an ultimate metaphysical unity. Buckler does make use of purely disjunctive devices like hypallage: "she felt the straddle of her husband in the tumbling night" (*Ox Bells* 125), which, by transposing the natural relationship between the elements in the syntactic unit, reinforces the strategy of disarticulation. He even at times mingles hypallage with other devices of displacement, such as transference, which, with its shifting of grammatical category, calls attention to linguistic and ontological flux: "The lake wakes innocently from dreams of drowning and the tombstones grandfather the slopes of distance" (*Ox Bells* 211). But the overwhelming majority of his disjunctive devices also serve conjunctive purposes. Parenthesis, as I have already shown above, is part of his incremental style. This technique of adding adjacent assertions introduced by parentheses, dashes, or simply commas, allows a statement to interrupt and invade another syntactically independent unit. It breaks up the syntactic development of the sentence, but encloses and includes all the while opening out. On a larger scale of augmentation and addition, there is the device of counterpoint, the alternation or comingling of several distinct isotopies or universes of discourse. One illustration is the extensive passage near the end of *The Mountain and the Valley* in which Anna grieves after having provoked her husband Toby into leaving her. Through recurrent use of parenthesis, her brooding over the "present" abandonment is layered, doubled, superimposed upon an earlier childhood abandonment, when her brother David left her behind:

He was gone.

> But I don't care, she thought defiantly...("I don't care....I don't care..." she'd said to David the night they asked him on the sleighing party, but not her.) Your face won't hit me any more. I can step over things too. ("I don't want to go anyway," she'd said to David, "I got lots of other things to do....") (235)

The counterpoint continues, weaving together episodes that are perceptibly separate, spatially and temporally distant. But the disorder is only an apparent one, for the contrapuntal juxtapositions ultimately serve a unifying function, serving to link and fuse disparate elements. They reveal an underlying psychological "truth" and trigger an ethical reflection on loyalty, commitment, and pride.

Also apparently contributing to the dynamics of flux and chaos are the rhetorical figures based on the resemblances of form or sound, such as the play on homonyms or paronomasia rain/rein, that I have already cited. In *Ox Bells*, Bucker foregrounds discourse by making it perceptible. He shows that language is alive, by playing simultaneously on both form and sound. Metaplasms, metagrams, or anagrams are favourite devices. There is the sequence of the child playing with the alphabet blocks, transforming "thing" to "think" (37), a sequence that bears witness to the plasticity of language. There is the following linguistic play triggering a reflection on the infinite diversity of the cosmos: "Plow, cow, crow...rock, cock, clock...everything, animate or inanimate, cast a different shadow of itself as its context varied" (20), or on the human reaction to the awesomeness of death: ("Tears," "stare," they have the same letters) (131).

These altered configurations do with sound and form what metaphor does with imagery: they superimpose another notion onto the signifiers, allow other words to be read into them. In the end, they serve not only to branch out (*"different* shadow," *"varied* context"), but also to channel inwards (*"same* letters"). Just so does the artistic Paul jot down in his scribbler anagrammatical signifiers that concretize by their form and sound oppositions and similarities in the (often metaphysical) notions signified: "Word game: Words, sword. Rose, sore. Love, vole. Live, evil. Life, file. Death, hated. Stud, dust....Ah yes, but: Penis, spine. Our cage, courage. Earth, heart..." (*Cruelest Month* 273).

If metaplasms and anagrams function like metaphors, another favourite device, antonomasia, functions metonymically—is in fact a subcategory of synecdoche. Obeying a strategy of displacement from the particular to the general, from an individual to a group or category, antonomasia is rife in Buckler's texts. All of the actors in *Ox Bells and Fireflies* are universal, allegorical types. There is the mythical, idyllic setting of Norstead and the first person narrator: "I'll call the village 'Norstead,' the boy 'I.' They stand for many" (3). who at times shifts to the second person, taking on the bodies and points of view of the old and the young, of sons and fathers. There are the inhabitants of the village: "I'll call the people of Norstead family and neighbors. They stand for many too" (19). The device is foregrounded in the chapter "A to Z," in which Buckler methodically inventories and describes the inhabitants of Norstead, from App to Zeb, conveniently named after all the letters of the alphabet, and thus clearly marked as *exempla*. This device, too, carries a ramifying strategy leading from the one to the many, but it simultaneously triggers a strategy of inclusion, a movement from the many to the underlying, universal One.

Along with the rhetorical figures serving both conjunctive and disjunctive functions in an irreconcilable tension, generating flux only to transform chaos back into system, there are figures that are dominantly conjunctive. A device like chiasmus—"cloud-shaped rocks and rock-shaped clouds" (*Ox Bells* 232), reproduces visually on the page, with its criss-cross syntactic order, the correspondences or similarities in the universe. The zeugma and its atypical yoking, associates, even fuses, two disparate elements toward a common denominator. The examples "dinnertime or death," "doubt and heartburn (*Ox Bells* 204, 193), or "not death but bunions,"[19] yoke the abstract and the concrete, the sublime and the trivial. The zeugmas are indeed what Henri Morier calls the resolution of an ontological antithesis. They set up a relationship of tense opposition yet alliance between the spiritual and the material, between the body and the soul, and by so doing, they re-establish a certain balance. *Synaesthesia*, the correspondence between the different sense perceptions, establishes certain equivalences that are not founded on any element that can be grasped by deduction, either logical or linguistic, for it does not carry the function of communication. What logical or linguistic link indeed can be found in "the green smell of the white willows?" (*Ox Bells* 41). The absence of deductive link, in fact, makes it a favourite strategy of blurring, of con/fusion with modernist writers such as Faulkner. In the space of a mere two lines in *Light in August*, Faulkner introduces several sense analogies into a scene of anamnesis (which I shall examine further on): *"How can he be so nothungry and I smelling my mouth and tongue weeping the hot salt of waiting in my eyes tasting the hot steam from the dish"* (217, Faulkner's emphasis).

Buckler's correspondences, like Faulkner's, can function by comparison, as does the simile, or by substitution, with the same formal structure as the metaphor. His perceptive analogies offer us "the pure ringing smell of sun and sky" (230), or a "yellow smell," "pointed smell," "round smell," even "laughing smell" (*Ox Bells* 41). The analogy can fuse up to three different senses, as in the sentence from which the very title is derived: "I hear the ox bells cool as glint in the swamp" (41). Michel Le Guern's remark that a writer's system of correspondences bears the mark of his or her unique universe, throws light on Buckler's heavily recurrent use of sense analogy. In a letter to his editor, Buckler himself links "the translatability of the senses one into the other" with "the inter-locking and cross-pollination of all things tangible or intangible."[20] In addition to carrying the writer's philosophical perception of the universe, the sense analogies also foreground with "ontological vehemence" the paradise of the senses explored in previous chapters.

Among the most striking rhetorical figures that have a conjunctive function is that of anamnesis, which rhetoricians define as the reminiscences of a past event substituted for the expression of a present feeling or idea. These remembered events or flashbacks are re-experienced in the present by the protagonist and the receiver, and serve to throw light on the character's actions or motivations. Henry James once again comes to mind, when he declares in his preface to *The Portrait of a Lady* that the centre of interest lies in "this projection of memory upon the whole matter of the growth, in one's imagination, of some such apology for a motive" (vi). James does indeed equate memory and experience in his heroine's "meditative vigil" (xvii): "She could *live* it over again" (429). In Buckler's work, the example I gave above of Anna and the reliving of a past abandonment that sheds light on a present one also fits the definition adequately. But Buckler goes further than that. Through anamnesis, he conquers Time, fusing past and future into an "eternal and unaging present" (*Cruelest Month* 266).

When discussing ex-stasis in chapter 3, I evoked David's "complete translation to another time" (*Mountain* 289). Here the writer insists on the origin/ality of the experience:

> It is not a *memory* of that time: there is no echo quality to it. It is something that deliberate memory (with the changed perspective of the years between changing the very object it lights) cannot achieve at all. It is not a returning: you are there for the first time, immediately. No one has been away, nothing has changed—the time or the place or the faces. The years between have been shed. There is an original glow on the faces, like on the objects of home. It is like a flash of immortality. (289, Buckler's emphasis)

That flash of immortality is the glimpse of the essence or is-ness of things. It is the ecstatic contact with the *noumenon*, or absolute Unity beyond our senses, the epiphanic realization that "we are only that one eye of the world which looks out from all knowing creatures" (Schopenhauer 121). David is far from being the only protagonist to undergo such a "translation," Buckler's manipulated version of the flashback. We have seen how in *The Cruelest Month*, the glimpse of the deer projects Bruce through time and beyond: "his mind's leap was backward. Through time and time again, until it left him standing looking at the first deer he'd ever seen. One morning on the road to school. He saw it clearer than the one before his eyes. His deeper eye was back completely on that wide, wide day" (266). The narrative voice in *Ox Bells* explains that such voyages cannot be trusted to the memory, but to the heart, which once in a while "leaps of its own accord—through the skin, through the flesh, through the bone—straight back to the pulse of another time, and will take all of you with it. You are not seeing this place again through the blurred telescope of the mind: you are standing right there" (21). As does Proust, the voice of the older narrator muses upon what causes these leaps, positing various triggers such as "a slat of light surprising the dust on an empty chair" (21). In the case of the synaesthetic passage from Faulkner quoted above, the trigger back to childhood is closer to the famous "madeleine": it is the taste and smell of a dish of "peas cooked with molasses" (217) that catalyzes "sight":

> I'll know it in a minute, I have eaten it before, somewhere. In a minute I *will* memory clicking knowing *I see I see I* more than

> *see hear I hear I see my head bent I hear the monotonous dogmatic voice which I believe will never cease going on and on forever and peeping I see the indomitable bullet head the clean blunt beard they too bent and I thinking How can he be so not hungry and I smelling my mouth and tongue weeping the hot salt of waiting my eyes tasting the hot steam from the dish.* (*Light* 217, Faulkner's emphasis)

In *Ox Bells and Fireflies* we witness just such a "translation," when the eye of the mind fuses with the physical eye. We can remark the significant use of the verbs "to be" and "to see," and of the present tense:

> in one translocation after another, changing as swiftly as one sense can grasp the lead from another, I *am* back where....
>
> I *see* the unshed rain in the bundled clouds, thinking its troubled thoughts when I have none.
>
> For this *is* the day I have fished all afternoon in the boat with my father on the sunstruck lake that lulled the insistence out of everything. (39, Buckler's emphases)

Time is elastic, both expanding and contracting. Such play with time, with flashbacks that are re/lived rather than re/membered, is evocative of the writer Buckler so emulated: Faulkner. Each chapter of *Light in August*, to continue with the same example, begins in the "present" and is followed by a flashback, which in turn is followed by an anterior flashback whose end corresponds to the beginning of the first flashback. Time is compressed: thirty years are "obliterated" (422), cease to exist. The contraction is such that past, present and future are interchangeable, fused into one. In the peas and molasses sequence, the voice from the past "will never cease going on and on forever." But meanwhile, time also expands, slows and stops. Space and distance are distorted, mobility and immobility fused: a wagon "seems to *hang suspended* in the middle distance *forever and forever*, so *infinitesimal* is its progress" (5-6). Time is placed under the sign of the paradox: a train "has an effect of *terrific nomotion*. Yet it does move, *creeping terrifically*" (417). The blurring of movement with stasis extends to the blurring of movement in the world and in the mind: "He looked at the stranger. When he did so, he saw the waitress again and he ran again. He *actually* moved now" (202). Joe's "seeing" and "running" correspond to Bruce's "deeper eye" in *The Cruelest Month*, which sees the image in his mind "clearer than the one before his eyes" (266). Buckler's and Faulkner's explorations of time through memory are simultaneous explorations of knowledge, perception, and apperception, and of how they interrelate. Perhaps the most remarkable synthesis of these preoccupations is Faulkner's oneiric re/construction of an orphanage shrouded in the past: "Memory believes before knowing remembers. Believes longer than recollects, longer than knowing even wonders. Knows remembers believes a corridor in a big long garbled cold echoing building" (*Light* 111). Even the use of the gerund—a favourite device of both writers—is significant, for as opposed to the neutral noun "knowledge," the gerund "knowing" implies the present (and future) continuation of the past, a fusion as it were. Both writers' use of anamnesis is Schopenhauerian, corresponding to the philosopher's call to artists to become "a pure, willess, painless, timeless subject of knowledge" as well as a "mirror of the essence of the world" (Schopenhauer 102, 109).

Just as anamnesis is a conjunction of two periods in time, the rhetorical figure of metonymy is a conjunction of two semantic fields. Metonymy is a trope that implies a transfer which—unlike the metaphor—is based not on substitution or analogy, but on a discursive, logical link, implying an appurtenance or relationship of inclusion. The first chapters of this section have demonstrated that Buckler's way of thinking, of perceiving the world, are ultimately metonymical, that his texts ceaselessly trace the links between cause and effect, abstract and concrete, physical and moral, object and place, container and contained, sign and thing. Consequently, I shall go on here to examine that other trope that also fulfills a heuristic function—the metaphor.

Laurie Ricou has already remarked the disjunctive and conjunctive functions of Buckler's abundant imagery, pointing out "the multiple interconnections implied by Buckler's similes" (688), and the fact that his "massed similes and metaphors move the mind *in so many directions at once* that the reader is left…almost entranced" (691). But he also remarks that images "are often run together in celebration of a perfect, if irrational, unity" (691). The transfer or yoking involved in metaphor is predominantly conjunctive, for it discloses hidden analogies, unsuspected similarities, grounded as it is in the apperception of the same in the different. Yet, as we shall see, the process involves interaction rather than substitution. The metaphor is the most condensed form of imagery, having—unlike simile—only one phore or vehicle. At the same time, it is the most elaborate form, for the marks of analogy have been erased, and the transfer from one meaning to another stems from a personal operation based on an impression or interpretation. The epiphora—the transfer, transposition, or unifying process—assimilates heteroclitic ideas through apperception, through insight, the domain of vision, of transcendent intuition and imagination, that, as Aristotle points out in *Poetics,* cannot be taught. The metaphor's more concise form, which elides the initial ramifying step of analogy, its outward movement, is undeniably more conjunctive than the simile. If there is an effect of amplification, it is paradoxically produced by a process of reduction. Owen Barfield defines the metaphor as "a deliberate yoking of unlikes by an individual artificer" (81), but it never resolves the tension between the same and the other, between re/semblance and dis/semblance. Marcus Hester judiciously remarks that it harmonizes a theory of *tension* and a theory of *fusion*—the aporia central to Buckler's textual production. Allowing that seeing the same in the other is to see the similar, the similar in the metaphorical statement is perceived in spite of the difference or antithesis that remains unresolved.

The metaphor plays a key role in Buckler's heuristic writing process, which, as demonstrated in the previous chapters, consists in Unity in Variety—in opposing and uniting the identical and the different. The heavy use of personification which, as Dupriez points out, relies on metaphors of action denoting persons—and which no reader can fail to notice in all of Buckler's texts—is but one manifestation. The metaphoric process corresponds to his world view for, as Ricoeur argues, it is a strategy of shifting, of deviation with respect to established use, a dynamic agent of marvellous transformation, dismantling or destroying a previous categorization in order to construct a new domain on its ruins (251). It destructures ordinary language only to reconstruct it on another, superior plane. The device allows the receiver to see one thing under the aspect of another, or to see together, in the same category, what the ordinary gaze does not or cannot associate.

The gap that is leapt with such extreme concision can startle by deviating from received perceptions: Ricoeur's *para-doxa* (39). It may partly account for irritation with what Keefer calls Buckler's "acutely figurative prose," when she declares with a simile of her own that reading his "intolerably problematic, contradictory, fraught" texts is "like trying to drink out of a shattered glass" (222). The zone of Buckler's unusual metaphorical junctions, like the rearrangement inherent in *muthos,* is submitted both to reality and to fabulous invention, to restitution and to a displacement toward a higher sphere. The tension between the coexisting fusion and contradiction is what engenders meaning. The heteroclitic intersection necessarily carries an ontological dimension. This ontological dimension is inseparable from the metaphor's poetic function—the substance of the message—of symbolizing one thing through another. As Ricoeur argues, the figure adds nothing to the description of the world but, by infusing into the heart of the symbolized element, the emotions attached to the symbolizing one, does add something to the way that we feel about it (241). Unlike simile, whose function is generally to improve communication by providing additional clarification, the metaphor is not enclosed in the logical sphere of communication, but contains the dynamics of a subjective, emotional interpretation that, as Michel Le Guern points out, cannot be easily refuted—corresponding to *movere,* the rhetorical function of persuading or moving the receiver (74-6). For Le Guern observes that we can argue with a comparison, or can reject a simile because we reject the reasoning behind the analogy. We can even refuse to acknowledge the correspondence upon which a symbol is founded. But the metaphor escapes rational criticism and prevents the censure of logic from repelling the emotional movement that it seeks to share; this is why it is perfectly appropriate to Buckler's heuristic texts.

Almost all metaphors, according to Le Guern, express a value judgment, because the associated images that they introduce trigger an emotional reaction. The metaphor in fact contains to a small degree all the functions of language categorized by Roman Jakobson in *Essais de linguistique générale.* The phatic function remains unmodified, but the referential function of the proper term is attenuated in the metaphorical term, and the poetic function concerning the substance of the message is not a determining factor. Le Guern argues that the metalinguistic function centring the discourse on a code allows the formation of the metaphor but does not generate it. He goes on to add that what engenders the metaphor is the emotive function, centred on the locutor, and the conative function, oriented toward the receiver. Above all, the metaphor serves to express an emotion or a feeling that it seeks to share.

This function is nowhere more visible than in Buckler's dynamic metaphors, a term that Le Guern uses to designate a series of linked metaphors, each of which triggers the next. The following extract from *The Cruelest Month*, which is the continuation of the passage revolving around Rex's oncoming attack of migraine, illustrates how Buckler imprints upon his metaphors a movement that engenders transformation. By virtue of correspondences grasped by the intellect, the metaphor escapes from the stasis of symbol or allegory, and adds emotional charges one after the other, creating a feeling in the receiver that no logical explanation could produce.

> Little networks of spider-rope were stretched in every direction. Nothing quite attached anywhere, or quite touching anything else—but everything tightened to just within its breaking point. The ropes chafed against his thoughts, though never quite enough to rupture their skin. Little telegraph systems were set up, and the ache ceaselessly tapped out the message of its own tirelessness along them. The circuits snagged but never quite snapped. Little battering rams were pressed against his temples, but never quite split them open. Weights that themselves ached for being suspended by their own arms were not quite attached to his eyelids. Every nerve in his head was tied up and suspended in the position of prisoners who can't quite touch their feet to the ground. A million little suction cups pressed everywhere there was blood, drawing it upward against a downward pull, and whitening it. Two blunt thumbs pressed against the arteries in his throat without quite choking them off. (167)

We note the minimalist approach consisting in the paratactic accumulation of main clauses, little or no subordination, no syntactic link from statement to statement. The abstract network of pain is concretized by a series of physical objects: ropes, telegraph systems, battering rams, suction cups. The device of concatenation ("nothing quite" leading to a series of "never quite" which in turn modulate into "can't quite" and "without quite"), involves liminal terms that evoke a twilight zone between presence and absence. Like the dynamic metaphors, it suggests the shades of feeling and experience that are beyond the capacity of language to express.

The metaphor's capacity to trigger an emotional response in the receiver makes it the ideal vehicle for meditation. It is through the metaphor, after all, that the mystics express the inexpressible, translating into language what lies beyond language. Le Guern remarks how the metaphor of religious language constitutes a sort of intermediary between the transcendental reality that language cannot express, and the daily experience of human, material reality (72-3). Buckler's search for the *noumenon* springs to mind, particularly when Le Guern declares the metaphorical process to be similar for the poet who wishes to translate into words a grasp of the universe that lies beyond common logic and common language (72). The aim of the metaphorical process is, through the intermediary of language, to go beyond the language of simple logical information to attempt to transmit information of a higher order (Le Guern 72). Bearing witness to this higher truth is what Ricoeur terms the existential function of the metaphor (313).

When David and his father are working together on the farm in a passage that recycles material from the short story "The First Born Son," focalization rests first on Joseph, then on David. The extended metaphors in which the ontological and epistemological questioning of the implied author superimposes itself upon the running thoughts of his protagonists reflect two antagonistic but coexisting visions of the world. Buckler introduces what will be Joseph's paean to the land and to a pastoral way of life with an extended metaphor contrasting and weaving the cultural spheres of language and music as not only modes of expression, but as lenses or filters shaping our perception:

> His feelings weren't word-shaped, like David's. There was no page in his mind or heart where their tracery was legible to himself. But they made a tune in him just the same. He couldn't write the notes that made it up, if he tried. But whether he could translate them into words or not, the notes were there. (*Mountain* 156)

Not only does Buckler map out the world in metalinguistic terms, implying that David sees the world through language, but he even distinguishes between the oral and the written, between speech and print, which can be considered to be representative of the passage from *parole* to *langue* as organized system. If, as implied by the negatives, David's thoughts are word-shaped, his mind a transcribed page that he can (re)read, Joseph's belong to the universal, non-semantic language of music ("tune," "notes"), and the hymn that follows is a litany to a rural way of life that is the manifestation of the sacred. The litany is more elaborate in "The First Born Son," with Martin, the father, singing the glories of "the brown waves of earth" (*Rebellion* 19), the "whole green wind [which] is full of leaves and growing," the "thunder-frown of the sky," or the way "sleep's drowsy wind blow[s] out the candles of thought" (21). Joseph's litany, albeit "not word-shaped," is paradoxically imbued with imagery ending with a synaesthetic fusion of metaphor and simile: "My life *tastes* like fresh bread" (*Mountain* 157). The final co-mingling of simile and metaphor sings the eternal cycle of time/lessness, forever moving on, yet forever the same: "The days *roll* down the week *like* a wheel. Then it is Sunday and *the wheel is* still" (157). The neverending repetition that for Joseph has a taste of heaven, is the pivot around which revolves David's antithetical stance. The young man, who feels the attraction of the city, describes the patient, labouring oxen and their monotonous stride. Buckler transforms the beasts into a metaphor for an archaic, brutish way of life in which the human spirit is not only *not* elevated but dragged downwards, trapped by the basest material clay: "They held their heads down, drawing the heavy rocks. Their eyes saw only the ground" (158). The sacred has become the brutish.

As far back as Aristotle, even in the face of irremediable dispersion, it was an essence, or impossible ideal of a world that had regained its unity, which was expected to regulate human quests and acts (Aubenque 402). Merleau-Ponty's "*chair*," Joyce's "thing-ness" and Buckler's "is-ness" echo Aristotle's *ousia*, or substance, which designates both sublunar realities and divine reality. They correspond to the analogical aristotelician stance positing an ordered cosmos in which everything can be traced back to an essence, a first principle. Thomas Aquinas's doctrine of analogy also sought to define the horizontal relationship of all categories to the substance, and the vertical relationships of all created things to the Creator. Buckler's young protagonists David and Effie are united in just such a search for analogies:

> She was rubbing the soft knobs of a squaw-weed blossom against her chin.
>
> "Dave," she said, "what does it feel like? Feel it."
>
> He felt the blossom, "Moths?" he said.
>
> "Yes," she cried. "Moths—it does, doesn't it?"

> They always felt an instant closeness when both saw the same likeness of something else in what to others was never more than just the thing it was. (*Mountain* 109)

Aquinas's doctrine of analogy rejects one unique causality, for that would engender only the Same, but posits that analogy is what prevents language from dislocating, and that similitude in causality is what resists dispersion of logical classifications that could only end in silence. Ricoeur comments on Aquinas's *Summa theologica*, explaining that in the play between Telling and Being, Telling is on the point of succumbing to the weight of the heterogeneity of being and of beings. But Being itself relaunches Telling by virtue of the subterranean continuities that confer upon Telling an analogical extension of its significances (352). This is the play that Buckler signals in the escalating metalinguistic epilogue of *The Mountain and the Valley*, in which David hears the "swarming multitude of all the voices it was physically impossible to attend to" (291), the voices becoming "suddenly infinite," each one fanning "at the touch of thought into another infinite divisibility" (292), until David feels he has "run into a cluster of floating cobwebs" (294). The heterogeneity of all the beings to be accounted for is dizzying, and their calling out to be told quickens, rendered by the homely concrete similes "[i]t was like the woodsaw gaining such speed that the teeth disappeared" (295), or "like a stream forking in the sand," or the technological but homely simile "like the chicken-wire pattern of atoms" (296). David succumbs to the sheer weight, mass, and number of the variety and diversity of things waiting to be heard and told:

> They had a *double* accusing, because of themselves *and* of the things they mirrored. They were shapeless and infiltrate through each other. Their fluctuate form was not traceable in space or boundable by time. It was broader than space, and faster than time, and not containable by definite quantity in either. But each one was exactly as it was, just the same... (297, Buckler's emphases)

The "frenzied forking" can ultimately end only in silence, for Telling cannot cope with "the crushing screaming challenge of the infinite permutations of the possible...the billion raised to the billionth power" (297). But, echoing Thomas Aquinas, Being itself relaunches Telling by virtue of the subterranean continuities that confer upon Telling an analogical extension of its significances. The process takes place, of course, when David stands at the top of the metaphorical mountain overlooking the equally metaphorical valley:

> He stood there, looking down over the mountain and the valley, and it was as if the sun-shadow passed swiftly over all the voices as the sun-shadow had swept across the road.
>
> I will *tell* it, he thought rushingly: that is the answer.
>
> I know how it is with everything. I will put it down and they will see that I know. (298, Buckler's emphasis)

The fact that David equates knowing and telling is significant. That a sign can intend one thing without ever ceasing to intend another is "precisely what makes language an instrument of knowing," argues W.M. Urban (112).

The metaphor is a trope that, like irony, generates double vision, or even stereoscopic vision with its aptitude for cumulation, for the "accumulated intension" of words, according to Urban, is the source of fertile ambiguity and of the symbolic power of language, allowing the writer to name realities for which language has, and can have, no proper term. For Ricoeur remarks that all analogy ultimately designates the movement from the visible to the invisible, arguing that the most well-known forms of metaphor linking the animate and the inanimate, the abstract and the concrete, do not obey a logical order but an ontological one. He adds that whether we ponder the metaphorical nature of metaphysics or the metaphysical nature of the metaphor, we are in the presence of one same movement that carries words and things somewhere beyond, or *meta* (366). Along with Buckler's recurrent metaphor of the sun, for example—as in the extract above—can be found the metaphors of light, of the gaze, of the eye, of the circle, already examined in chapter 3. They draw the receiver toward a metaphysical unifying system, for they are figures of idealization, from Plato's *eidos* to Hegel's Idea. Buckler's metaphors are an inherent part of his speculative discourse, his setting up of fundamental principles and concepts. But concepts arrest and fix, while what Ricoeur terms the "métaphore vive" goes beyond in a leap of the imagination (384).

Reminding us of Saussure's distinction between *langue* (language as organized system or code) and *parole* (the concrete individual act of language), Ricoeur heuristically contrasts the conventional or stock metaphor, with the "live" or original metaphor: "la métaphore vive" (156). He remarks that the metaphor stems from the polysemic structure of language, and that even if the new metaphor is an act of *parole*, it becomes incorporated into the code when it ceases to be an innovation, becomes a stock metaphor and then a cliché. The lexicalized dead metaphor is the last step in the cycle *parole/langue*. These distinctions synthesize notions on imagery stemming from thinkers from Emerson to Merleau-Ponty. As I pointed out in the introduction, Emerson in "The American Scholar" criticizes the writers who "feed unconsciously upon the language created by the primary writers of the country," arguing that in this case "new imagery ceases to be created" and "a paper currency is employed when there is no bullion in the vaults" (38). Emerson's bullion and paper currency anticipate Ricoeur's live and dead metaphors, as they do Merleau-Ponty's distinction—using almost the same imagery—between "parole parlante," creation in its nascent state, and "parole parlée," which benefits from already available meanings like a fortune already acquired (*Phénoménologie* 229). Merleau-Ponty gives the live or original metaphor a maieutic role, arguing that the metaphor is the *locus* of the gestation of meaning and even of the genesis of the world (241-245). Ricoeur argues that live metaphors do not describe the world—they create a new vision of the world. For semantic innovation is a creative manner of responding to the question posed by things, which requires work, an effort of *parole* over *langue* that confronts both words and things. At stake is a re/description or new way of accounting for the universe of representations (161).

Buckler's metaphorical network carries the vision of the universe that I examined in chapter 4. It transmits the perception of a world (de)ciphered and (re)ordered through *logos*. Let us look again at that more complex form of analogy, the proportional metaphor, in which Bruce envisages sharing his life with his lover Sheila: "She'd be there, to put meaning within the bare lines of him...someone to whom his name and his face would not be just a scrambled hieroglyph, but reading" (*Cruelest Month* 211). The analogy made between love and the Rosetta stone sets up a multilateral system of interconnections in which Bruce is to Sheila what Egyptian script was to Champollion, and the understanding between a man and a woman equivalent to the decoding of a cipher. Reading, being able to connect the signifier and the signified, is the ultimate metaphor for making sense of the world. This explains why the writer's metaphysical quest is dominantly depicted in metalinguistic terms. Metalinguistic metaphors abound in all of Buckler's texts, nowhere more clearly than in the extended metaphor of death in *The Cruelest Month*. The X-ray or "photograph of death" (176) that Paul receives in the Montreal hospital is both visual text and script, and metamorphoses into a ubiquitous cipher of doom covering the surface of all things. Paul reads the message "[o]ff the walls and the floor and his hands and his feet" (177). The writer seems to be searching for ultimate meaning embodied by some sort of logical unifying system linking all the components of the cosmos just as it links the components of the system of language/*langue* for those who attempt to pierce its logic: "He read the part where it had all the words in it starting with 'n,' the most remoreseless of all letters, the one that infects every syllable it helps to form" (177). Mingling his voice with that of the protagonist, Buckler seeks to articulate through an extended metalinguistic metaphor, followed by a concrete metaphor modified by a series of imagery, the manner in which a human comes to grips with his or her own mortality:

> This was not a noun, with a noun's face. It was a faceless verb. He couldn't tell if it was transitive or intransitive. All he could grasp was its *ad*verbial shadow.
>
> …You were slewed around, with eyes in your back—facing all that had or hadn't happened to you: a gallery with subtly shifted emphases, at once totally communicative and totally deaf; but numinously distinct in some opalescent light like the sun's high drawing water over a high wall of trees in the primaeval secrecy before a change of weather. (178, Buckler's emphasis)

Identifying the word is the equivalent of finding the original Word; it allows the protagonist to grasp his place in the cosmos, in the order of things. Through the rhetorical figure of *dubitatio*, giving the effect of orality, Paul searches, tests, hesitates, rejects, before the final epiphany:

> Reverberating? Was that its note? No. Muting? No. Cueing? No. Hinting?…Lurking?…
>
> He gave it up. He couldn't do it here, when the monotone of

> strangeness hummed like invisible tuning bars between the lines of the message and its meaning. Home, he thought. There I can capture it. Where the trees and the house and the sky will help translate it for me. Each in its own particular hand, as familiar as a wife's.
>
> And then, suddenly, without conscious bidding, there was a pulse-thump of recognition and the verb's name flashed across his vision like a bulletin.
>
> The verb was "notify"!
>
> That was the way it went! You drifted along, with all perceptions swaddled in a cirrus of hopes and forgetfulness and hearsay and excuses; then all at once you were precisely *notified*. Of *everything*. And you stood there with the implacable registered letter in your hand and there'd be no more swaddling cirrus ever again. (179, Buckler's emphases)

The metaphor of a registered letter that terminates all "drifting," (underscored by the lexical fields of vagueness and ambiguity), emanating from some sort of giant cosmic post office, and the corresponding analogy Paul has scribbled into a notebook of ideas for a potential book—"Each man switchboard of uncompleted calls" (273)—fit in well with the baroque conception of death that I examined in chapter 6. Paul's epiphany, and this startling, rather grotesque way of revealing the grand design is a variant of another heuristic metaphor, that of Saint Paul's: "For now we see through a glass, darkly; but then face to face" (1 Corinthians 13:12).

While Le Guern claims that the metaphor modifies the very substance of language (66), Ricoeur specifies that at the heart of the acquired innovation is the "twisting" ("torsion") of words (289). The new state of things is necessarily perceived through the "thickness" of the dislocated former state of things, for it is in the very resistance of the previous word usage, of former categories and classifications, that a stereoscopic vision is created. Such resistance at times stems from the weight of a stock or even dead metaphor that Buckler twists or revives in various manners. Playing with the conventional image "the mind's eye," the writer uses cacology—twisting or doing violence to standard usage—to call attention to its original value. He resemanticises the component eye, giving it back its original literal weight. First, he gives the mind hands instead of an eye: "The hands of his mind were paralyzed" (*Cruelest Month* 272). Then he puts the metaphorical eyes in contiguity with "real" eyes, and finally gives the eyes hands: "His mind's eye telescoped its beam downward to synchronize with the beam of his physical eyes, and his eyes began again to manipulate things like hands" (272). Attributing hands to eyes is a recurrent tactic: a little later, when Paul looks out the window, the author pointedly states "[h]is eyes touched the trees...his eyes touched them like hands" (274). This imagery reinforces the philosophical stance discussed in the first chapter, equating the visible and the tangible. But giving eyes hands also gives us a fresh gaze on the logic of attributing eyes to the mind. It reactivates the physicality of the dead metaphor and triggers a reflection on language and its signifying system. The body continues to be dismembered and recombined. The eyes of the mind become the eyes of thoughts, in another startling reflection on writing, when Paul describes the notes that he has jotted down as being "merely the pencil drawings of thoughts with their eyes left out" (273). Later his glance falls "on a sentence that all at once had eyes" (274). It is significant that the sentence that "sees" is a metaphor establishing parallels of similitude and opposition, a mirror relationship as it were, between humans and those organic beings so often selected as their counterparts in works of art: "People, shedding their leaves at the moment of leaving, never leaf out the same again; but a re-leafing tree is exactly the friend of last year" (274). Another destabilizing tactic is to reverse in a way the device of personification. In contrast to the heavily recurrent houses and homely objects with human faces and attributes, Buckler disconcerts by giving humans the qualities of objects: "Faces with their blinds up...or like pianos with no music open on them" (*Cruelest Month* 273), or the heart that "flaps on its hinges, like a derelict gate" (*Ox Bells* 84).

At times, Buckler's imagery is so curious that it verges on the conceit. This device, characteristic of seventeenth-century metaphysical poets and later exploited by modernists, violently yokes dissimilar images and heterogeneous ideas together. While such intricate, unusual, or far-fetched metaphors are a favourite device of T.S. Eliot, as in the opening lines of "The Love Song of Alfred J. Prufrock," the conceit in Buckler's texts, while always startling, sometimes fails to convince. The elements seem to have nothing in common, and their conjunction feels strained. They make up a part of what Keefer calls

Buckler's "verbal binges" or "wildcatting with words," the "verbal vivisection" causing the reader to be "jostled and jerked, not led, through the narrative" (206). The reader, for instance, cannot fail to wonder at the appropriateness of some similes in *The Cruelest Month*,[21] such as the one describing Bruce and Sheila's first lovemaking: "longing distended in them like a horse's nostril" (209). Others, however, are breathtakingly effective. The image can be simplicity itself: the deer "as collisionless" as the light (*Cruelest Month* 264). Or it can be quite complex. By gaining access to Morse the writer's thoughts through a paratactic, hypnotic style giving us the impression of a stream of consciousness, we learn that the boy Morse used to inhabit the clean, beautiful, natural world of Minnesota forests in which "the ax more beautiful like swimming than the gun is beautiful like Christmas" (*Cruelest Month* 80). The elaborate, apparently dislocated structure of the simile is based on the intricate proportional metaphor and its four components, but disconcerts with its blend of noun and gerund, abstract and concrete. The "proportional simile" is extended further and shifts to a striking, grotesque metaphor in which we learn that Morse has been corrupted by the world of words, that he has "lost his clean beautiful axe somewhere and all he has to cut a path with is the beat-up sickle he's twisted his tongue into" (80). Other conceits resonate in the mind through the skilful combination of what Fontanier calls inanimate but physical things and inanimate but purely moral or abstract things. Among the ones that we have already seen is the simile describing the death of a soldier in "Thanks for Listening"—and in which we can once again appreciate the Faulkneresque use of gerunds: "I saw all the hearing and the seeing and the touching go out of him like a breeze that dies in the air quicker than running."[22] Or there is the yoking in the short story "Another Christmas," poetic in its elaborate simplicity, describing the boy's first pair of skates, "[g]leaming and clean like speed itself" (*Rebellion* 33). Perhaps one of the most remarkable conceits is the one we have seen describing the old man in "Man and Snowman" storming the future, attempting to penetrate time and to see beyond, only to meet up with "a wall blanker than smoke, a nowhere louder than silence, a stare whiter than zeroes" (*Window* 63). Unlike the strained effects of much of the imagery in *The Cruelest Month*, this conceit carries an effect of naturalness and simplicity, all the while fusing the solid and the ethereal, the abstract and the concrete, different forms of absence experienced through space, sound, and colour, the (in)tangible with the (un)seen and the (un)heard, an intellectual concept (zero) with sight made visible and palpable.

According to Schlegel, the conceit is elaborated through wit (*Witz*) or imagination. He argues that through this faculty of synthesizing and catalyzing, one can attempt to grasp the flux or infinite becoming of the universe, to fuse the physical and mental realms by uniting two opposed phenomena or ideas. Buckler in just this manner connects incongruous elements, creating fertile relationships and engendering an alertness to resemblances and analogies elsewhere. We readers find ourselves, like the narrator of *Ox Bells and Fireflies*, staring "into the eye of everything. Flesh or plant or matter" (45).

# Conclusion

Writers such as Margaret Atwood and Margaret Laurence have acclaimed Ernest Buckler to be an innovator, calling him "one of the *pathbreakers* for the modern Canadian novel" and "a genuine *pioneer* in Canadian writing."[1] Why should a large number of Canadian writers, critics, and readers consider that Buckler has "broken ground" (Primrose 8) in the world of Canadian letters, that he has created a distinctive literature? The themes on which the author writes are certainly not new—they have preoccupied artists and thinkers since antiquity. Buckler's writing is a crossroads characterized by simultaneous tension and fusion between the old and the new, one that propulses nineteenth-century cultural stances into twentieth-century modernism. The writer's *oeuvre* is grounded in platonic, Renaissance, and Romantic currents of thought, yet the aesthetic philosophy that he elaborates not only connects Canadian literature to international modernist tendencies, but anticipates and even paves the way for certain postmodern concerns.

---

Note is on p. 248.

His writing is grounded in phenomenological and ontological concerns that can be traced back beyond Emersonian transcendentalism and the European Romantic movement to idealists who in turn owe an immense debt to Renaissance and medieval thinkers and, ultimately, to Aristotle and Plato. Buckler's work essentially stages a confrontation of ontological and linguistic antitheses. Both the linguistic and the philosophical dimensions of his texts are placed under the sign of paradox and aporia. The reader is constantly confronted with a cohesive yet irreconcilable tension between the Multiple and the neoplatonic prototype of the One: the dynamics of his writing involve creating simultaneously a web of ramifications that generate an expanding cross-network of analogies and a corresponding but inverse movement from the Many to the One. The entire textual production with its rhetorical and metaphorical networks strains toward a metaphysical unifying system, transmitting the perception of a world de/ciphered and re/ordered through *logos*, and exploring the interspace where subject and object are joined by language. Whether we consider the metaphorical nature of Buckler's metaphysics or the metaphysical nature of his metaphors, we are in the presence of one single movement that carries words and things somewhere beyond, or *meta* (Ricoeur 366). Yet even the ontological idealism contains an underlying current of materialism that can be considered problematic. The materialist currents of thought that undermine in an endless dialectic the writer's idealist stance not only echo other modernist writers seeking the essence behind thing and thought, but eventually inflect Canadian postmodernism with a materiality not to be found in that of the United States.

Buckler's *oeuvre* is rooted in an organicist view of the universe that the Romantics transmitted to the modernists—a view in which the grand is contained in the small, the abstract in the concrete, and the universal in the particular. However, the Romantic, idealist quest for the *noumenon* that is apprehendable through the power of the imagination is tempered by the modernist conception of ambivalence, even liminality, derivative of a philosophical stance: the impossibility in front of the fertile flux of the universe of perceiving—let alone articulating—the essence of reality.

Buckler's rhetorical and discursive practices, which enclose and include while opening out, reflect an aesthetic theory founded simultaneously on chaos and system, and on the fluctuating manner in which they have been perceived throughout history. On the one hand, we find a Schlegelian celebration of infinite abundance and diversity, a ramifying web branching outward through strategies of disorder, displacement, disarticulation, accumulation, and amplification. These strategies of chaos are confronted yet never reconciled with the conjunctive dynamics straining toward synthetic resolution or unity. On the other hand, the writer's aesthetic philosophy is anchored in the world view constructed by scholasticism, which persisted throughout the Renaissance and beyond, positing that beauty emanates from the supernatural connections that exist between the object and a perfectly regular, admirably designed cosmos. Such an aesthetic philosophy is by definition rooted in an ethical vision positing the interconnectedness of beauty and utility, and in turn implying a didactic dimension.

Buckler does share with modernist writers their fascination with the mechanisms of language, and their quest for surprising, unusual, or curious ideas, figures, and words. His formalistic, often outrageously baroque innovations, like theirs, serve to stretch or bend language to create new concepts, or to acknowledge concepts that *langue* as system can only express periphrastically. His stylistic acrobatics, like theirs, calls attention to linguistic and ontological flux. Yet his prose is both cipher and hermeneutic instrument with which to read and interpret the cipher of the world. Buckler's rhetorical strategies are an inherent part of his speculative discourse, his setting up of fundamental principles and concepts that are of universal and timeless concern. The moral dimension of his work, the preoccupation with the rhetorical functions of *docere* and *movere* (teaching and moving or persuading) as well as of *placere* (pleasing) are perhaps what set him off from his fellow modernists who, despite their interest in Renaissance notions linking art with the good and the useful, explore language in a hermetic fashion that tends to exclude any preoccupations with mass or popular culture, or any pretentions of instructing.

For Buckler's semantic innovations are part of his heuristic texts' creative manner of responding to the question posed by things. Already anticipating the postmodern tendency to cross traditional generic boundaries and to combine modes, Buckler shares many traits with the postmodern writing that is simultaneously a reaction to yet a continuation of modernism. Breaking away from the common modernist stance, he believes that art finds its meaning within a social framework. His frequent recourse to forms of fable, *exemplum*, and allegory as well as his predominantly metonymic and metaphorical modes of process generally aim to underscore an underlying lesson. Postmodern writers, with their political questioning and their social commitment, are also interested in both language and the world. Convinced of the moral and political dimensions of art, and committed to anchoring literature in the community, they cannot fail to be responsive to his production. On one level, Buckler's explorations of time, memory, knowledge, truth, and perception, are all central preoccupations in postmodern writing as well. But beyond that, his manner of connecting incongruous elements and engendering an alertness to resemblances and analogies elsewhere, cannot fail to strike a chord in contemporary sensibilities. For Buckler's *oeuvre* anticipates the way postmodern art tends to celebrate diversity yet to seek and disclose hidden or unsuspected analogies, rooted in the apperception of the similar in the Other.

The author of what Alden Nowlan proclaimed in the 1950s to be one of the "finest novels in the English-speaking world" (French, "Ernest Buckler") was, by the 1970s, already relatively neglected, to the consternation of critics such as William French and Claude Bissell. The loss of interest—both on the part of readers and of critics—can be imputed to changing sensibilities and aesthetic trends. Buckler's romanticism and idealism began to be viewed as old-fashioned. His focus on the domestic, on familial relationships and community ties, strongly grounded in a firm ethical stance, was perceived as overly sentimental and morally earnest by a society in which sentiment was no longer valued and a moral outlook suspect. Today, literary tastes are ready to acknowledge the worth of this writer and to appreciate the way in which he blends the universal and the particular, staging the universal concerns of the romantics and the modernists with the stunning particularities of modernist and postmodern discursive techniques. In Buckler's *oeuvre*, Canadian literature finds a meeting-point of multiple currents of thought and of aesthetic practices that are increasingly relevant. In addition, the postmodern interest in exploring and shattering the frontiers of language should lead today's readership to rediscover "Canada's least-known best writer" (Bissell, "Prose").

# Notes

## Introduction

1 Barbara Wickens, "From Reviled Art to Revered Icons," *Maclean's*, 8 May 1995, 15.
2 From the *Toronto Star*, qtd. in Allan Fotheringham, "The 'Old Boys' of Canadian Art Can't Win," *Maclean's*, 4 May 1996, 84.
3 Peter Mellon suggests that the myth of a reactionary establishment hostile to innovative artists was exaggerated, and that the Group's paintings were on the whole well received and quickly became popular. But the "nauseating colors" attack was made by the *Toronto Star* in 1932, over fifteen years after the Group began unofficially to work together. Even admitting that such attacks were not typical, they carried weight and authority precisely because they were voiced by official, opinion-forming organs like major newspapers.
4 Margaret Atwood, letter to Claude Bissell, 9 August 1982, Ernest Buckler Manuscript Collection, Thomas Fisher Rare Book Library, University of Toronto (hereafter BMC).
5 Margaret Laurence, tribute to Buckler sent to Claude Bissell and included in Bissell's "Ernest Buckler Presentation—Mountainlea Lodge, Bridgetown," 11 September 1982, BMC.

6 Buckler, "My First Novel," undated typescript, p. 4, BMC. The text which Buckler prepared and read for the CBC in 1953 but never published, was subsequently included in Cook, ed., *Ernest Buckler,* 22-27.
7 In this essay, entitled "The Transcendentalist," Emerson explains that the transcendentalist "believes in miracle, in the perpetual openness of the human mind to new influx of light and power; he believes in inspiration, and in ecstasy" ( 90).
8 John Rackliffe, letter to Buckler, 27 September 1961, BMC.
9 Bissell, "Ernest Buckler: Rural Intellectual," typescript of lecture at Carleton University, n.d., p. 11, BMC.
10 "Supplementary Answers to Questionnaire," undated typescript, p. 1, BMC. Certain references make it clear that it was written at the time of the publication of *Ox Bells and Fireflies* (1968).
11 Buckler, letter to Harry Brown, 30 June 1969, BMC.
12 Buckler, handwritten notes about writing, BMC. This phrase is found under another remark under the title "Esquire" and is clearly meant to be eventually used as material for an opinion piece.
13 Tribute dated 15 August, 1982 from William French to Buckler sent to Claude Bissell to be read during the celebration organized by Bissell in Bridgetown, 11 September 1982, BMC.
14 Apart from Janice Kulyk Keefer's heuristic analysis of Buckler's *oeuvre* in *Under Eastern Eyes*, there has been little analysis of *The Cruelest Month* with the exception of the introduction by Alan R. Young in the 1977 paperback edition of the novel, further developed in his monograph *Ernest Buckler*, and the brief commentary of Robert D. Chambers in *Sinclair Ross and Ernest Buckler*. Similarly, Keefer, Young, and Chambers, as well as Andrew Seaman in "Fiction in Atlantic Canada" and John Orange in *Ernest Buckler and His Works*, are among the few to discuss *Ox Bells and Fireflies*. *Nova Scotia: Window on the Sea*, has not been analyzed, and Buckler's short stories have on the whole been dismissed as mere embryos of *The Mountain and the Valley*, which incorporates much of this earlier material.

## Chapter 1

1 The *Halifax Gazette*, founded in 1751, was Canada's first newspaper, preceding by 12 years the *Quebec Gazette*. The first performance of a play by a Canadian author took place in Halifax in 1774. The first Canadian university was the Anglican King's College, founded in Windsor, Nova Scotia in 1802, preceding the founding of Montreal's McGill (1821), Toronto's King's College (1827), and Kingston's Queen's College (1830). The first film production company (the Bioscop Company) in Canada was also founded in Halifax in 1902. It notably produced a series of short features for the CPR, intended to attract immigrants from Great Britain.
2 Margaret Laurence, tribute to Buckler sent to Claude Bissell and included in Bissell's "Ernest Buckler Presentation—Mountainlea Lodge, Bridgetown," 11 September 1982, BMC.

# Notes                                                                     235

3  qtd. in French, "Ernest Buckler: a Literary Giant Scorned?" (23). Furthermore, in a letter to the mayor of Bridgetown paying tribute to Buckler in anticipation of the 11 September ceremony, Nowlan stated, "I have said in print before and will say here again that *The Mountain and the Valley* is not just the finest novel yet written in Canada, but among the finest novels in the English-speaking world," 1 September 1982, BMC.

4  The opening sentence of Buckler's essay "My First Novel" (typescript, BMC), clearly proclaims: "What I happen to be is a farmer who writes, not a writer who farms."

5  A review of *The Mountain and the Valley* pointed out that there were "very few Canadian novels dealing with farm life" and that this was surprising "in view of the fact that the farming population of Canada [was] about sixteen percent of the total population." "Impressive First Novel by A Maritime Farmer," unsigned review in "The Bookshelf...," *Montreal Star*, 20 December 1952.

6  Entry in Buckler's private journal dated 1 January 1937, typescript, BMC.

7  Buckler, "Excerpts from a Life," undated typescript, BMC.

8  Buckler, *Three's a Crowd*, typescript, BMC.

9  Buckler, *Four on a Match, a Radio Comedy*, undated typescript, p. 23, BMC.

10  Buckler, letter to Rachel Grover, 19 October 1972, BMC.

11  *By Sun and Candlelight* (originally "Late Victory," crossed out in pencil), typescript, p. 37, BMC.

12  Here too, there are striking parallels with W.O. Mitchell that the reader may want to pursue by consulting Sheila and David Latham's book on Mitchell, *Magic Lies*.

13  Buckler, "Puss in the Corner," undated typescript, pp. 2 and 3, BMC.

14  In a virulent journal entry, the young Buckler calls the clergy "that lichen on the face of civilization," places ministers next to rats as "the lowest form of life," and claims that one should "disinfect after them, as one would after malaria mosquitoes." Buckler's journal, 18-19 October 1936, BMC.

15  For excellent overviews of the critical reception of Ernest Buckler's works, see John Orange, "Ernest Buckler, an Annotated Bibliography," Orange, *Ernest Buckler and His Works*, and Pell.

16  An MA thesis subsequently analyzed the Carlylean strains in *The Mountain and the Valley*, notably its parallels with *Sartor Resartus*, and eventually led to the publication of an article. See Westwater.

17  Entry in Buckler's private journal, 1 January 1937, typescript, BMC.

18  Copies of these essays are available in BMC.

19  Buckler, letter to Francis Brown, 16 December 1963, BMC.

20  Claude Bissell, Introduction to "Ernest Buckler: Rural Intellectual," typescript for lecture at Carleton University, BMC, n.d. p.6.

21  When the Atlantic Monthly Press in Boston expressed interest in his short story "The Harness," calling it "extraordinarily well-organized and well-written," Buckler answered gratefully, explaining that he farmed all day and did all of his writing at night, and that everyone in his community regarded

his writing as merely "a harmless eccentricity": Buckler, letter to the Atlantic Monthly Press, 31 July 1950, BMC.
22 Buckler, letter to John Bennett, 28 May 1952, BMC.
23 Quoted both by French, "Ernest Buckler" 23, and by Percy, 11.
24 "My First Novel," typescript, p. 4, BMC.
25 Buckler, letters to Josephine Rogers, 25 January 1969, and to Ernest Dobbs, 7 February 1969, and 7 July 1969, BMC.
26 The opening sentence of Buckler's "My First Novel," BMC.
27 "Supplementary Answers to Author's Questionnaire," BMC. Entire chunks of his musing about himself are reproduced almost intact in *Whirligig*.
28 Buckler, letter to William Raney of Henry Holt and Co., 15 September 1952, BMC.
29 One can detect resonances with Emerson's essay "Nature," which is quoted in the epigraph of chapter 3, focusing on Buckler's ontological commitment.
30 Buckler, letter to William Raney, 15 September 1952, BMC.
31 In a letter to Claude Bissell dated 16 December 1961, Buckler confessed: "Dickens bored me to yawns. Thackeray to tears," qtd. in Bissell, *Ernest Buckler Remembered*, 36.
32 Buckler, letter to Ted Bentley, 9 September 1937, qtd. in ibid., 36.
33 Buckler, letter to Arnold Gingrich, 12 December 1966, BMC.
34 Buckler, letter to Don Cameron, 25 May 1969, BMC.
35 Buckler, letter to Bill Raney, 7 September 1953, BMC.
36 Buckler, letter to Diane Mew, 11 May 1963, BMC.
37 Diane Mew, letter to Buckler, 15 May 1963, BMC.
38 Buckler, letter to Don Cameron, 25 May 1969, BMC.
39 Buckler, letter to Margaret Laurence, 10 June 1974.
40 Buckler, letter to Pamela Frye, 9 December 1970, BMC.
41 Buckler, letter to Margaret Atwood, 29 September 1972, BMC.
42 Buckler, letter to Atwood, 5 May 1971, BMC.
43 Buckler, letter to Atwood, 29 September 1972, BMC.
44 Buckler, letter to Max Ferguson, 10 June 1968, BMC.
45 Manuel Komroff, letter to Buckler, 29 December 1939, BMC.

## Chapter 2

1 Six years is the figure that Buckler himself gave in the piece "My First Novel," which was broadcast on the CBC on 2 December 1953, and which was subsequently published in Cook, ed., *Ernest Buckler*. But as Alan Young has pointed out, the gestation period was actually much longer ("Genesis"). Claude Bissell places it at around ten years, in *Ernest Buckler Remembered*.
2 Jonathan Leff, letter to E. Buckler, 4 March 1952, BMC.
3 Buckler, letter to William Buckley of Henry Holt and Co., 12 January 1953, BMC.
4 Dudley Cloud, letter to Buckler, 4 May 1951, BMC.
5 Ibid.
6 Cloud, letter to Buckler, 11 May 1951, BMC.

# Notes

7. Ivan Von Auw Jr, letter to Buckler, 23 July 1951, BMC.
8. Ivan Von Auw Jr, letter to Buckler, 20 August 1951, BMC.
9. In this letter to Claude Bissell dated 4 January 1972, Buckler reproduced in almost exactly identical terms a complaint he had formulated in an early critical piece published in *Esquire*. Bissell quotes from the letter in his Carleton lecture "Ernest Buckler: Rural Intellectual," undated typescript, BMC, pp. 2 and 23, as well as in the article "Ernest Buckler."
10. Sinclair Ross, letter to Buckler, 3 September 1976 (qted by Bissell, in Carleton lecture "Ernest Buckler: Rural Intellectual," pp 13-14).
11. The self-proclaimed Faulknerian writer Javier Marìas quotes Faulkner as saying "I prefer silence to sound, and the image produced by words is formed in silence. The thunder and music of prose take place in silence," *William Faulkner, un entusiasmo*, Alfaguara, 1997, qtd. in William Faulkner, "né d'une esclave noire et d'un caïman," *Le Monde*, 3 octobre 1997, p. III, my translation.
12. Letter from Maureen McManus of Henry Holt & Co., announcing the 27 October date of publication and quoting part of the review of the New York *Library Journal*'s October issue, 2 October 1952, BMC.
13. William Arthur Deacon, "Every Little Movement Has a Meaning All Its Own," *Globe and Mail*, 29 November 1952.
14. David Anderson Ramsey, "First Novel of Brilliant New Writer," *The Charlotte News*, 22 November 1952.
15. David A. Ramsey, letter to Buckler, 21 October 1952, BMC.
16. Buckler, letter to Bill Raney, 7 September 1953, BMC.
17. Unsigned review, "Fiction of the Week," *Boston Sunday Post*, 26 November 1952.
18. Unsigned review, "Hardy Like a Farmer," *Miami Herald*, 14 December 1952.
19. Buckler, letter to Pamela Frye, 15 May 1970, BMC.
20. Buckler, letter to Don Cameron, 14 May 1970, BMC.
21. Buckler, "My First Novel," p. 4, BMC.
22. Buckler, letter to McClelland, 12 October 1963, BMC.
23. Dudley Cloud, letter to Buckler, 4 May 1951, BMC.
24. Buckler, letter to Harold Ober Associates, 23 May 1951, BMC.
25. To earn money for university, the young Buckler had worked for several summers at an elegant resort in this area of Connecticut.
26. Letter to Henry Holt and Company Inc., 3 September 1952, BMC.
27. Worksheets on *Nova Scotia: Window on the Sea*, BMC.
28. Letter to Claude Bissell, 8 September 1969, qted in C. Bissell, *Ernest Buckler Remembered*, p. 40.
29. Buckler, letter to John Rackliffe, 31 January 1962, BMC.
30. Ivan Von Auw, Jr, letter to Buckler, 30 October 1959, BMC.
31. Robert Lescher of Henry Holt and Co., Inc., letter to Ivan Von Auw, 4 January 1960, BMC.
32. Ivan Von Auw, Jr, letter to Buckler, 13 April 1961, BMC.
33. Buckler, letter to Ivan Von Auw, Jr, 20 March 1961, BMC.
34. Ivan Von Auw, Jr, letter to Buckler, 24 May 1961, BMC.
35. John Rackliffe, letter to Buckler, 27 September 1961, BMC.

36 Ibid.
37 Bissell, letter to Jack McClelland, 18 March 1963, BMC.
38 Both reviews were quoted by Buckler in a letter to Hiram Haydn, editor of Harcourt, Brace and World, 19 February 1966, BMC.
39 Ibid.
40 Ivan Von Auw Jr, letter to Buckler, 3 October 1963, BMC.
41 Letter from the New American Library of World Literature Inc. to Buckler, 2 September 1964, BMC.
42 Llewellyn Howland, letter to Buckler, 31 August 1965, BMC.
43 Hiram Haydn, letter to Buckler, 16 March 1966, BMC.
44 Jack McClelland, letter to Ivan Von Auw, 11 May 1962, BMC.
45 Buckler, letter to Henry Holt and Co., 3 September 1952, BMC. (The novel referred to in the final sentence is clearly *The Mountain and the Valley*.)
46 "Supplementary Answers to Author's Questionnaire," undated typescript, BMC, p. 2. Although the questionnaire is undated, the references clearly place the date around the 1968 publication of *Ox Bells and Fireflies*.
47 Buckler, letter to Josephine Rogers, 30 June 1967, BMC.
48 Ivan Von Auw Jr, letter to Buckler, 25 April 1967, BMC.
49 Jack McClelland, letter to Buckler, 2 October 1967, BMC.
50 Allen Klots Jr, letter to Josephine Rogers, 16 October 1967, BMC.
51 Julian P. Muller, letter to Ruth Bond of Collins-Knowlton-Wing, 14 September 1967, BMC.
52 Anne MacDermot, letter to Josephine Rogers, 21 August 1967, BMC.
53 Buckler, letter to Josephine Rogers, 30 December 1967, BMC.
54 Angus Cameron, letter to Ernest Buckler, 31 January 1968, BMC.
55 Cameron, letter to Buckler, 1 February 1968, BMC.
56 Ibid.
57 Ibid.
58 Buckler, letter to Cameron, 29 February 1968, BMC.
59 Cameron, letter to Buckler, 3 April 1968, BMC.
60 Buckler, letter to Cameron, 6 April 1968, BMC. In the letter which is typed, Buckler crossed out in pencil the phrase "heighten its penumbra" and replaced it with "also give it nimbus."
61 Kenneth C. Bolton, "Bolton on Books," *Regina Leader-Post*, February 1969.
62 Qtd. in William French, "Ernest Buckler: a Literary Giant Scorned?"
63 John McClelland, letter to Buckler, 31 March 1969, BMC.
64 Mary Williams Ward, "Books," *The Wellington*, 21 December 1968, and Shirley Sullivan, *The Houston Post*, 24 November 1968.
65 James S. Richmond, "Evocative Spirits, Diverse But Choice ," *Savannah News*, 23 February 1969.
66 Qtd. in French, "Ernest Buckler," 13.
67 Among the numerous accounts of the incident is the mention in Buckler's letter to John Orange, 11 February 1970, BMC.
68 Buckler, letter to Angus Cameron, 14 May 1970, BMC.
69 Buckler, letter to Cameron, 10 March 1972, BMC.

70  Buckler, letter to Pamela Frye, 19 January 1971, BMC.
71  Buckler, letter to Hans Weber, 23 September 1970, BMC.
72  Conversation between Buckler and Hans Weber, Tape 2 (reel to reel), recorded 13 December 1968, Ernest Buckler Collection, Public Archives of Nova Scotia.
73  Pamela Frye, letter to Buckler, 10 March 1970, BMC.
74  Buckler, letter to Pamela Frye, 16 March 1970, BMC.
75  Pamela Frye, letter to Buckler, 25 January 1971, BMC.
76  Jo Rogers, letter to Buckler, 3 March 1971, BMC.
77  Jo Rogers, letter to Buckler, 14 March and 27 July 1972, BMC.
78  Claire Booss, letter to Buckler, 29 November 1972, BMC.
79  Buckler, letter to Hans Weber, 1 February 1973, BMC.
80  Robert Chambers, letter to Jack McClelland, 4 September 1974, BMC.
81  Jack McClelland, letter to Buckler, 26 June 1974, BMC.
82  Ibid.
83  Eileen Herbert Jordan, letter to Buckler, 29 October 1947.
84  We have seen how the Atlantic Monthly Press refused to publish *The Mountain and the Valley* because a novel of more than 100,000 words could not be sold for less than $3 (Dudley Cloud, letter to Buckler, 4 May 1951, BMC).
85  It was not until 1991 that the complete text was published by McClelland & Stewart. Cf Schieder, 47-48, and Mitchell, 9.
86  Buckler, letter to W.O. Mitchell, 16 December 1950, BMC.
87  Buckler, letter to Michael Wardell, 9 June 1956, BMC.
88  Buckler, letter to McKenzie Porter, 15 September 1951, BMC.
89  When the Boston-based Atlantic Monthly Press expressed interest in the short story "The Harness," Buckler wrote them a grateful letter explaining the hardships of working on a farm all day, writing at night, and living in a social environment that regarded writing as only "a harmless eccentricity." Buckler, letter to the Atlantic Monthly Press, 31 July 1950, BMC.
90  B.K. Sandwell, letter to Buckler, 11 December 1941, qtd. in Bissell, *Ernest Buckler Remembered*, 56.
91  B.K. Sandwell, letter to Buckler, 27 September 1943, qtd. in Bissell, *Ernest Buckler Remembered*, 56.
92  Buckler, letter to Margaret Laurence, 11 October 1974, BMC.
93  Buckler, letter to McClelland, 11 September 1974, BMC.
94  Buckler, letter to Bissell, 25 April 1975, qtd. in Bissell, *Ernest Buckler Remembered*, 57.
95  W.O. Mitchell, letter to Buckler, 19 July 1948, qtd. in Bissell, *Ernest Buckler Remembered*, 59.
96  Buckler quoting Bissell to Hans Weber, 18 November 1971, BMC.
97  Bissell, letter to Jack McClelland, 22 October 1973, BMC.
98  Buckler, letter to Josephine Rogers, 25 June 1972, BMC.
99  Buckler, letter to McClelland, 19 April 1977, BMC.
100 Buckler, "The Eruption of Albert Wingate," *Atlantic Advocate*, November 1956, 27.
101 Buckler, "The Dragnet," *Whirligig*, October 1938, 26-27; 33; "Casting Suspicion on an Adage," *Saturday Night*, 14 December 1940, p. 41.

102 Buckler, letter to Jack McClelland, 10 July 1974, BMC.
103 "Shakespeare Wrote Bacon or Seen Through Different I's," unedited typescript, BMC.
104 Ibid.
105 Jack McClelland, letter to Buckler, 11 October 1973, BMC.
106 Josephine Rogers, letter to Buckler, 21 July 1972, BMC.
107 Louis MacKendrick, "Pretension punctured in prose and verse," *Windsor Star*, 5 November 1977.
108 Ken Adachi, *Toronto Star*, 28 October 1977.
109 Gerald Huntley, "The Book Shelf," *Brantford Expositor*, 8 October 1977.
110 Dorothy Bishop, "A Humorist and 'Sculptor of Words,'" *Ottawa Journal*, 19 November 1977.
111 Buckler, letter to Max Ferguson, 10 June 1968, BMC.

## Chapter 3

1 This quote from "Nature," the first essay in Emerson's book *Nature* (13), undoubtedly inspired Buckler's synecdochic clash between the squash and the sonnet in "Muse in Overalls," *Whirligig*, 86.
2 David Perkins points out in his Introduction to Shelley that the publication of Shelley's *Poetical Works* with notes in 1839 by Mary Shelley sparked wider interest for the poet, who after 1850 became more popular than the celebrated Byron. Critics as well as writers such as Browning and Tennyson saw in his work a sort of gospel. Yeats classified *Prometheus Unbound* among the "sacred" books of the world. For Matthew Arnold, Shelley was an "angel, beating in the void his luminous wings in vain" (*English Romantic Writers*, 957), and in his search for an aesthetic philosophy, James Joyce's protagonist in *Portrait of the Artist* cites Shelley as an authority (193).
3 Author questionnaire addressed to Crown Publishers, New York, BMC.
4 Supplementary Answers to Author's Questionnaire, undated typescript, p. 3, BMC.
5 Buckler, letter to Harry Brown, 31 January 1969, BMC.
6 "Snow Apples," typescript, pp. 2-3, BMC. Cf also "The Orchard," *Review* 3 (1978) 29. Apart from the emphasis on "selves," which disappears, what is cut in the published version is the weak sentence "It was as if, if I spoke my own name, it would have no response."
7 Among the countless mirror metaphors that Schopenhauer makes, apart from the quotations made above, we find the assertions that "the world as idea is a mirror which reflects the will. In this mirror the will recognises itself in ascending grades of distinctness and completeness," or that "[l]ife, the visible world, the phenomenon, is only the mirror of the will" (176, 177).
8 "The world is my idea" is significantly the opening sentence in his chief work, *The World as Will and Idea*.
9 I use this term, which literary critics and social scientists since Arnold Van Gennep's study *Les Rites de passage* (1908) have used to designate a borderland or threshold, in the more precise sense given it by Linda Hutcheon, who

argues in *Splitting Images* that a liminal zone opens up a new space, a place of paradox, where new things can happen.

10 The concentric patterns of Ellen's rug seem to be the materialization of the Chain of Being, which Emerson evokes in the epigraph to later editions of *Nature* as "A subtle chain of countless rings/The next unto the farthest brings."

11 This preoccupation is clear in the journal entry dated 9 February 1935 which describes the work being completed on the oil painting "Fir Tree and Sky": "I am painting a sky. A big tree butts up into it on one side, and there is a slope in the corner with pines. These are only to give distance. The subject is sky. There is to be one sweeping movement through the whole air, an ascending movement, high and fathomless. The movement must connect with each part, taking great care with the articulation. A movement floating up. It is a study in movement, designed movement—very subtle" (170).

12 Steve McCaffery, *Every Way Oakley*, (Edmonton: privately printed 1978), qtd. in Barbour, "Transformations," 49.

13 Buckler, "Would You Know It If You Fell Over It?" unpublished typescript, BMC.

14 Although Buckler italicizes the noun "feelings," I would like to emphasize for our purposes here the use of the preposition "behind."

15 This piece on Buckler (typescript, p. 1, BMC) was sent on 2 August 1983 to Jack Kapica, book editor at the *Globe and Mail*. After Bissell wrote again on 25 September to say that he had just seen Buckler, who was ill and whose writing days were "over," he insisted that the piece he had written would "stand whatever the fates [had] in store" (BMC). The piece was finally published on the day that Buckler's funeral services were held. Claude Bissell, "His Prose."

16 "Car nommer un objet, c'est s'arracher à ce qu'il a d'individuel et d'unique pour voir en lui le représentant d'une essence ou d'une catégorie," in Merleau-Ponty, *Phénoménologie*, 205.

17 Coleridge claims to have restored the words "intuition" and "intuitive" to their original sense: "'an intuition,' says Hooker, 'that is, a direct and immediate beholding or presentation of an object to the mind through the senses or the imagination.'—Thus geometrical truths are all intuitive, or accompanied by an intuition." *Principles*, 442.

18 "En tant que l'imagination est spontanéité, je l'appelle aussi quelquefois imagination productive, et je la distingue par là de l'imagination reproductive dont la synthèse est uniquement soumise à des lois empiriques, à celles de l'association, et qui par conséquent, ne contribue en rien à l'explication de la possibilité de la connaissance à priori et pour cette raison n'appartient pas à la philosophie transcendentale, mais à la psychologie," Kant, *Critique de la raison pure*, trans. Tremesaygues et Pacaud Alcan, 1927, 151-52.

19 We shall see more closely in the following chapters the ontological and aesthetic parallels with modernist poet Francis Ponge.

20 Whoever has seen a performance by Gould cannot fail to be struck by the trance-like state that he fell into as he played, head back, mouth open, eyes

staring into the face of the absolute. In various interviews and letters, this master of pianistic technique and of electronic technology referred to what he called ecstatic experience, that moment in time when one goes beyond the mechanical means of performance and stands outside of oneself to find a special view of the work of art, Robarts and Guertin.

21 Buckler, "Indian Summer," unpublished typescript, BMC.
22 Buckler, "Indian Summer," BMC.
23 As I have pointed out, Buckler, for whom mathematics was the ultimate metaphor for perfection, and who saw "the whole world as a vast equation in the mind of God that only the supreme artist can hope to solve," (Bissell, 1984), is not wholly in agreement with this stance, and aligns himself more with Husserl, who elaborated from a study of numbers his theory of eidetic reduction, the mental operation that disengages the essence of things. Although Buckler's sequence in the novel is steeped in structural irony, the epiphanic projection back into the past at the end of the novel has David reproducing the moment in his childhood when he realized that mathematics was the unifying code to the universe: "he tried the arithmetic problem that was three grades ahead of him. He tried it several ways, and then he saw that the number he was dividing with this time was the same odd one (139) as the denominator in the fractional part of the answer at the back of the book. *Everything inside his mind was gathered up in one great shiver of unity*. He knew he'd be the most famous mathematician there ever was..." (290, emphasis mine).
24 The proleptic phrase "It was so beautifully simple" is followed by a series of jejune assertions imbued with structural irony that Buckler had already made extensive use of in the early unpublished short stories "No Matter Which People Are There" and "Would You Know It If You Fell Over It?" We read: "When he grew up he'd be the best fiddle player in the whole world. He knew he'd be the most famous mathematician there ever was...suddenly he knew he'd be the most wonderful dancer that people had ever seen" (290-91).
25 Pamela Frye, letter to Buckler, 25 January 1971, BMC.
26 "So What and the Seven Paradoxes," typescript, undated, p. 12, BMC.
27 "By Guess or By God," typescript, undated, p. 3, BMC.
28 Qtd. in C. Bissell, Introduction "Ernest Buckler: Rural Intellectual," typescript of lecture at Carleton University, n.d., BMC.

## Chapter 4

1 "The Orchard," *The Review* No. 3, 1978, p. 29.
2 Emerson points out that Homer's words are as admirable as Agamemnon's victories, and that the poet "does not wait for the hero or sage, but, as they act and think primarily, so he writes primarily what will and must be spoken" (170).
3 Critics have long debated Buckler's ironic intention with respect to his protagonist's writerly ambitions and death. The irony, both structural and dramatic, is inscribed in the text, but those who welcome a sign of authorly

intention to confirm their own interpretation can fall back on Buckler's numerous exegetical declarations. To support Douglas Barbour's argument for the ironic dimension, Alan Young in "A Note" judiciously refers to a letter from Buckler to Dudley Cloud meant as a rebuttal to the negative readers' reports of *The Mountain and the Valley*, in which Buckler wrote: "it was the crucial irony of the whole set-up that the writing business was just another instance of his fatal self-deluding blinding by transports of enthusiasm (as illustrated also in the "best fiddler business," the best soldier, the man who had gone everywhere and done everything...." Buckler insists that David's death was to be "the crowning point of the whole dramatic irony (and of course, the most overt piece of symbolism in the book), that he should finally exhaust himself climbing the mountain, and...achieve one final transport of self-deception: that he would be the greatest writer in the whole world" (15 May 1951). Furthermore, in a letter to his agent Harold Ober asking him to enter the novel in the Harper Prize Novel Contest, Buckler also insists on how at the very moment of David's death, the protagonist "achieves one last transporting self-delusion" which creates "an authentic and crowning dramatic irony" (23 May 1951).

4 For a more complete analysis of this short story, see Dvorak, "Ernest Buckler."
5 Reminiscent of Emily Carr's "one sweeping movement" that "connect[s] with each part," Buckler's texts often seek Unity through movement. In the unpublished short story "The Christmas That Faced Both Ways," that is how the boy narrator captures a moment of transcendence: "the bicycle and I and movement had become a single fluid" (typescript, p. 13, BMC).
6 "My First Novel," BMC.
7 In the supplementary answers to the author's questionnaire upon the publication of *Ox Bells and Fireflies* (undated, BMC), Buckler claims to find outdoor work "not work at all, but the most restorative of holidays from the taxations of the page."
8 "By Sun and Candlelight," typescript, p. 37; holograph drafts of *Whirligig*, BMC, (emphases mine).
9 "No Matter Which People Are There," unpublished typescript, p. 16 (discarded original ending), BMC.
10 An earlier version of my analysis was published under the title "Buckler's Grammatical Universe."
11 Endlaw is the owner's anagram for Walden. It would be enlightening to include Thoreau in the constellation of American influences on Buckler. Readers might wish to consult the article by Clara Thomas.
12 For different forms of sign systems that also communicate ideas, Saussure gives as examples the language of the deaf, which operates with gestural units, military signals, symbolic rites, even protocol or etiquette. See *Cours*, 33-34.
13 As Saussure points out, wholly arbitrary signs accomplish more effectively the mandate of a semiological system, which explains the success of language (*Cours*, 101). But Benveniste argues that not all other signifying systems can

be put on the same plane as language in that to hold a place in a semiological relation they require the mediation of discourse, and actually presuppose language, which produces and interprets them (*Problèmes 2:* 50).

## Chapter 5

1. An admirer of the Roman philosopher Lucretius, Ponge emulated in his own fashion the didactic poem *De rerum natura* expounding on Epicurus's atomist theory of the universe.
2. "Mais au fond ce qui importe, n'est-ce pas de saisir le noeud? Lorsque j'aurai écrit plusieurs pages, en les relisant j'apercevrai l'endroit où se trouve ce noeud, où est l'essentiel, la qualité de l'oiseau." Ponge, *La Rage* 37.
3. Buckler's typed draft with holograph corrections of *Nova Scotia: Window on the Sea*, BMC. This earlier version actually underscores more effectively the place that the most humble objects, even those deemed noxious, hold in the universe. For the later modification obeys a logic of edulcoration—the "weeds" are replaced by "sky": "to put the fieldness back into the fields, the houseness back into the house, the skyness back into the sky, the roadness back into the road, the is-ness back into everything there is" (*Window* 111).
4. Buckler's adherence to Paul Ricoeur's concepts of ontological vehemence or ontological commitment are dealt with in chapter 3 above.
5. In a letter to Buckler dated 2 October 1952, Maureen McManus, in charge of publicity at Henry Holt, quotes part of the review of *The Mountain and the Valley* that appeared in the *Library Journal*'s October issue, praising "a style pregnant with beauty, amazing details and wealth of color, so that the reader lingers over each detail, to savor fully its significance and wonder about its aptness" (BMC).
6. As I have shown in the preceding chapters, Buckler, like Emerson, refuses the claims on truth of institutionalized religions. A sample of the anti-clerical free thinking that can be found in his scribblers appears in the one act play "Excerpts from a Life," which I evoked in chapter 1.
7. As Emerson pedagogically pointed out in the essay "Discipline," "Water is good to drink, coal to burn, wool to wear; but wool cannot be drunk, nor water spun, nor coal eaten" (*Nature* 48-49).
8. These two writers are exemplary of the fact that what was still medieval in England was elsewhere in Europe already the Renaissance, notably in full flower in the fourteenth century in Italy.
9. Request to the Canada Council, 20 October 1965, BMC.
10. Buckler, letter to Angus Cameron, of Alfred A. Knopf, 10 February 1968, BMC.
11. Supplementary answers to author's questionnaire, BMC.
12. Notes for *Fireflies and Freedom* and *The Cruelest Month* respectively, BMC.
13. "Would You Know It If You Fell Over It?" typescript, BMC.
14. This description of migraine is but one of many in Buckler's works. Perhaps the most remarkable, excruciatingly developed one is contained in chapter 19 of *The Cruelest Month*, in which Rex, tempted to put a bullet through his head to end the pains, wonders if they might not "come back like maggots to ache-eat his brain away even after it was dead" (168).

15 Already one of his earliest unpublished short stories, entitled "The Widow," a rather clumsy narration, contains an aching, meditative coda on loss and grief and forgetting, ending with the metaphorical lines: "For the loneliness of contentment is emptier than the loneliness of loss and to have stored one's long Gethsemanes is to have furnished one's empty house. There is tragedy in the death of a stranger whom one cannot miss—there is rust in a long laugh and there is immortality only in an ache" ("The Widow," typescript, BMC).
16 This perhaps explains why a certain number of Buckler's stories which were rejected for publication needed little transformation to be broadcast as radio plays on the CBC.
17 Buckler seems to echo Friedrich Schlegel who saw life itself as *Spiel* or play. His declaration in the *Dialogue of Poetry*, "We demand that events, men, in short the play of life, be taken as play and be represented as such" (89), in turn echoes Friedrich Schiller's affirmation that a human is only wholly human "when he is playing" (80).
18 Buckler, letter to Francis Brown, 16 December 1963, BMC.
19 Buckler, letter to McKenzie Porter, 15 September 1951, BMC.
20 "The Balance," typescript, BMC.
21 "Snows of Christmas, Snows of Spring," typescript, 10, BMC.
22 Buckler, letter to Ivan Von Auw Jr, of Harold Ober Associates, 20 March 1961, BMC.
23 "The Music Goes Round and Round," typescript, BMC.
24 Buckler, "Nettles Into Orchids," *Atlantic Advocate*, August 1961, 70-71.
25 Buckler, "Nettles Into Orchids," typescript manuscript, 6, BMC.
26 The patient, who is a writer, consults the psychiatrist beacause of a secret conviction that he would be a great doctor. In the resolution of the short story, we learn that the psychiatrist, who has dissuaded him from his desire is secretly convinced that he himself would be a great writer.
27 "The Doctor and the Patient," *Atlantic Advocate*, July 1961.
28 Buckler, "The Educated Couple," typescript manuscript, p. 12, BMC.

## Chapter 6

1 Angus Cameron, letter to Buckler, 31 January 1968, BMC.
2 Anne MacDermot, letter to Josephine Rogers, 21 August 1967, BMC.
3 Request to the Canada Council, 20 October 1965, BMC.
4 Buckler, letter to Josephine Rogers, 30 June 1967, BMC.
5 Buckler, "There Was a Devil in the Village," *New York Times Book Review*, 19 August 1962, 5.
6 Buckler, "And to the Artist a Towering Mountain was the Supreme Challenge," *New York Times Book Review*, 28 October 1962, 4.
7 Buckler, "A Case of Departure Sickness," *New York Times Book Review*, 11 September 1966, 4.
8 Arthur Rimbaud, letter to Georges Izambard, in *Oeuvres*, 344.
9 The very design of Ovid's ironically didactic poem *Ars Amatoria* or *The Art of Love* (a treatise with rules and examples for the "nice" conduct of illicit

affairs, such as "Don't visit her on her birthday: it costs too much" [i, 403]) presupposes an audience to whom love is one of the minor peccadilloes of life, and the joke is to treat it seriously.

10  *Pan I: Colline; Pan II: Un de Baumugnes; Pan III: Regain.*

11  This is in direct contrast to the sordid "scalding and scraping" and melting down of the lard in Thomas Hardy's *Jude the Obscure* (1896), which follows an abattoir description shot through with negative terms and ending with an explicit value judgment of the "dismal, sordid, ugly spectacle." Hardy makes it clear that Jude and his wife have taken the life of a living creature: the description ends with "the white snow, stained with the blood of [their] fellow-mortal" (111, 112).

12  Buckler, "Notes on David and Effie (for *The Mountain and the Valley*)," typescript, p. 6, BMC. Buckler's emphasis.

13  Also rooting his study in Panofsky's work, Alan Young too has remarked that the "intelligent pastoralist is aware that Death is one of the inhabitants of Arcadia, and that the mortals who live there may well be ignorant (rather than innocent), coarse and brutish (rather than noble), and frustrated and impatient (rather than calm and contemplative) ("Pastoral" 220).

14  Victor Turner, *The Forest of Symbols: Aspects of Ndembu Ritual*, cited in Claire Harris, "Poets in Limbo" in Neuman and Kamboureli, 125.

15  Buckler, letter to Angus Cameron, 14 May 1970, BMC.

16  In *The Mountain and the Valley*, the reader finds out immediately in a parenthetical narratorial comment the narrative twist to be conveyed by the ending: "(this wouldn't come out till the end—yes, *yes*, that was the way to do it) he was…sick; he'd never been *any*where" (260).

17  "Thanks for Listening," undated typescript, p. 1, BMC. The modification in the fragmented embedded story in *The Mountain and the Valley* is revelatory of an edulcoration process: Buckler has substituted the less graphic "face" for "flesh": "Maybe you didn't recognize me sometimes because a face looks different with the blood on the outside" (*Mountain* 260).

18  In the later fragments of the story embedded into *The Mountain and the Valley*, Buckler cuts the simile short, eliminating the extension ("that dies in the air") that in turn branches out into a second simile, or rather conceit ("quicker than running"). The simple and rather banal result—"I saw all the hearing and the seeing and the touching go out of him like a breeze" (262)—could stem from a desire to simplify his earlier style or could be meant to illustrate that David, the aspiring writer, has not yet honed his craft. The latter hypothesis seems to fit in well with the ironic self-satisfaction of the protagonist at his sole (and seemingly final) draft: "He tore the pages out of the scribbler and read them over. He sat there, with the luxurious feeling of being spent with accomplished expression" (263).

19  Untitled and undated letter, Box 12: Early plays, sketches, poetry, BMC.

20  Buckler, "The End Came Quietly At…," unpaginated, undated typescript, second draft, BMC.

21  "The Snowman," undated typescript, p. 1, BMC.

22 This passage is kept almost in its integral version in *Window on the Sea*, 53.
23 This is another indication that "The Snowman" was written much earlier, for the sixtieth birthday of the original typescript has become the seventieth in *Window on the Sea*—a result, no doubt, of Buckler's taking into account the recent lengthening of life expectancy.

## Chapter 7

1 James Joyce is notably dubbed "the greatest modern connoisseur in the theory and practice of rhetorical forms" by the rhetorician Bernard Dupriez (xix).
2 The device is easily illustrated by the way Morse describes Endlaw in *The Cruelest Month*: "You feel as if you are stepping into the very domicile of peace. And yet—an odd acceleration. As if the natural drift of all things interpersonal develops here with the short-cut pace of shipboard or dream..." (11-12).
3 "Hacking at the Parsnips: *The Mountain and the Valley and the Critics*," typescript, p. 13, BMC. The article went on to be published in *The Bumper Book*. Metcalf. ed., Toronto: ECW, 1986.
4 *Cacophony* in the sense of a too frequent repetition of the same letters or syllables, and *tautophany* as a form of cacophony due to excessive alliteration (the evaluation as to what constitutes "too frequent" and "excessive" belonging, of course, to the zone of the subjective).
5 "Supplementary Answers to Author's Questionnaire," typescript, p. 1, BMC. (Although the typescript is undated, certain references indicate it was written for the publication of *Ox Bells and Fireflies*.)
6 Buckler, letter to Harry Brown, 30 June 1969, BMC.
7 Laurie Ricou has pointed out how, rather than using imagery to make abstractions more concrete, Buckler resorts to imagery made up of "[i]nsubstantial and transitory things" such as "shadows, breeze, breath, smoke, light, cloud, fog, mist, snow, and the colours of grey, white and twilight" (691).
8 "Supplementary Answers to Author's Questionnaire," p. 3, BMC.
9 "Excerpts from a Life," undated typescript, pp. 29-30, BMC.
10 The reader of the opening pages of *Light in August* or *Absalom, Absalom!* encounters the curious adjectives "creakwheeled" and "pinewiney" (*Light* 5), the nouns "hearing-sense" and "unamaze," and, as a good illustration of the device of transference, the verb "would abrupt" (*Absalom* 5-6).
11 Ivan Von Auw Jr of Harold Ober Associates had already criticized Buckler's recurrent recourse to *transference*, objecting to the way he used "thwart" as a noun and "sentinel" and "cuneiform" as transitive verbs, and wondering what "thicked" meant. He warns Buckler that these kinds of sentences cannot be read out loud. (Von Auw to Buckler, 29 October 1959, BMC). In his response dated 30 October, Buckler defends his choices and points out: "How many sentences of Faulkner, James, Bowen et al. could possibly be read out loud?" Although he protests that he is not in their league, we can see which writers he brings up as measuring sticks.
12 John Rackliffe, letter to Buckler, 27 September 1961, BMC.

13 Buckler, letter to John Rackliffe, 14 October 1961, BMC.
14 Quoted by Angus Cameron in a letter to Buckler, 1 February 1968, BMC.
15 Ibid.
16 Buckler, letter to Angus Cameron, 10 February 1968, BMC.
17 Ricou judiciously notes the "hypnotic magic of the lists" and their "trance-like effect" (688), arguing that "[m]agic is as important as meaning" (687).
18 Dupriez disregards this subcategory of enumeration, but it is deemed a useful distinction by Morier and Robrieux, and is most useful in analyzing Buckler's textual strategies.
19 "By Guess or By God," undated typescript, p. 3, BMC. This philosophical essay is discussed in chapter 3.
20 Buckler, letter to Angus Cameron, 10 February 1968, BMC.
21 For his second novel, Buckler deliberately sought out curious effects. In a scribbler in which he jotted down notes for *The Cruelest Month*, he reminded himself in a section entitled "Devices" to "couple odd adjectives with unlikely nouns: eg. 'affable trees" (Buckler's scribbler, holograph notes for *The Cruelest Month*, BMC).
22 "Thanks for Listening," undated typescript, p. 1, BMC.

## Conclusion

1 Letter from Margaret Atwood to Claude Bissell, 9 August 1982, BMC, and tribute from Margaret Laurence to Buckler sent to Bissell and included in Bissell's "Ernest Buckler Presentation—Mountainlea Lodge, Bridgetown," 11 September 1982, BMC; emphases mine.

# Works Cited

### Archival Sources

Ernest Buckler Collection. Public Archives of Nova Scotia.
Ernest Buckler Manuscript Collection. Thomas Fisher Rare Book Library, University of Toronto, (hereafter BMC).

### Works by Buckler

"The Accident." *Chatelaine* May 1960: 38-39ff.
"Against the Terror, the Spirit of Sisyphus." Rev. of *The Golden Notebook*, by Doris Lessing. *New York Times Book Review* 1 July 1962: 4.
"Alden Nowlan: An Appreciation." Rev. of *Miracle at Indian River*, by Alden Nowlan. *Fiddlehead* 81 (August-October 1969): 46-47.
"Always Old Ending." *Trinity University Review* June-July 1934: 246-49.
"Always Old Ending." *Trinity University Review* October 1934: 16-21.
"And to the Artist a Towering Mountain Was the Supreme Challenge." Rev. of *The Hidden Mountain*, by Gabrielle Roy. *New York Times Book Review* 28 October 1962: 4, 18.

"Another Christmas." 1949. Rpt. in *The Rebellion of Young David* 29-34.
"Another Man." *Ox Bells and Fireflies* 251-63.
"Anti-Paintings of What Wasn't There." Rev. of *White Figure, White Ground,* by Hugh Hood. *New York Times Book Review* 1 November 1964: 5.
"Anything Can Happen at Christmas." *Chatelaine* December 1957: 66-68.
"The Balance." Original manuscript in BMC.
"The Bars and the Bridge." Original manuscript in BMC.
"The Best Place to Be." *Graduate* (University of Toronto) 1977: 32-33.
"Blame It on the Snow." *Star Weekly* (*Toronto Daily Star*) 21 December 1957: 22-23.
"Buckler, Like the Brook." The Sound and the Fury column. *Esquire* November 1934: 10.
"By Any Other Name—A Holiday Romance." *Atlantic Advocate* June 1957: 48, 79-80.
"By Guess or By God." Original manuscript in BMC.
"A Case of Departure Sickness." Rev. of *The Road Past Altamont,* by Gabrielle Roy. *New York Times Book Review* 11 September 1966: 4-5.
"Casting Suspicion on an Adage." *Saturday Night* 14 December 1940: 41.
"Choose Your Partners." *Atlantic Advocate* August 1962: 62-64ff.
"The Christmas That Faced Both Ways." Original manuscript in BMC.
"Cleft Rock, with Spring." 1957. Rpt. in *Rebellion of Young David* 126-32.
"The Clumsy One." 1950. Rpt. in *Rebellion of Young David* 53-64.
"The Concerto." *Atlantic Advocate* February 1958: 65-67.
*The Cruelest Month.* 1963. Toronto: McClelland and Stewart, 1977.
"The Darkest Time." *Canadian Home Journal* May 1958: 31, 64-66.
"David Comes Home." *Collier's* 4 November 1944: 24.
"Dictionaries of the Blood: Bless You, Kate Reid." *Globe and Mail* 23 October 1976: 6.
"The Doctor and the Patient." *Atlantic Advocate* July 1961: 65-66.
"Down to the Sea to Prove Himself a Man among Men." Rev. of *Ultramarine,* by Malcolm Lowry. *New York Times Book Review* 14 October 1962, 5.
"The Dragnet." *Whirligig* October 1938: 26-27, 33.
"The Dream and the Triumph." 1956. Rpt. in *Rebellion of Young David* 67-81.
"The Echoing Hills." *Atlantic Advocate* May 1958: 75-77.
"The Educated Couple." *Weekend Picture Magazine* 7 June 1952: 18ff.
"The End Came Quietly At." Original manuscript in BMC.
"The Eruption of Albert Wingate." *Atlantic Advocate* November 1956: 27-29. Rewritten as "Marriage, TV Style" in *Whirligig* 93-98.
"Excerpts from a Life." Original manuscript in BMC.
"The Finest Tree." *Saturday Night* 1 January 1944: 17.
"The First Born Son." 1941. Rpt. in *Rebellion of Young David* 18-27.

"The Fish Crisis Needs a Minister Who Knows Skate from Flounder." *Saturday Night,* 27 September 1947: 20-21.
"Forever Ernest." *Esquire* October 1948: 139.
"Four on a Match." Original manuscript in BMC.
"Glance in the Mirror." 1957. Rpt. in *Rebellion of Young David* 133-8.
"Goin' Crazy, Pal? Just Try on a Sanity Quiz to See if Any of Your Marbles Are Chipped and Ready to Fall Apart." *Globe and Mail* 19 November 1977: 10.
"Goodbye, Prince." *Canadian Home Journal* December 1954: 6-7ff.
"Guilt on the Lily." *Atlantic Advocate* August 1963: 61-69.
"The Harness." G. Rimanelli and R. Ruberto, eds. *Modern Canadian Stories.* Toronto: Ryerson, 1966: 137-47.
"A House, a House, My Kingdom for a House." *Globe and Mail* 1 January 1977: 10.
"How to Write an Artistic Novel." *Saturday Night* 3 May 1941: 25.
"Humble Pie." *Advertiser* May 1960: 7, 25-26.
"In Case of Emergency." *Atlantic Advocate* August 1957: 69-72.
"Last Delivery before Christmas." 1953. Rpt. in *Rebellion of Young David* 97-113.
"Last Stop before Paradise." *Maclean's* 1 June 1949: 22-23, 49.
"The Late Bus." *Advertiser* May 1964: 1, 19-20.
"The Line Fence." 1955. Rpt. in *Advertiser* May 1963: 13, 22-23.
"A Little Flag for Mother." *Farm Journal* May 1963: 69-70.
"Long, Long after School." 1959. Rpt. in *Rebellion of Young David* 122-26.
"A Man." *Ox Bells and Fireflies* 234-40.
"Man and Snowman." *Window on the Sea* 49-57, 60-63.
*The Mountain and the Valley.* 1952. New Canadian Library Intro. Claude Bissell. McClelland and Stewart, 1985.
"The Mouths of Babes." *Atlantic Monthly* July 1954: 90-91.
"The Music Goes Round and Round." Original manuscript in BMC.
"My First Novel." Original manuscript in BMC.
"Nettles into Orchids." *Atlantic Advocate* August 1961, 70-71.
"Night Journey of the Soul." Rev. of *A State of Siege,* by Janet Frame. *New York Times Book Review* 11 September 1966: 5.
"No Matter Which People Are There." Original manuscript in BMC.
"Non!" *Atlantic Advocate* September 1961: 59-60, 62-63.
"No Second Cup." *Trinity University Review* December 1933: 74-76.
"Notable Spring Fiction." Rev. of *They Wanted to Live,* by Cecil Roberts. *New York Herald Tribune Books* 2 April 1939: 16.
*Nova Scotia: Window on the Sea.* Photographs by Hans Weber. Toronto: McClelland and Stewart, 1973.
"Novels Distinctive in Substance and in Integrity." Rev. of *The Keepers of the House,* by Shirley Ann Grau, and *Next Door,* by Johanna Moosdorf. *Los Angeles Times Calendar* 12 April 1964: 22.

"On the Third Day." *Saturday Night* 24 April 1943: 33.

"One Quiet Afternoon." *Esquire* 1940: 70, 199-201.

"One Sweet Day." *Atlantic Advocate* January 1962: 49-51, 53.

"The Orchard." *Review* 3 (1978): 28-29.

"An Ornithological Travelogue." Rev. of *The Peregrine Falcon*, by Robert Murphy. *Los Angeles Times Calendar* 2 February 1964: 20.

"Our Shield and Our Buckler." The Sound and the Fury column. *Esquire* June 1938: 194.

*Ox Bells and Fireflies: A Memoir*. 1968. New Canadian Library Intro. Alan Young. Toronto: McClelland and Stewart, 1974.

"Penny in the Dust." 1948. Rpt. in *Rebellion of Young David* 3-7.

"People Survive Somehow." Rev. of *An Unofficial Rose*, by Iris Murdoch. *New York Times Book Review* 20 May 1962: 5.

"A Present for Miss Merriam." 1952. Rpt. in *Rebellion of Young David* 81-97.

"The Quarrel." 1949. Rpt. in *Rebellion of Young David* 41-53.

"The Rebellion of Young David." 1951. Rpt. in *Rebellion of Young David* 7-17.

*The Rebellion of Young David and Other Stories*. Ed. Robert Chambers. Toronto: McClelland and Stewart, 1975.

"School and Me." *Maclean's* 1 September 1949: 30ff.

"Seven Crows a Secret." *Reader's Digest* February 1969: 64-68.

"A Sign of the Times." *National Home Monthly* July-August 1950: 11, 32.

"Snow Apples." Original manuscript in BMC.

"The Snowman." Original manuscript in BMC.

"Snows of Christmas." Original manuscript in BMC.

"Snows of Spring." Original manuscript in BMC.

"A Sort of Sign." *Ladies' Home Journal* May 1945: 36-37.

"So What and the Seven Paradoxes." Original manuscript in BMC.

"The Stars Were Bright." Original manuscript in BMC.

"Summer Stock." *Weekend Picture Magazine* 9 February 1952: 30-31.

"Surely the Queen Merits Conservation No Less Than Does the Dolphin." *Globe and Mail* 26 February 1977: 6.

"Thanks for Listening." Original manuscript in BMC.

"There Was a Devil in the Village." Rev. of *The Rain Bird*, by Sara Lidman. *New York Times Book Review* 19 August 1962: 5.

"This Side of Paradise, Nova Scotia (Home Is Where You Hang Your Heart)." Preface by Gregory Cook. *Maclean's* September 1973: 40-41.

"To Sleep, Perchance? No, It's Never Lights Out for the True Insomniac." *Globe and Mail* 23 July 1977: 10.

"Unto the Hills." Original manuscript in BMC.

"What I Like or Don't Like on Canadian TV." *Liberty* July 1957: 11.

"What Is *Coronet*?" *Coronet* 25 January 1938: 191-94.

*Whirligig*. Intro. Claude Bissell. Toronto: McClelland and Stewart, 1977.
"The Widow." Original manuscript in BMC.
"The Wild Goose." 1959. Rpt. in *Rebellion of Young David* 115-21.
"A Woman." *Ox Bells and Fireflies* 243-50.
"Would You Know It if You Fell Over It?" Original manuscript in BMC.
"Yes, Joseph, There Was a Woman; She Said Her Name Was Mary." *Saturday Night* 8 December 1945: 48-49.
"You Could Go Anywhere Now." 1946. Rpt. in *Rebellion of Young David* 34-38.
"You Wouldn't Believe Me." *Saturday Night* 6 December 1947: 48-49.

### Works about Buckler

Adachi, Ken. Rev. of *Whirligig*. *Toronto Star* 28 October 1977.
Barbour, Douglas. "David Canaan: The Failing Heart." *Studies in Canadian Literature* 1 (winter 1976).
_____. "Transformations of (the Language of) the Ordinary: Innovation in Recent Canadian Poetry." *Essays on Canadian Writing* 37 (spring 1989).
Beresford-Howe, Constance. "More Canadian Classics!" *Montrealer* 36:1 (January 1962).
Bickerstaff, Isaac. "Running Blue Noses." Rev. of *Nova Scotia: Window on the Sea*. *Books in Canada* July-September 1973.
Bishop, Dorothy. "A Humorist and 'Sculptor of Words.'" *Ottawa Journal* 19 November 1977.
Bissell, Claude. "Ernest Buckler: His Prose Reads Like Poetry." *Globe and Mail* 7 March 1984.
_____. *Ernest Buckler Remembered*. Toronto: U of Toronto P, 1989.
_____. Introduction to *The Mountain and the Valley*. Toronto: McClelland and Stewart, 1961.
_____. Introduction to *Whirligig*. Toronto: McClelland and Stewart, 1977.
_____. "Letters in Canada, 1952: Fiction." *University of Toronto Quarterly* 22 (April 1953).
_____. "A Masterly Return to Innocence and Wonder." Rev. of *Ox Bells and Fireflies*. *Globe and Mail* 9 November 1968.
_____. Rev. of *The Cruelest Month*. *Dalhousie Review* 43 (winter 1963-64).
Blake, Fran. "Dignity, Truth in Buckler Tale." *Boston Herald* 25 December 1952.
Bolton, Kenneth. "Bolton on Books." *Regina Leader-Post* January 1969.
Butler, John. "The Short Stories of Ernest Buckler: The Family Stories." MA thesis, BMC, n.d.
Cameron, Don. "A Conversation with an Irritated Oyster." *Conversations with Canadian Novelists*. Vol. 1. Toronto: Macmillan, 1973.
_____. "Don Cameron Interviews Ernest Buckler." *Quill and Quire* July 1972.
_____. "Letter from Halifax." *Canadian Literature* 40 (spring 1969).

Chambers, Robert D. "Notes on Regionalism in Modern Canadian Fiction." *Journal of Canadian Studies* 11:2 (spring 1976).

———. *Sinclair Ross and Ernest Buckler*. Toronto: Copp Clark; Montreal: McGill-Queen's UP, 1975.

Chapman, Marilyn. "The Progress of David's Imagination." *Studies in Canadian Literature* 3 (summer 1978).

Cook, Gregory M., ed. *Ernest Buckler*. Critical Views on Canadian Writers, no. 7. Toronto: McGraw-Hill Ryerson, 1972.

———. Preface to Buckler, "This Side of Paradise, Nova Scotia (Home Is Where You Hang Your Heart)." *Maclean's* September 1973.

Deacon, William Arthur. "Every Little Movement Has a Meaning All Its Own." *Globe and Mail* 29 November 1952.

———. "In Buckler Country, Neighbour Is a Holy Word." Rev. of *Nova Scotia: Window on the Sea*. *Globe and Mail* 2 June 1973.

Dooley, D.J. "*The Mountain and the Valley*: The Uncreated Word." *Moral Vision in the Canadian Novel*, by D.J. Dooley. Toronto: Clarke, Irwin, 1979.

Dvorak, Marta. "Buckler's Grammatical Universe." *Commonwealth* 20: 1 (autumn 1997).

———. "Ernest Buckler: Canada's 'Another-time-and-space-builder.'" *The Short Story in Postcolonial Literatures in English*. Ed. Jean-Pierre Durix, André Vial. Atlanta, GA: Rodopi, 2001.

———. "Ernest Buckler's *The Mountain and the Valley*: 'Broader than Space, Faster Than Time'." *Etudes canadiennes / Canadian Studies* 36 (1994).

Fee, Margery. "Ernest Buckler's *The Mountain and the Valley* and That Dangerous Supplement." *Ariel* 19:1 (January 1988).

"Fiction of the Week." *Boston Sunday Post* 26 November 1952.

French, William. "Buckler in an Unbuttoned Mood Plays a Little Ragtime, but Not Always Well." *Globe and Mail* 15 October 1977.

———."Ernest Buckler: A Literary Giant Scorned?" *Globe and Mail* 24 June 1972.

———. "Just Blame Enthusiasm for Flaws." Rev. of *The Rebellion of Young David and Other Stories*. *Globe and Mail* 19 April 1975.

"Hardy Like a Farmer." *Miami Herald* 14 December 1952.

Huntley, Gerald. "The Book Shelf." *Brantford Expositor* 8 October 1977.

James, Irene. "Under One Roof." *Montreal Gazette* 5 October 1963.

Kertzer, J.M. "The Past Recaptured." *Canadian Literature* 65 (summer 1975).

Lockhead, Douglas. Rev. of *Nova Scotia: Window on the Sea*. *University of Toronto Quarterly* 44 (summer 1975).

MacDonald, Bruce F. "Word-Shapes, Time and the Theme of Isolation in *The Mountain and the Valley*." *Studies in Canadian Literature* 1 (summer 1976).

MacKendrick, Louis. "Pretension Punctured in Prose and Verse." *Windsor Star* 5 November 1977.

Mathews, Lawrence. "Hacking at the Parsnips: *The Mountain and the Valley* and the Critics." *The Bumper Book*. Ed. John Metcalf. Toronto: ECW, 1986.

Merlin, Milton. "Translation to Another 'Time' Told." *Los Angeles Times* 16 November 1952.

Noonan, Gerald. "Egoism and Style in *The Mountain and the Valley*." *The Marco Polo Papers One: Atlantic Provinces Literature Colloquium*. Ed. Kenneth MacKinnon. Saint John, NB: Atlantic Canada Institute, 1977.

Orange, John. "Buckler Revisited." *Journal of Canadian Fiction* 16 (1976).

———. "Ernest Buckler." *Profiles in Canadian Literature*. Vol. 2. Ed. Jeffrey M. Heath. Toronto: Dundurn, 1980.

———. "Ernest Buckler, an Annotated Bibliography." *The Annotated Bibliography of Canada's Major Authors*. Vol. 3. Ed. Robert Lecker and Jack David. Toronto: ECW, 1981.

———. *Ernest Buckler and His Works*. Toronto: ECW, 1995.

Pacey, Desmond. "Earthy Idyll." *Canadian Literature* 40 (spring 1969).

Pell, Barbara. *A Portrait of the Artist: Ernest Buckler's* The Mountain and the Valley. Canadian Fiction Studies 31. Toronto: ECW, 1995.

Percy, H.R. "Sleight of Heart." *Books in Canada* May 1984.

Porterfield, Waldon. "A Fresh Warm Pastoral Novel of Nova Scotia." Rev. of *The Mountain and the Valley*. *Milwaukee Journal* 14 December 1952.

Primrose, Tom. "Western Round-up." *Albertan* January 1969.

Ramsey, David A. "First Novel of Brilliant New Writer." Rev. of *The Mountain and the Valley*. *Charlotte News* 22 November 1952.

Richmond, James S. "Evocative Spirits, Diverse but Choice." *Savannah News* 23 February 1969.

Ricou, Laurence. "David Canaan and Buckler's Style in *The Mountain and the Valley*." *Dalhousie Review* 57:4 (winter 1977-78).

Sartwell, Frank Jr. "*The Mountain and the Valley*, by Ernest Buckler." *Washington Star* 9 November 1952.

Schieder, Rupert. "A Classic Restored." *Books in Canada* 21:1 (February 1992).

Seaman, Andrew Thompson. "Fiction in Atlantic Canada." *Canadian Literature* 68-9 (spring-summer 1976).

Spettigue, D.O. Rev. of *The Rebellion of Young David and Other Stories*. *Queen's Quarterly* 82 (winter 1975).

———. "The Way It Was." *Canadian Literature* 32 (spring 1967).

Sullivan, Shirley. Rev. of *Ox Bells and Fireflies*. *Houston Post* 24 November 1968.

Tallman, Warren. "Wolf in the Snow, Part One: Four Windows onto Landscapes." *Canadian Literature* 5 (summer 1960).

Van Rys, John. "Diminishing Voice in Buckler's *The Mountain and the Valley*." *Studies in Canadian Literature* 20:1 (1995).
Wainwright, Andrew. "Fern Hill Revisited: Isolation and Death in *The Mountain and the Valley*." *Studies in Canadian Literature* 7:1 (1982).
Ward, Mary Williams. "Books." *Kansas Wellington* 21 December 1968.
Weir, Lorraine. "Country Cuteness." *Canadian Literature* 80 (spring 1979).
Wellejus, Ed. "The Bookshelf." *Times* (Erie, PA) 9 February 1969.
Westwater, Sister A.M. "Teufelsdrock Is Alive and Doing Well in Nova Scotia: Carlylean Strains in *The Mountain and the Valley*." *Dalhousie Review* 56 (summer 1976).
Willmott, Glenn. "On Postcolonial Modernism: The Invisible City in *The Mountain and the Valley*." *American Review of Canadian Studies* 25 (1995).
Young, Alan. *Ernest Buckler*. Toronto: McClelland and Stewart, 1976.
_____. "The Genesis of Ernest Buckler's *The Mountain and the Valley*." *Journal of Canadian Fiction* 16 (1976).
_____. Introduction to *The Cruelest Month*. Toronto: McClelland and Stewart, 1977.
_____. Introduction to *Ox Bells and Fireflies: A Memoir*. Toronto: McClelland and Stewart, 1974.
_____. "A Note on Douglas Barbour's 'David Canaan: The Failing Heart' (*SCL*, Winter 1976)." *Studies in Canadian Literature* 1 (summer 1976).
_____. "The Pastoral Vision of Ernest Buckler in *The Mountain and the Valley*." *Dalhousie Review* 53:2 (summer 1973).
_____. Rev. of *The Rebellion of Young David and Other Stories*. *Dalhousie Review* 55 (summer 1975).
_____. Rev. of *Whirligig*. *Fiddlehead* 116 (winter 1978).

**General Works**

Aristotle. *La Poétique*. Trans. Roselyne Dupont-Roc, Jean Lallot. Paris: Seuil, 1980.
Aubenque, Pierre. *Le Problème de l'être chez Aristote. Essai sur la problématique aristotélicienne*. Paris: Presses Universitaires de France, 1962.
Bakhtin, Mikhail. *Rabelais and His World*. Trans. Hélène Iswolsky. Bloomington: Indiana UP, 1984.
Barfield, Owen. *Poetic Diction: A Study in Meaning*. New York: McGraw-Hill, 1964.
Barthes, Roland. "Introduction à l'analyse des récits." *Communications* 8 (1966).
Benveniste, Emile. *Problèmes de linguistique générale*. Vol. 1. Paris: Gallimard, 1966.
_____. *Problèmes de linguistique générale*. Vol. 2. Paris: Gallimard, 1974.
Bergson, Henri. *Oeuvres*. Intro. H. Gouhier. Paris: Edition de centenaire, 1959.
Berkeley, George. *An Essay towards a New Theory of Vision*. 1705. *The Complete Works*. Ed. M.R. Ayers. London: Everyman, 1975.

Blake, William. *Auguries of Innocence: Blake's Poetry and Designs*. Ed. M.L. Johnson and J.E. Grant. New York: Norton, 1979.
Butler, Samuel. *Satires and Miscellaneous Poetry and Prose*. Ed. R. Lamar. Cambridge, 1929.
Caillois, Roger. *Les Jeux et les homme, le masque et le vertige*. Paris: Gallimard, 1958.
Cameron, Don. "W.O. Mitchell: Sea Caves and Creative Powers." *Conversations with Canadian Novelists*. Vol. 1. Toronto: Macmillan, 1973.
Carr, Emily. *Hundreds and Thousand: The Journals of Emily Carr*. Toronto: Clarke, Irwin, 1966.
Chaucer, Geoffrey. *The Canterbury Tales: The Works of Geoffrey Chaucer*. Ed. F.N. Robinson. 2nd ed. Boston: Houghton Mifflin, 1957.
Coleridge, Samuel Taylor. *Biographia Literaria*. In *English Romantic Writers*. Ed. David Perkins. New York: Harcourt, Brace and World, 1967.
_____. *On the Principles of Genial Criticism*. In *English Romantic Writers*. Ed. David Perkins. New York: Harcourt, Brace and World, 1967.
Derrida, Jacques. "Mythologie blanche (la métaphore dans le texte philosophique)." *Poétique* 5 (1971).
Ducrot, Oswald, and Tzvetan Todorov. *Dictionnaire encyclopédique des sciences du langage*. Paris: Seuil, 1972.
Dupriez, Bernard. *A Dictionary of Literary Devices: Gradus, A-Z*. Trans. and adapted by Albert W. Halsall. Toronto: U of Toronto P, 1991.
Eco, Umberto. *Art et Beauté dans l'esthétique médiévale*. Trans. Maurice Javion. Paris: Bernard Grasset, 1997.
Emerson, Ralph Waldo. *The Complete Essays and Other Writings of Ralph Waldo Emerson*. Ed. Brooks Atkinson. New York: Random House, Modern Library, 1940.
_____. *Essays and English Traits by R.W. Emerson*. Ed. Charles W. Eliot LLD. New York: P.F. Collier and Son, Harvard Classics, 1909.
_____. *Nature*. 1836. Ed. Kenneth Walter Cameron. New York: Scholars' Facsimiles and Reprints, 1940.
Faulkner, William. *Absalom, Absalom!* 1936. Harmondsworth, UK: Penguin, 1987.
_____. *Light in August*. 1932. New York: Modern Library, 1968.
Fontanier, Pierre. 1821, 1827. *Les Figures du discours*. Paris: Flammarion, 1977.
Forster, E.M. 1907, 1922. *The Longest Journey*. New York: Vintage Books, Random House, 1962.
Foucault, Michel. *Les Mots et les choses*. Paris: Gallimard, 1966.
Francastel, Pierre. *Histoire de la peinture*. Paris: Editions Gonthier, 1983.
Frye, Northrop. *Anatomy of Criticism*. Princeton, NJ: Princeton UP, 1957.
_____. Conclusion. *The Literary History of Canada: Canadian Literature in English*. Ed. Carl F. Klinck. Toronto: U of Toronto P, 1965.

Gingrich, Arnold. *Nothing but People: The Early Days at Esquire—A Personal History, 1928-1958.* New York: Crown Publishers, 1971.
Giono, Jean. *Pan III: Regain.* 1930. Paris: Bernard Grasset, 1989.
Greimas, A.J. *Sémiotique.* Paris: Hachette, 1979.
Hamon, Philippe. "Texte et Idéologie." *Poétique* 49. Paris: Seuil, 1982.
Hardy, Thomas. *Jude the Obscure.* 1896. Middlesex: Penguin, 1979.
Hester, Marcus B. The Meaning of Poetic Metaphor. LaHaye: Mouton, 1967.
Huizinga, Johan. *Homo ludens, Essai sur la fonction sociale du jeu.* 1938. Trans. C. Seresia. Paris: Gallimard, 1951.
Hunter, Lynette, ed. *Toward a Definition of Topos.* London: Macmillan, 1991.
Hutcheon, Linda. *Splitting Images: Contemporary Canadian Ironies.* Toronto: Oxford UP, 1991.
Jakobson, Roman. *Essais de linguistique générale.* Paris: Editions de Minuit, 1963.
James, Henry. *The Portrait of a Lady.* 1881, 1908. Harmondsworth, UK: Penguin, 1977.
Jones, D.G. "Myth, Frye, and Canadian Writers." *Canadian Literature* 55 (winter 1973).
Joyce, James. *A Portrait of the Artist as a Young Man.* 1916. London: Granada, 1977.
_____. *Ulysses.* 1922. New York: Vintage, 1986.
Kant, Immanuel. *Critique de la raison pure.* Trans. Tremesaygues and Pacaud. Paris: Alcan, 1927.
Keats, John. *John Keats: The Complete Poems.* Ed. John Barnard. 2nd ed. Middlesex: Penguin, 1977.
Keefer, Janice Kulyk. *Under Eastern Eyes: A Critical Reading of Maritime Fiction.* Toronto: U of Toronto P, 1987.
Latham, Sheila, and David Latham, eds. *Magic Lies: The Art of W.O. Mitchell.* Toronto: U of Toronto P, 1997.
Le Guern, Michel. *Sémantique de la métaphore et de la métonymie.* Paris: Larousse, 1973.
Lévi-Strauss, Claude. *Anthropologie structurale.* Paris: Editions Plon, 1958.
_____. *Le Cru et le Cuit.* Paris: Plon, 1964.
_____. *L'Origine des manières de table.* Paris: Plon, 1968.
Lewis, C.S. *The Discarded Image.* Cambridge: Cambridge UP, 1964.
MacMechan, Archibald. *Headwaters of Canadian Literature.* Toronto: McClelland and Stewart, 1974.
Mansfield, Katherine. *Selected Stories.* Ed. D.M. Davin. Oxford: Oxford UP, 1981.
Mellon, Peter. *The Group of Seven.* Toronto: McClelland and Stewart, 1970.
Mellor, Anne K. *English Romantic Irony.* Cambridge: Harvard UP, 1980.
Merleau-Ponty, Maurice. *L'Oeil et l'esprit.* Paris: Gallimard, 1964.
_____. *Phénoménologie de la perception.* Paris: Gallimard, 1945.

———. *Le Visible et l'invisible*. Paris: Gallimard, 1964.
Mitchell, Barbara. "The Long and the Short of It: Two Versions of *Who Has Seen the Wind*." *Canadian Literature* 119 (winter 1988).
More, Sir Thomas. *Utopia*. 1516. Ed. J. Churton Collins. Oxford: Clarendon, 1964.
Morier, Henri. *Dictionnaire de poétique et de rhétorique*. Paris: Presses Universitaires de France, 1961.
Moss, John. *Patterns of Isolation in English-Canadian Fiction*. Toronto: McClelland and Stewart, 1974.
Neuman, Shirley, and Smaro Kamboureli, eds., *A Mazing Space: Writing Canadian/Women Writing*. Edmonton: Longspoon/NeWest, 1986.
Panofsky, Erwin. *L'Oeuvre d'art et ses significations, essais sur les arts visuels*. Trans. Marthe and Bernard Teyssèdre. Paris: Gallimard, 1969.
Perkins, David, ed. *English Romantic Writers*. New York: Harcourt, Brace and World, 1967.
Ponge, Francis. *Le parti pris des choses, Douze petits écrits, Proêmes*. 1942, 1926. 1948. Paris: nrf/Gallimard, 1967.
———. *La rage de l'expression*. 1952. Paris: nrf/Gallimard, 1976.
Ricoeur, Paul. *La Métaphore vive*. Paris: Seuil, 1975.
Rimbaud, Arthur. *Œuvres*. Ed. Suzanne Bernard. Paris: Garnier, 1960.
Robarts, John, and Ghyslaine Guertin eds., *Glenn Gould: Selected Letters*. Toronto: Oxford UP, 1992.
Robrieux, Jean-Jacques. *Eléments de Rhétorique et d'Argumentation*. Paris: Dunod, 1993.
Rousseau, Jean-Jacques. *Essai sur l'origine des langues*. Paris: Copedith, 1970.
Saussure, Ferdinand de. *Cours de linguistique générale*. Paris: Payot, 1969.
Schiller, Friedrich. *On the Aesthetic Education of Man in a Series of Letters*. Trans. Elizabeth M. Wilkinson and L.A. Willoughby. Oxford: Clarendon, 1967.
Schlegel, Friedrich. *Dialogue on Poetry and Literary Aphorisms*. Trans. Ernst Behler and Roman Struc. University Park: Pennsylvania State UP, 1968.
Schopenhauer, Arthur. *The World as Will and Idea*. 1818. Ed. David Berman. Trans. Jill Berman. London: J.M. Dent, Everyman, 1997.
Shelley, Percy Bysshe. *A Defence of Poetry*. In *English Romantic Writers*. Ed. David Perkins. New York: Harcourt, Brace and World, 1967.
———. *Prometheus Unbound*. In *English Romantic Writers*. Ed. David Perkins. New York: Harcourt, Brace and World, 1967.
Sollers, Philippe. "Ponge en abîme." *Le Monde des Livres* 1:5 (February 1999).
Staines, David, ed. *The Canadian Imagination: Dimensions of a Literary Culture*. Cambridge: Harvard UP, 1977.
Thomas, Clara. "New England Romanticism and Canadian Fiction." *Journal of Canadian Fiction* 2:4 (fall 1973).

Urban, W.M. *Language and Reality*. New York: Macmillan, 1961.
Van Gunsteren, Julia. *Katherine Mansfield and Literary Impressionism*. Amsterdam: Rodopi, 1990.
Waterston, Elizabeth. *Survey: A Short History of Canadian Literature*. Toronto: Methuen, 1973.
Weschler, Lawrence. "The Art World." *New Yorker* 9 July 1984.
Wordsworth, William. *The Prelude*. In *English Romantic Writers*. Ed. David Perkins. New York: Harcourt, Brace and World. 1967.

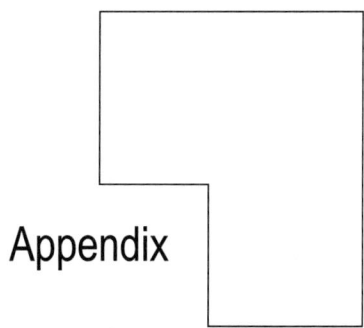

# Appendix

### Full-Length Published Works

*The Mountain and the Valley*. New York: Henry Holt, 1952. Toronto: Clarke, Irwin, 1952. New Canadian Library edition, intro. Claude Bissell. Toronto: McClelland and Stewart, 1961.

*The Cruelest Month*. Toronto: McClelland and Stewart, 1963.

*Ox Bells and Fireflies: A Memoir*. New York: Knopf, 1968. Drawings by Walter Richards. Toronto: McClelland and Stewart, 1968. New Canadian Library edition, intro. Alan Young. Toronto: McClelland and Stewart, 1974.

*Nova Scotia: Window on the Sea*. Photographs by Hans Weber. Toronto: McClelland and Stewart, 1973.

*The Rebellion of Young David and Other Stories*. Ed. Robert Chambers. Toronto: McClelland and Stewart, 1975.

*Whirligig*. Intro. Claude Bissell. Toronto: McClelland and Stewart, 1977.

## Published Short Stories

"No Second Cup." *Trinity University Review* December 1933: 74-76.

"Always Old Ending." *Trinity University Review* June-July 1934: 246-49.

"Always Old Ending." *Trinity University Review* October 1934: 16-21.

"One Quiet Afternoon." *Esquire* 1940: 70, 199-201. Echoes in *The Mountain and the Valley*.

"The First Born Son." *Esquire* July 1941: 54-55, 114. Rpt. in D. Pacey ed., *A Book of Canadian Stories*. Toronto: Ryerson, 1950. 192-203; M.O. Nowlan, ed. *The Maritime Experience*. Toronto: Macmillan, 1975. 33-44; A. Hale and S. Brooks, eds. *Nearly an Island: A Nova Scotia Anthology*. St. John's: Breakwater, 1979. 139-50; *Rebellion of Young David* 18-27. Embryo of chapter 24 of *The Mountain and the Valley*.

"Another Christmas." *Saturday Night* 20 December 1941: 25. Rpt. in *The Rebellion of Young David* 29-34.

"On the Third Day." *Saturday Night* 24 April 1943: 33.

"The Finest Tree." *Saturday Night* 1 January 1944: 17.

"David Comes Home." *Collier's* 4 November 1944: 24.

"A Sort of Sign." *Ladies' Home Journal* May 1945: 36-37.

"Yes, Joseph, There Was a Woman; She Said Her Name Was Mary." *Saturday Night* 8 December 1945: 48-49.

"You Could Go Anywhere Now." *Saturday Night* 2 November 1946: 28-29. Rpt. in *Rebellion of Young David* 34-38.

"You Wouldn't Believe Me." *Saturday Night* 6 December 1947: 48-49.

"Penny in the Dust." *Maclean's* 15 December 1948: 18-19, 44. Rpt. in C.F. Klinck and R.E. Watters, eds. *Canadian Anthology*. 2nd ed. Toronto: Gage, 1966. 324-28; G.H. Green and G. Sylvestre, eds. *A Century of Canadian Literature*. Toronto: Ryerson, 1967. 318-22; J. Hodgins and W.H. New, eds. *Voice and Vision*. Toronto: McClelland and Stewart, 1972. 77-80; D. Daymond and L. Monkman, eds. *Literature in Canada*. Vol. 2. Toronto: Gage, 1978. 172-77; *Rebellion of Young David* 3-7.

"The Quarrel." *Maclean's* 15 January 1949: 5-6ff. Winner of *Maclean's* fiction contest. Rpt. in L.F. Hannon, ed. *Maclean's Canada*. Toronto: McClelland and Stewart, 1960. 146-51; *Rebellion of Young David* 41-53.

"Another Christmas." *Saturday Night* 20 December 1949: 25. Rpt. in *Chatelaine* July 1959: 65-68; *Rebellion of Young David* 29-34.

"A Sign of the Times." *National Home Monthly* July-August 1950: 11, 32.

"The Clumsy One." *Maclean's*, 1 August 1950: 8-9, 28-30. Rpt. in *Rebellion of Young David* 53-64.

"The Rebellion of Young David." *Maclean's* 15 November 1951: 22-23, 36-38. Rpt. in *Rebellion of Young David* 7-17. Echoes and a fragment in *The Cruelest Month*. Published under original title "The Harness" in G. Rimanelli and

R. Ruberto, eds. *Modern Canadian Stories*. Toronto: Ryerson, 1966: 137-47.
"Summer Stock." *Weekend Picture Magazine* 9 February 1952: 30-31.
"The Educated Couple." *Weekend Picture Magazine* 7 June 1952: 18ff.
"A Present for Miss Merriam." *Chatelaine* December 1952: 8, 36-39. Rpt. in *Rebellion of Young David* 81-97.
"Last Delivery before Christmas." *Chatelaine* December 1953: 11ff. Rpt. in *Rebellion of Young David* 97-113.
"Goodbye, Prince." *Canadian Home Journal* December 1954: 6-7ff.
"The Line Fence." *Country Gentleman (Better Farming)* February 1955: 32-33ff. Rpt. in *Advertiser* May 1963: 13, 22-23.
"The Dream and the Triumph." *Chatelaine* November 1956: 13ff. Original title "Mary Redmond." Rpt. in *Rebellion of Young David* 67-81.
"The Eruption of Albert Wingate." *Atlantic Advocate* November 1956: 27-29. Rewritten as "Marriage, TV Style" in *Whirligig* 93-98.
"Glance in the Mirror." *Atlantic Advocate* January 1957: 53, 55. Rpt. in *Rebellion of Young David* 133-38.
"By Any Other Name—A Holiday Romance." *Atlantic Advocate* June 1957: 48, 79-80.
"In Case of Emergency." *Atlantic Advocate* August 1957: 69-72.
"Cleft Rock, with Spring." *Atlantic Advocate* October 1957: 89-91. Rpt. in *Rebellion of Young David* 126-32.
"Anything Can Happen at Christmas." *Chatelaine* December 1957: 66-68.
"Blame It on the Snow." *Star Weekly (Toronto Daily Star)* 21 December 1957: 22-23.
"The Concerto." *Atlantic Advocate* February 1958: 65-67.
"The Bars and the Bridge." *Family Herald* 24 April 1958: 17. Reappears, slightly modified, as "A Man" in *Ox Bells and Fireflies* 234-42.
"The Darkest Time." *Canadian Home Journal* May 1958: 31, 64-66.
"The Echoing Hills." *Atlantic Advocate* May 1958: 75-77.
"The Wild Goose." *Atlantic Advocate* October 1959: 91-95. Rpt. in B.L. McEvoy, ed. *Stories from Across Canada*. Philadelphia: Lippincott, 1967. 70-78; *Rebellion of Young David* 115-21.
"Long, Long after School." *Atlantic Advocate* November 1959: 42-44. Rpt. in *Rebellion of Young David* 122-26.
"The Accident." *Chatelaine* May 1960: 38-9ff.
"Humble Pie." *Advertiser* May 1960: 7, 25-26.
"The Doctor and the Patient." *Atlantic Advocate* July 1961: 65-66.
"Nettles into Orchids." *Atlantic Advocate* August 1961: 70-71.
"One Sweet Day." *Atlantic Advocate* January 1962: 49-51, 53.
"Choose Your Partners." *Atlantic Advocate* August 1962: 62-64ff.

"A Little Flag for Mother." *Farm Journal* May 1963: 69-70. Reappears as "A Woman" in *Ox Bells and Fireflies* 243-50.
"Guilt on the Lily." *Atlantic Advocate* August 1963: 61-69.
"The Late Bus." *Advertiser* May 1964: 1, 19-20.
"The Harness." See "The Rebellion of Young David" (1951).
"A Man." *Ox Bells and Fireflies* 234-40.
"Another Man." *Ox Bells and Fireflies* 251-63.
"A Woman." *Ox Bells and Fireflies* 243-50.
"Seven Crows a Secret." *Reader's Digest* February 1969: 64-68. Chapter 1 of *Ox Bells and Fireflies*.
"Man and Snowman." *Window on the Sea* 49-57, 60-63.
"The Orchard." *Review* 3 (1978): 28-29.

## Unpublished Short Stories

"Appointment with Harry." The narrative encounter of a woman and an escaped Nazi.
"The Balance." Early variant of "Another Man" in *Ox Bells and Fireflies*. The story of an outsider: a man who never married.
"By Accident, or A Pocketful of Rue." Early variant of "The Accident" (1960) and the unpublished story "The Christmas Order." A boy who thinks he caused his father's death resents his new stepfather, but finally arrives at a reconciliation.
"By Any Other Name." Early variant of "By Any Other Name—A Holiday Romance" (1957). A man masquerades as his namesake bestselling author to see how it feels to be a celebrity; he falls in love with a woman who sees through him before he confesses.
"By Guess or By God." Original manuscript in BMC.
"A Catch in It." A vulnerable young singer searches for his place in the world; a reflection on artists and on what sets them apart.
"Children." A slight variant of the unpublished stories "The Day before Never" and "Hares and Hounds." Embryo of the David-Effie relationship in *The Mountain and the Valley*. The Mark and Laura episode cut out of *Ox Bells and Fireflies*.
"The Choice." A poor young man, who leaves the farm to go to medical school, is torn between two young women whom he loves equally but who are from different social backgrounds.
"The Christmas Order." Early variant of "Last Delivery before Christmas" (1953) and the unpublished story "By Accident."
"The Christmas That Faced Both Ways." A fuller version of the unpublished story "Goodbye, Prince." A boy yearns for a colt, but is given a bicycle.
"The Dark Valley." War and love between a pilot and an ambulance driver.

"The Day before Never." A variant of the unpublished stories "Children" and "Hares and Hounds."

"The End Came Quietly At...." Embryo of "Man and Snowman" (1973) and the unpublished story "The Snowman." A blend of essay, poetry, and fiction exploring old age and death.

"Five on a Match." An early variant of the radio plays "Huldah's Hunch" and *Four on a Match*. A romantic game of musical chairs with two roommates and twin sisters.

"God Was Good." A melodrama with war as a backdrop.

"Goodbye, Prince." A simpler, narrative version of the more contemplative unpublished story "The Christmas That Faced Both Ways."

"Hares and Hounds." A variant of the unpublished story "Children," with a more explicit, phallic ending.

"In Times Like These." An early variant of "A Sign of the Times" (1950).

"Indian Summer." Embryo of chapter 38 of *The Mountain and the Valley*.

"The Invisible Trapeze." Published as "The Darkest Time" (1958).

"It Was Always Like That." Cain and Abel resonances in a story of a young man who kills his brother.

"It Was That Tune." A writer estranged from his wife, in the manner of "Glance in the Mirror" (1957); further resonances with the unpublished story "The Choice."

"The Locket." Echoes found in *The Mountain and the Valley* (the story of Ellen and the sailor initiated in chapter 3).

"Mary Redmond." Original title of "The Dream and the Triumph" (1956). A homage to his mother, in the manner of the fictional essay "A Little Flag for Mother," which reappears as "A Woman" in *Ox Bells and Fireflies*.

"Miss Merriam's Christmas." Early variant of "A Present for Miss Merriam" (1952).

"The Music Goes Round and Round." The allegorical story of a broken cog that almost wrecks a car's transmission.

"No Future There." Early variant of "The First Born Son" (1941).

"No Matter Which People Are There." Embryo of David in *The Mountain and the Valley*.

"One Sweet Day." A variant of the unpublished story "The Music Goes Round and Round."

"Plot for Hollywood, or Three's a Crowd." Embryo of the radio play *Three's a Crowd*.

"Possibly Sentimental." Love, war, and a *quid pro quo*.

"Puss in the Corner." Accepted by *Esquire* but never used. Later appears as "Education at Mimi's" in *Whirligig*.

"Return Trip to Christmas." Early variant of "Anything Can Happen at Christmas" (1957).

"The Ring." Early, almost identical variant of "Cleft Rock with Spring" (1957).

"A Singing in the House." Original, more complete version of "Yes Joseph, There Was a Woman; She Said Her Name Was Mary" (1945).

"Short Circuit: A Satirical Revue." A round moving from one character to another throughout the globe, through the device of a $2 bill exchanging hands.

"Should Auld Acquaintance." A man meets an old flame; a reflection on choice and commitment.

"Snow Apples." Early variant of "The Orchard" (1978).

"The Snowman." Early variant of "Man and Snowman" (1973).

"Snows of Christmas, Snows of Spring." Early variant of "Another Man" in *Ox Bells and Fireflies*.

"A Sort of Sign." A young woman, a sailor, and the sea.

"The Stars Were Bright." Early, more complete variant of "Yes Joseph, There Was a Woman; She Said Her Name Was Mary" (1945). Adapted into the play *A Singing in the House*.

"Strange Compass." A young couple gets lost as the winter night falls.

"The Tablecloth." A variant of "The Quarrel" (1949).

"Thanks for Listening." Reappears in chapter 37 of *The Mountain and the Valley*.

"Three Little Words." A detective story set in Alaska.

"The Tie." Rejected story to be turned into a play.

"The Trains Go By." Reworked into chapter 39 of *The Mountain and the Valley*.

"The Trap." A variant of the unpublished story "No Matter Which People Are There."

"Unto the Hills." A young Frenchman during the Resistance is shot by German soldiers.

"Why Must It Sound Like a Cowboy Song?" The death of a friend told in the second-person singular.

"The Widow." A lyrical meditation on grief.

"Would You Know It If You Fell Over It?" The story of a gifted child; an ontological reflection on transcendence and failure.

"You Could Always Go Home Now." Early variant of "You Could Go Anywhere Now" (1946).

"You Wouldn't Believe Me." A separating couple reconciles.

### Radio and Television Drama

"Excerpts from a Life." A one-act play in four scenes, originally a first attempt at a novel.

"Choose Your Partners, or Artist's Life." A 30-minute television comedy.

*Four on a Match: A Radio Comedy.* (30mm) Broadcast by the CBC, *The Canadian Theatre of the Air*, 10 July 1941.

"Huldah's Hunch, or Love in a Quadrilateral." A radio comedy based on the unpublished short story "Five on a Match."

*Three's A Crowd.* Broadcast by the CBC, *The Canadian Theatre of the Air*, 29 May 1942.

*The Stars Were Bright.* (30mm) CBC version, December 1954; radio play, CBC-Halifax, December 1959. Adapted from Buckler's unpublished short story of the same name.

*A Singing in the House.* Produced by John Hobday, Halifax Theatre, 22 December 1960. Final title of the adaptation of the unpublished story "The Stars Were Bright."

*By Sun and Candlelight.* (30 mm) Broadcast on CBC-Halifax, *Play of the Month*, June 1961, for the 100th anniversary of Elizabeth Barrett Browning's death.

*The Accident.* Produced by John Hobday, Halifax Theatre, 31 August 1961. Adapted from Buckler's short story of the same name (1960).

*Doctor and the Patient.* CBC, *Stories with John Drainie*, 29 May 1964. A 15-minute adaptation of the short story "The Doctor and the Patient" (1961).

*Christmas in Canada: Cantata for Chorus and Narrator.* Music by Keith Bissell, text by Ernest Buckler. World premiere December 1967, Halifax, commissioned by the PEI Centennial Commission, and performed by the Confederation Centre Choir. Broadcast on the CBC, 25 December 1968 (produced by Michael Cass-Beggs, narrated by Paul Hecht).

### Selected Essays (published)

"Buckler, Like the Brook." The Sound and the Fury column. *Esquire* November 1934: 10.

"Think Dos Passos Opaque." The Sound and the Fury column. *Esquire* March 1937: 178.

"What Is *Coronet?*" *Coronet* 25 January 1938: 191-94. Winner of *Coronet*'s essay contest.

"Our Shield and Our Buckler." The Sound and the Fury column. *Esquire* June 1938: 194.

"The Dragnet." *Whirligig* October 1938: 26-27, 33.

"Notable Spring Fiction." Rev. of *They Wanted to Live,* by Cecil Roberts. *New York Herald Tribune Books* 2 April 1939: 16.

"How to Write an Artistic Novel." *Saturday Night* 3 May 1941: 25.

"The Fish Crisis Needs a Minister Who Knows Skate from Flounder." *Saturday Night* 27 September 1947: 20-21.

"Forever Ernest." *Esquire* October 1948: 139.

"Last Stop before Paradise." *Maclean's* 1 June 1949: 22-23, 49.

"School and Me." *Maclean's* 1 September 1949: 30, 44, 47-48.

"My First Novel." Undated typescript read by Buckler on CBC radio, 1953. The text was subsequently included in Gregory Cook, ed. *Ernest Buckler.* Toronto: McGraw-Hill Ryerson, 1972, along with "My Second Book" and "My Third Book."

"The Mouths of Babes." *Atlantic Monthly* July 1954: 90-91.

"What I Like or Don't Like on Canadian TV." *Liberty* July 1957: 11.

"Non!" *Atlantic Advocate* September 1961: 59-60, 62-63.

"People Survive Somehow." Rev. of *An Unofficial Rose*, by Iris Murdoch. *New York Times Book Review* 20 May 1962: 5.

"Against the Terror, the Spirit of Sisyphus." Rev. of *The Golden Notebook*, by Doris Lessing. *New York Times Book Review* 1 July 1962: 4.

"There Was a Devil in the Village." Rev. of *The Rain Bird*, by Sara Lidman. *New York Times Book Review* 19 August 1962: 5.

"Down to the Sea to Prove Himself a Man among Men." Rev. of *Ultramarine*, by Malcolm Lowry. *New York Times Book Review* 14 October 1962: 5.

"And to the Artist a Towering Mountain Was the Supreme Challenge." Rev. of *The Hidden Mountain*, by Gabrielle Roy. *New York Times Book Review* 28 October 1962: 4, 18.

"An Ornithological Travelogue." Rev. of *The Peregrine Falcon*, by Robert Murphy. *Los Angeles Times Calendar* 2 February 1964: 20.

"Novels Distinctive in Substance and in Integrity." Rev. of *The Keepers of the House*, by Shirley Ann Grau, and *Next Door*, by Johanna Moosdorf. *Los Angeles Times Calendar* 12 April 1964: 22.

"Anti-Paintings of What Wasn't There." Rev. of *White Figure, White Ground*, by Hugh Hood. *New York Times Book Review* 1 November 1964: 5.

"A Case of Departure Sickness." Rev. of *The Road Past Altamont*, by Gabrielle Roy. *New York Times Book Review* 11 September 1966: 4-5.

"Night Journey of the Soul." Rev. of *A State of Siege*, by Janet Frame. *New York Times Book Review* 11 September 1966: 5.

"Alden Nowlan: An Appreciation." Rev. of *Miracle at Indian River*, by Alden Nowlan. *Fiddlehead* 81 (August-October 1969): 46-47.

"This Side of Paradise, Nova Scotia (Home Is Where You Hang Your Heart)." Preface by Gregory Cook. *Maclean's* September 1973: 40-41. Rpt. as "My Places of Peace" in *Reader's Digest* October 1977: 12, 14.

"Dictionaries of the Blood: Bless You, Kate Reid." *Globe and Mail* 23 October 1976: 6.

"The Best Place to Be." University of Toronto *Graduate* Sesquicentennial Issue 4, no. 3 (March 1977): 32-33. Rpt. in *Whirligig* 10-13.

"A House, a House, My Kingdom for a House." *Globe and Mail* 1 January 1977: 10.

"Surely the Queen Merits Conservation No Less Than Does the Dolphin." *Globe and Mail* 26 February 1977: 6.

"To Sleep, Perchance? No, It's Never Lights Out for the True Insomniac." *Globe and Mail* 23 July 1977: 10.

"Goin' Crazy, Pal? Just Try on a Sanity Quiz to See if Any of Your Marbles Are Chipped and Ready to Fall Apart." *Globe and Mail* 19 November 1977: 10.

### Selected Essays (unpublished, undated)

"Ah, the Tears Behind Art: Satire." On writer's block.

"By Guess or By God." Humorous metaphysical speculation.

"The Hearse-and-Bogey-Doctor: Satire." A fuller variant of "My Dream Doctor." Resonances with the short story "The Doctor and the Patient" (1961).

"My Dream Doctor." On how to write a chapter in one's sleep.

"A Patient Looks at His Doctor, or Let's Ventilate the Lamaserie." Metafiction.

"The Proof of the Pudding, or I'll Take Yoga." Ironic essay criticizing Dale Carnegie's *Winning Friends and Influencing People*.

"So What and the Seven Paradoxes." Ontological/epistemological speculation.

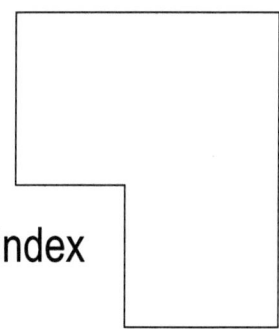

# Index

**Note:** Bold face indicates most significant discussions of topics.

*Advertiser, The*, 53
Aeschylus, 26
agents. *See* correspondence
allegory. *See* rhetoric
*American, The*, 54
anacoluthon. *See* rhetoric
analogy, 9, 11, 73, 77, 102, 113, 117, 119, 125, 130, 197, 201, 204, 207, 216, 219; sense analogy, 103, 195, **211**, 214-15, 219-22, 224, 227, 230, 232. *See also* synaesthesia
anamnesis, 76, 206-209, 211-14
anaphora. *See* rhetoric
Anderson, Sherwood, 191, 198
antithesis. *See* rhetoric
antonomasia. *See* rhetoric/metonymy
aporia, 7, 8, 11, 67, 83, 91, 111, **113**, 116, 150, 182, 185, 194, **195-97**, 210, **215**, 230-31

apperception, 22, 91, 72-74, 95, **96-100**, 214-15, 232
Aquinas, Thomas, 9, 128-29, 132, 219-21
Arcadia, 10, 15, 76, 79, 128, **153-89**, 246
Aristotle, 9, 22, 127-28, 131-33, 146, 152, 215, 219, 230
Arnold, Matthew, 240
*Atlantic Advocate*, 19, 52-53, 57
Atwood, Margaret, 2, 27-28, 229. *See also* correspondence
Augustine, Saint, 132, 135-36
Austen, Jane, 26
Austin, John, 88

Bakhtin, Mikhail, 180-82
Barbour, Douglas, 241, 243
Barfield, Owen, 215
baroque, 173, 224, 231
baroquism. *See* rhetoric

271

Barrett, Elizabeth, 19
Barthes, Roland, 66-67
Baudelaire, Charles, 86
Beckett, Samuel, 36
Bellow, Saul, 193
Benveniste, Émile, 7, 102-103, 107, 113, **119**, 243-44
Beresford-Howe, Constance, 1-2
Bergson, Henri, 83
Berkeley, George, 77, 96
Bissell, Claude, 2, 5, 6, 16, 23, 26, 27, 35, 44, 56, 58, 83-84, 105, 130, 192-94, 232, 233, 236, 241, 242. *See also* correspondence
Bissell, Keith, 43
Blake, William, 69-70. *See also* Romanticism
*Books in Canada*, 24
Braque, Georges, 80
Browning, Robert, 19, 240
Bruce, Charles, 16, 192
Butler, John, 52
Butler, Samuel, 154-55
Byron, George Gorden, Lord, 68, 240. *See also* Romanticism

cacology. *See* metaphor
cacophony. *See* rhetoric
Caillois, Roger, 144
Callaghan, Morley, 19
Cameron, Don, 5, 40-41, 55-56, 64-65, 70, 74, 114-15. *See also* correspondence
Camus, Albert, 27
Canada Council, 24, 132, 154
Capote, Truman, 41
Carlyle, Thomas, 63, 71, 235. *See also* Romanticism
Carman, Bliss, 3, 21, 88
carnival, 180-82
Carr, Emily, 80, 88, 109-10, 241, 243
Cather, Willa, 33
CBC, 2, 17-19, 24, 55, 234, 236, 245
Chambers, Robert, 20, 50, 54, 151, 234. *See also* correspondence
*Chatelaine*, 19, 53, 54, 55, 142
Cicero, 135

circle. *See* metaphor
Clark, Joan, 15
classicism/neoclassicism, 10, 137-38, **173**, 175, 181, 189
Coleridge, Samuel Taylor, 7, 63, **70**, 86, 95, 108. *See also* Romanticism
*Collier's*, 19, 54
concatenation. *See* rhetoric
conceit. *See* rhetoric
Cook, Gregory, 49, 234, 236. *See also* correspondence
Cornell, Katherine, 21
*Coronet*, 23
**correspondence,** 146
  **publishers**
    Atlantic Monthly Press, 235-36
      Dudley Cloud, 31, 239, 243
    Clarkson Potter
      Claire Booss, 57
    Dodd, Mead, 41
    Harcourt, Brace & World
      Hiram Haydn, 38
      Julian Muller, 41
    Henry Holt & Co., 34-36, 40
      William Buckley, 30
      Jonathan Leff, 30
      Robert Lescher
      Maureen McManus, 32, 244
      William Raney, 24-26, 32
    Knopf
      Angus Cameron, **42-43**, 46, 55-56, 133, 154, 179, 200, 211
    Little, Brown
      Llewelyn Howland, 38
    McClelland and Stewart,
      Pamela Frye, 27, 33, 46-48, 96
      **Jack McClelland,** 34, **37-39**, 41, 44, 50, 54, 57-59
      Diane Mew, 26, 27
      John Rackliffe, 4-5, 36, 37, 199
    New American Library of World Literature, 38
    Scribner's
      Anne MacDermot, **41-42**
  **magazine publishers/editors,**
    *Esquire*, 23

Arnold Gingrich, 26
Manuel Komroff, 28
*Macleans*
　W.O. Mitchell, 52-53, 55
*Saturday Night*
　B.K. Sandwell, **52, 54**
**agents**
　Collins-Knowlton-Wing
　　(Little, Brown)
　　Josephine Rogers, 24, 41,
　　　49, 57, 59, 154, 155
　Harold Ober Assoc., 34, 243
　Ivan Von Auw Jr., 31, 36,
　　38-39, 41, 147, 247
**critics/writers/artists**
　Margaret Atwood, 27, 28, 229,
　　233
　Claude Bissell, 32, 37-38, 55,
　　56
　Harry Brown, 5, 45, 70, 194,
　　234
　Don Cameron, 26, 27, 34
　Robert Chambers, 50
　Max Ferguson, 28, 60
　Margaret Laurence, 27, 54, 23
　W.O. Mitchell. *See*
　　correspondence/magazine
　　editors
　Alden Nowlan, 235
　John Orange, 45
　Sinclair Ross, 32
　Hans Weber, 46, 49, 56
*Country Gentleman*, 54
Coward, Noël, 17, 22, 35
***Cruelest Month, The***, 4-5, 16, 22,
　26-27, 34-39, 55, 78, 89-93,
　113-26, 139-40, 147-48, 150,
　199-202, 204, 209, 211-14,
　222-26, 234, 244, 248
cubism, 80, 82
cummings, e.e., 19

Dante, Alighieri, 26
Davies, Robertson, 17, 28
Day, Frank Parker, 15
Deacon, William Arthur, 32
Derrida, Jacques, 11

Dickens, Charles, 25
*docere*, 231
Dooley, D.J., 192-93
Dos Passos, John, 19, 28
drama, 17-19, 23-24, 55, 115, 245
Dreiser, Theodore, 19, 28
Dryden, John, 27
Dupriez, Bernard, 196, 203, 215,
　247-48

Eco, Umberto, 82-83, 131-32
*eidos*, 83, 126-27, 221
*eikos*, 7, 66, 73, 83
Eliot, T.S., 4, 26-27, 191, 225. *See also*
　modernism
Emerson, Ralph Waldo, 3-4, 7, 8, 10,
　25, 63-67, 70-73, 75, 78-79, 83-
　84, 87, 88-90, 94, 103, 106, 110,
　113-16, 130-31, 133-36, 145, 163,
　194, 222, 230, 234, 236,
　240-42, 244. *See also* transcen-
　dentalism
empiricism, **22, 64**
epanalepsis. *See* rhetoric/repetition
epiphany, 8, 76, 83, 88-92, 108-109,
　125, 140, 204, 206-207, 212,
　223-24, 242
epistemology, 8, 9, 22-23, **77, 99-100**,
　139, 196, 214, 218
*Esquire*, 19, 23, 28, 99
*Et in Arcadia ego*, 10, 154, **173-82**,
　185
Evans, Edith, 21
*Everywoman*, 54
*exemplum*, 140-42, 176, 203-204, 232
ex-stasis/ecstasy, 8, 84, **88-96**,
　168-69, 206-207, 212-14, 241-42

*Family Circle*, 54
*Family Herald*, 42
*Farm Journal*, 42, 54
Faulkner, William, 4-5, 24, 26, 27,
　30, 32, 40, 82, 96, 191-193, 198,
　211, **212-14**, 226, 247. *See also*
　modernism
Fitzgerald, Scott, 19, 27, 30
Fontanier, Pierre, 226

form, 79, **82-88**, 105, 127, 131-32, 136, 154, 165, 167-71, 209
Forster, E.M., 6, 25, **65**, 81-82, 90, 191, 194
Foucault, Michel, 9, 99-100, **102-103**, 105
Four Horsemen, The, 82
Fragonard, J.H., 181
Francastel, Pierre, 80-81
Frege, Gottlob, 7, 9
French, William, 5, 20, 33, 44, 53, 59, 232, 234, 236
Frost, Robert, 44
Frye, Northrop, 9, 16, 21, **132**, 157

Garbary, Evelyn, 24
Gingrich, Arnold, 27. *See also* correspondence
Giono, Jean, 27, 155, 165
*Good Housekeeping*, 52, 54
Gould, Glenn, 88, 241-42
Guercino, 173, 181
Grey, Zane, 25
grotesque, 10, 97, 173, 175, **178-82**, 224, 226
grotesque realism, 180
Group of Seven, 1-3, 88, 233

Hamon, Philippe, 157
Hardy, Thomas, 26, 246
Harris, Claire, 246
Harris, Lauren, 3. *See also* The Group of Seven
Hegel, G.W. Friedrich, 11, 22, 102, 221
Hemingway, Ernest, 5-6, 19, 26, 28, 33, 182, 191. *See also* modernism
Hockney, David, 80
Hodgins, Jack, 15
Howse, Ernest, 21
Huizinga, Johan, 144
Hume, David, 96
Hunter, Lynette, 153
Husserl, Edmund, 79, 83, 242
Hutcheon, Linda, 141, 240-41
hypallage. *See* rhetoric

idealism, 8, 9, 11, 22-23, 25, 64-68, 72, 75-77, 94-96, 126, 149-50, 165-71, 221, 230, 232. *See also* neoplatonism
impressionism/post-impressionism, 82, 109, 201
Innis, Harold, 21
irony, 52-53, 146-47
   cosmic, 142
   dramatic, 147-48, 242-43
   structural, 95-96, 110, 140-42, 242-43
   self-deprecating, 141

Jakobson, Roman, 203, 216
James, Henry, 5-6, **26, 143**, 247, 211
Joyce, James, 4, 9, 32, 96, 128-29, 131-32, 191, 194, 197-98, 219, 240, 247. *See also* modernism
Juvenal, 154

Kafka, Franz, 27
Kant, Immanuel, 8, 22, 73, 85-86, 95, 96, 108, 241
Keats, John, 132
Keefer, Janice Kulyk, 16, 116, 122, 153, 174, 192-93, 215-16, 225-26, 234
King, Thomas, 15
Kingston, George Frederick, 21
Komroff, Manuel, 28

*langue/parole*, 7, 102-103, 105, 112, 198, 218, **221-23**, 231. *See also* metalanguage
Latham, David and Sheila, 235
Laurence, Margaret, 2, 16, 27, 50, 229, 233. *See also* correspondence
Lawrence, D.H., 33
Le Guern, Michel, 211, 216-18, 224
Leacock, Stephen, 16, 28, 59, 60
Lévi-Strauss, Claude, 157-58
Lewis, C.S., 9, 132, 138
Lewis, Sinclair, 19
Lidman, Sara, 155

# Index

liminality, 73-77, 159-60, 172, 217, 230, 240-241
Locke, John, 136
*logos*, 9, **103,** 107, 119, 125, 222, 230

MacDonald, Wilson, 21
*Maclean's*, 19, 20, 49, 54-55, 116
MacLennan, Hugh, 15, 21
MacMechan, Archibald, 4, 21
Mailer, Norman, 26
Mansfield, Katherine, 68, 73, 81-82, 191, 201
Maritime literature, 10, 15-16, 116, 153, 192, 234
Massey Commission, 4
materialism, 8, 11, 25, **64-67,** 76-77, 230. *See also* objectivity
Mathews, Lawrence, 193
McCaffery, Steve, 82
**McClelland, Jack,** 41, 46, 50. *See also* publishers/McClelland and Stewart, and correspondence
McLuhan, Marshall, 9, **132**
Mellon, Peter, 233
Melville, Herman, 155, 193
*memento mori*, 10, 173, 177-78, 182, 185
memory, 30, 51, 80, 85-86, 104, 108-109, **157,** 165-66, 170-71, 173-75, 203, 211-14, 232
Merleau-Ponty, 8, 10, **73-81,** 85, 93, 99-100, 219, 222, 241
metalanguage, 6-7, 9, **98-100,** 103, 105-106, 112-13, 116-17, **119, 122-26,** 134, 151, **216,** 218-19
**metaphor,** 5, 11, 25, 66, 89, 90-91, 97, 113-15, 124, 163, 192, 196, 197, 199, 205, 209-11, **214-25,** 232
 cacology, 96-97, 224-25
 circle, 73, 78-79, 84, 221, 241
 dynamic, 217
 extended metaphor (*See also* rhetoric/allegory), 125, 137, 218, 223-24
 ingestion, 158-59, 164-65, 169-70, 212-13

light, 95, 109-10, 221
mathematics, 83-84, 132, 242
metalinguistic, 103, 105, 119, 223
*métaphore vive*, 4, 10, 221-22
mirror, 72, 73, 78, 214, 240
objective correlative, 205
ocular, 72-73, 78, 213-14, 221, 224-25, 227
proportional, 123, 223-24, 226
stock/dead, 222, 224-25
metaphysical style, 44, 193, 225-26. *See also* rhetoric/conceit
metaphysics, 8, 22, 66, 76-79, 96, 99, 104, 111-12, 125, **131-32,** 194, 197, 208, 209, 221, 223, 230. *See also* ontology
metonymy. *See* rhetoric
*mimesis*, 172
mirror. *See* metaphor
Mitchell, W.O., 15, 16, 19, 20, 38, 52-53, 55, 64-65, 70, 74, 156, 235. *See also* correspondence
modernism, **4-6,** 9, 11, 16, 68, 74, 79, **81-82,** 85, 92, 85, 128, 131, 191, 194, 201, 211, 225, 229, 230, 232
More, Thomas, 155
Morier, Henri, 203, 248
***Mountain and the Valley, The,*** 1-2, 5-6, 7-8, 16, 17, 20, 22, 24-25, 30-34, 37, 44-45, 50, 64-67, 74, 78, 81-83, 88-89, 90, 92, 94, 95, 97-99, 107-108, 110-11, 129-31, 133-34, 136-37, 140, 153, 155, **161-70,** 176, 182, 192-96, 198-99, 203, **204-209,** 211-12, 218-21, 234-35, 239, 243, 246
*movere*, 216, 231
*muthos*, 172, 216
myth, 10, 15, 102, 154-72. *See also* Arcadia

Nash, Ogden, 57
Nathan, George John, 28
*National Home Monthly*, 51
neologisms, 198-99. *See also* rhetoric/neologistic compounds

neoplatonism, 7, 9, 64-65, 67-68, 127, 162, 194, 229-30. *See also* Idealism
nichol, bp, 82
*noema*, 203-204
Noonan, Gerald, 192
*noumenon*, 95, 153, 195, 218, 230
*Nova Scotia: Window on the Sea*, 9, 10, 16, 35, **46-51**, 69, 96, 112, 154, 179, **184-89**, 226-27, 234, 244, 247
Nowlan, Alden, 16, 232, 235. *See also* correspondence

objectivity, 64-67. *See also* materialism
O'Neill, Eugene, 27
ontology, 6, 9, **63-100**, 127-29, 131, 153, 194-95, 197, 199, 204, 206, 208, 210, 211, 216, 218, 221, 230-32, 241, 244
  ontological vehemence, **87-88**, 128, 204, 211
Orange, John, 234, 235. *See also* correspondence
*ousia*, 219
Ovid, 152, 154, 164, 245-46
***Ox Bells and Fireflies*** 2, 10, 16, 39-46, 51, 53, 55, 66-67, 69-76, 78-79, 84-87, 103-106, 112-13, 118, 128, 130, 134, 136, 139, 147, **154-64**, 174-82, 184, 192-94, 199-202, **208-13**, 225, 227, 234, 247

Panofsky, Erwin, 155, 181, 246
pantheism, 68-70
paradox, 10-11, 17, 76, 96, 116-17, 122-23, 150-51, **195**, 197, 213, **215**, 230, 241
parataxis. *See* rhetoric
parenthesis. *See* rhetoric
Parker, Dorothy, 19
*parole. See langue*
*parole parlante/parole parlée*, 10, 222
pastoral, 10, 15, 30, 40-42, 103-106, **153-65**, 171-72, 192, 218-19, 246
Pell, Barbara, 16, 88

perception, 7-8, 22-23, 64, 70, 72, **73-86**, 96-97, 99-100, 102, 108, 114, 130-31, 153, 205-208, **213-14**, **218-27**, **230-32**. *See also* vision
Percy, H.R., 24, 236
personification. *See* rhetoric
Phelps, Arthur, 32
phenomenology, 6, 64, 73-75, 79, 99, 194, 196, 201, 230
Philostratus, 154
Picasso, Pablo, 80, 128
*placere*, 231
Plato, 22, 83, 93, 126, 146, 221, 230
Plotinus, 94, 110. *See also* neoplatonism, idealism
Poe, Edgar Allan, 86
pointillism, 132-33, 200-201
polysyndeton. *See* rhetoric
Ponge, Francis, 9, **76-77**, **101**, 105, **128**, 194, 241, 244
postmodernism, 11, 16-17, 79, 81, 85, 183, 229-32
Pound, Ezra, 19, 191
Poussin, Nicolas, 10, 173-74
preciosity. *See* rhetoric
Prometheus, 164
Proust, Marcel, 26, 92, 95, 212
**publishers.** *See also* correspondence
  Atheneum Publishers, 38
  Atlantic Monthly Press, 31, 239
  Braziller, 38
  Clarke, Irwin, 30-31
  Clarkson Potter, 49
  Crown Publishers, 49, 69
  Dodd, Mead, 41
  Doubleday, 36
  Harcourt, Brace & World, 38, 41
  Henry Holt and Co., 30-31, 38
  Knopf, Alfred A., 42, 49, 153, 200, 202
  Little, Brown, 38, 52
  Macmillan, 30-31, 52
  McClelland and Stewart (*See also* McClelland, Jack), 1, 30-31, 37, 58, 97, 199
  New American Library of World Literature Inc., 38

# Index

Random House, 31, 38
Scribner's, 38, 41, 154
Viking, 46, 49
World Publishing, 38

Raddall, Thomas, 16
Rathbone, Basil, 21
*Reader's Digest*, 19, 33, 46, 49
**Rebellion of Young David, The**, 20, 36, 50-55, 78, 107, 109-12, 115, 130, 133, 142-43, 151, 168, 170, 175, 194, 218-19, 226
reception, 1, 8, 18-19, 23-24, **29-62**, 154, 191-93, 198-200, 239, 247
   *Cruelest Month, The*, 34-39
   *Mountain and the Valley, The*, 30-34
   *Nova Scotia, Window on the Sea*, 46-50
   *Ox Bells and Fireflies*, 39-46
   short stories, 50-56
   *Whirligig*, 56-60
*Redbook*, 54
Renaissance, 9, 86, 102, 128, 131-32, 136, 138, 146, 155, 177, 180, 229-31, 244
Reynolds, Joshua, 173
**rhetoric/rhetorical devices**, 11, **191-27**. See also **analogy, exemplum, irony, metaphor, paradox, synaesthesia**
   *accumulation*, 197, 201, **202**, 208, 231
      chaotic enumeration, 43, 84, 85, 87, 132, 162-63, 178, 185-86, **199-203**, 201-202
      concatenation, 159, 197, 201, 205-206, 217
      metabole, 197
      polysyndeton, 107, 171, 185, 186, 200, 205
      polyptoton, 196
      reiteration/repetition, 11, 47, 54, **204-208**, 219
         anaphora, 111, **207**
         epanadiplosis, 207-208
         epanalepsis, 147, 159, 197, 204, 206
         epiphora, 206, 207
         symploce, 207
      seriation, 197-98, 199
   allegory (*See also* extended metaphor), 137, 148, 203, 204, 217, 232
   *amplification*, 195, 202, 204, 215, 231
      counterpoint, 179, 208-209
      enumeration, 11, 86-88, 179, 180-81, 195, 197, 203, **204-208**
      *conglobatio*, **202-203**
      parenthesis, 110, **196, 208**
   anacoluthon, 120
   anagram (*See also* rhetoric/metaplasm), 209
   antithesis, 122, 148-49, 204, 210, 215, 219, 230
   asteismus, 120
   baroquism (*See also* rhetoric/preciosity), 198, 200
   cacophony, 194, 247
   celebration, 199
   chiasmus, 210
   compound words/neological compounds, 11, 89, 197, 198-199, **205-206**, 247
   conceit (*See also* metaphor, and rhetoric/baroquism/preciosity), 6, 189, 192, 197, 199, 225, **226-27**, 246
   *dubitatio*, 223
   hypallage, 197, 208
   metaplasm (*See also* anagram), 209
   metonymy, 203, 207, 210, **214**, 232
      antonomasia, 203, **210**
      synecdoche, 25, 43, 105, 132, 137, 148, 156, 177, 210, 240
   parachesis, 206
   parataxis, 120, 217, 226
   paronomasia, 197, 201, 209
   personification, 89, 215, 225
   preciosity (*See also* rhetoric/baroquism), 117-20, 122, 193, 199
      bomphilogia, 192;
      phoebus, 192

simile (*See also* metaphor), 197, 204, 205, 211, 214-16, 219, 226, 246
syllepsis, 19
tautophony, 194, 247
transference, 208, 247
verbigeration (*See also* rhetoric/baroquism), 200
zeugma, 97, 111, 179, 197, 210.
Richards, David Adams, 15
Ricoeur, Paul, 4, 10, 87-88, 172, 204, 215-16, 218, 220-22, 224, 230, 244
Ricou, Laurie, 192-93, 196-97, 214, 247-48
Rimbaud, Arthur, 156
Robarts, John (and G. Guertin), 242
Robbe-Grillet, Alain, 26
Roberts, G.D., 21
Robrieux, Jean-Jacques, 248
Romanticism, 8, 9, 11, 25, 63, 69, 86, 88, 95, 131, 134-35, 138, 157, 161, 181, 197, 229-30, 232
Ross, Sinclair, 16, 32, 50. *See also* correspondence
Roy, Gabrielle, 15, 16, 156

Sandburg, Carl, 44
Sappho, 26
*Saturday Night*, 17, 19, 20, **52**, **54**
Saussure, Ferdinand de, 7, 102-103, 113, 117-19, 243
Schiller, Friedrich, 245
Schlegel, Friedrich, 197, 200, 227, 231, 245
Scholasticism, 66, **131-32**, 135, 146, 231
Schopenhauer, Arthur, **72**, 73, 83, 94-95, 110, 141-42, 149-50, 212, 214, 240
Seaman, Andrew, 192, 194, 234
senses, 44, 74, 79, 90, 95, 165-67, 175, 178-79, 185, 196-97, 200-201, 203, 205; the visible and the tangible, 77-82. *See also* vision
Shakespeare, William, 26, 27, 149
Shaw, G.B., 27
Shelley, Mary, 240

Shelley, Percy Bysshe, 64, 68, 93, 128, 134-35, 138, 141, 150, 240. *See also* Romanticism
**short stories**, 19-20, 50-56, 78, 83-85, 92-93, 104, 106-107, 109-12, 115-16, 133, **139-52**, 168, 170, **182-89**, 218-19, 226-27, 234, 243, 245. *See also The Rebellion of Young David and Other Stories*
Snow, Michael, 80
Socratic, 22, 146
Spenser, Edmond, 83
Spinoza, Benedictus de, 22
Spirat, 11
Stein, Gertrude, 4, 5, 27, 82, 191, 198. *See also* modernism
Steinbeck, John, 33
synaesthesia, 11, 74, **77-82**, 149, 195, 197, 202, 205, 206, **210-12**, 219. *See also* senses, and sense analogy

Tallman, Warren, 192
tautophony. *See* rhetoric
Tennyson, Alfred, Lord, 240
Thackeray, William, 25
Theocritus, 155
*This Week*, 54
Thomas, Clara, 243
Thomas, Dylan, 26, 43
Thoreau, Henry David, 243
time, 72, 76, 88, 89, 92-93, 96, 98, 102, 124, 139, 154-67, 172-76, 183, 185-89, 205-209, 211-14, 219, 226-27, 231
transcendentalism, 3, 63-64, 66, 71, 88, 89, 91, 230, 234. *See also* Emerson
*Trinity University Review*, 19
Turner, Victor, 246

*ubi sunt*, 175
unpublished material, 8, 10, 17, 83, 84-85, 92-93, 96-99, 115-16, 139-42, 146-48, 154, **182-89**, 226, 242, 243, 245
Urban, W.M., 221

Utilitarianism, 136, 138
 aesthetics of Use, 10, 113-16, 121, **135-38**, 158-59, 231
Utopia, 155

Van Gennep, Arnold, 240-41
Van Gunsteren, Julia, 201
van Herk, Aritha, 15
Vanderhaeghe, Guy, 11
Varley, Frank, 3. *See also* The Group of Seven
Virgil, 155, 160, 173
vision, 66, 71-75, 77-87, 90, 103, 108-10, 127, 130-32, 158, 205-208, 215-16, **218-27**. *See also* perception

Wainwright, Andrew, 174
Weber, Hans, 16, 46-49, 54. *See also* correspondence

Welles, Orson, 21
Whalley, George, 9, 132
*Whirligig*, 16, 21, 23, 25, 50, 56-60, 96-97, 115, 151, 152, 236, 240
Whitman, Walt, 155
Wilde, Oscar, 152
Williams, Tennessee, 19
Wittgenstein, Ludwig, 7, 9
Wolfe, Thomas, 33, 193
*Woman's Day*, 54
Woolf, Virginia, 4, 82, 191. *See also* modernism
Wordsworth, William, 63, 68, 134, 157. *See also* Romanticism

Young, Alan, 50, 153, 191, 193, 234, 236, 243, 246

zeugma. *See* rhetoric